Lost Histories

*The Good, the Bad, and the Strange
in Early American Orthodoxy*

MATTHEW NAMEE

ANCIENT FAITH PUBLISHING
CHESTERTON, INDIANA

Published by:
Ancient Faith Publishing
A Division of Ancient Faith Ministries
1050 Broadway, Suite 6
Chesterton, IN 46304

Cover design by Samuel Heble
Cover images are used with permission from OrthodoxHistory.org and from the private collection of Holy Trinity Cathedral, Chicago, IL.
Interior images are used with permission from OrthodoxHistory.org.

ISBN: 978-1-955890-63-2

Library of Congress Control Number: 2024933360

For Catherine

Contents

Foreword

The V. Rev. Andrew Stephen Damick

M Y FRIENDSHIP WITH Matthew Namee, begun some twenty years ago when I was in seminary and he was an undergraduate student, was founded on our common love for the history of Orthodox Christianity in America. At the time, one of us reached out to the other through the internet to ask about a source for some piece of research. In the years since, we have swapped sources, told each other stories, run a history symposium, built the OrthodoxHistory.org website and social media, and worked together on more projects than I now can count.

Most notably for this volume, however, I had the opportunity to learn this history together with Matthew over the years. That is why I can say, as historian and then-dean of St. Vladimir's Seminary Fr. John Erickson said when he introduced Matthew as a conference speaker at SVS in 2009, that I don't know anyone who knows more about the history of Orthodox Christianity in America than Matthew does. No one else even comes close.

I do know that there are certain areas of this history that have their specialists, almost always focusing on the story of a particular jurisdiction. There are several books available that tell these stories. There are fewer that attempt to tell the story of the *whole* Orthodox community in America. Those that do tell this broader story essentially compile summaries of those other stories.

With so much attention spent on telling these larger stories—the establishment of archdioceses, saints' lives, the rise and fall of bishops, the building of major churches, and so forth—what is often left by the wayside are the details. Some of these details come from the lives of these prominent leaders, but other details concern the ordinary people who aren't usually included in such histories.

It is these details that Matthew has spent so much time gathering over the years, rescuing them from neglected archives, digging them out of old newspapers, looking them up in limited-run books long out of print. It is these forgotten finds that form the basis for this present book.

Yet if they are usually left out of the major histories, why publish them? Are they actually important? First of all, a good historian looks to the details to get the full picture. It is these apparently minor details which, taken together, told a story that resulted in that talk Matthew gave in 2009 at SVS—"The Myth of Unity and the Origins of Jurisdictional Pluralism in American Orthodoxy"—a paper that changed the course of American Orthodox historiography by radically revising some of its most basic assumptions that had been shared widely for decades.

Second, these stories are worth telling and publishing because they are not only interesting—and you will find some truly *interesting* tales in this book!—but because they give a more colorful, more fascinating picture of our Orthodox Christian forebears in America. I enjoy reading broad histories, but isn't it worth it to zoom in on the stuff that doesn't make it into those overarching summaries?

These stories are also worth telling because, together, they show that the histories of the various Orthodox jurisdictions and ethnicities in America have a lot more in common than just the things bishops do together and say to one another. That counts not only in stories that involve Orthodox people from different traditions interacting but in the truth that these stories belong to all of us, perhaps precisely because they don't really serve the interests of a particular jurisdiction.

Who would claim Agapius Honcharenko, for instance, in a jurisdictional history, except perhaps as a kind of embarrassing footnote? What about St. Tikhon's friendship with the Episcopal bishop Grafton, a story that does not establish any theology or method of ecumenism? Do we really need to remember the time St. Raphael was accused of pulling a gun on a police officer?

These stories and the many more that make up this book not only will interest American Orthodox Christians looking for more than the standard histories but also help to establish our common sense of identity. The identity of Orthodox Christians in America is not made up only of disparate tales of the establishment of jurisdictions in the wake of waves of immigration, nor does it consist purely of the holy lives of its saints. That identity is also constituted by the stories we share of Orthodox Christians—both "cradle" and "convert"—who are all grafted into Christ but also grafted into and, yes, *arising from* this American culture, trying to figure out what it means to be faithfully Orthodox in the New World.

Preface

THIS BOOK OWES its existence to three people, in reverse chronological order: my wife, Catherine, the great baseball author Bill James, and Bishop Basil of Wichita.

It was Bishop Basil who first sparked my love of church history. When I was twelve, he introduced me to St. Seraphim of Sarov and St. John Maximovitch—modern saints whose lives and wonders confirmed the truth of the entire Orthodox Faith. I dipped my toe into church history research by writing letters to people who knew St. John personally, and I was awed by the personal responses I got back. Then, when I was eighteen, I got my dream job: research assistant to the legendary baseball author Bill James, the father of sabermetrics. Bill taught me how to think and how to write, and in many ways, this book is my attempt to ape his brilliant storytelling, applying it to Orthodox history rather than baseball.

While working for Bill, I got access to ProQuest's digital newspaper archives via my membership in the Society for American Baseball Research. One day, it occurred to me that I could search for topics other than baseball. I searched for "Orthodox Church," and then "Tikhon," and then "Raphael Hawaweeny." I was gobsmacked by what I found: thousands upon thousands of turn-of-the-last-century newspaper articles about the early days of Orthodoxy in America. I had hit the mother lode, and I became obsessed with downloading every primary source I could get my hands on.

A year or so after this, my wife, Catherine, and I started dating. It is a testament to her grace and my idiocy that I spent hours every day digging through digitized old newspapers while my beautiful girlfriend waited patiently. We've now been married for eighteen years and have been blessed with seven amazing children. She also knows more than she ever wanted to about Fr. Ingram Irvine, Fr. Raphael Morgan, and all the other characters in this book. After law school, I went several years without writing about church history, and it was only because of Catherine's encouragement that I picked up my blog again in 2018. Without her support, there's no way this book would exist.

This book is not a meant to be a standard railroad-track history (if you're interested in that, check out Fr. John Erickson's *Orthodox Christians in America*). It's also not a compendium of saints' lives (for that, a great place to start is *Glorified in America*, from Holy Trinity Publications). And it's focused on Orthodoxy in the contiguous United States—what we now call the "Lower 48"—in the period from the Civil War through the end of World War I. There's not much here about Alaska (see *Orthodox Alaska* by the recently reposed Fr. Michael Oleksa), and the past century gets only a brief mention in the epilogue.

This book is more of a cabinet of curiosities—a collection of stories, in roughly chronological order, meant to give you a window into the early days of Orthodoxy in the United States. It's full of saints, yes, but of charlatans too. The stories about saints aren't hagiographic or even strictly biographical; in fact, I'm deliberately trying to avoid too much overlap with books like *Glorified in America*. So instead of a life of St. Tikhon, you'll learn about how his younger brother fell in love with an Italian opera singer in San Francisco and died of a broken heart. Saint Raphael gets a lot of attention in this book because he's a personal favorite of mine, and also because there are so many amazing things to tell you about him—perhaps the wildest being his involvement in a gunfight on the streets of Brooklyn, which led to his arrest on charges that he'd pulled a gun on a police officer. But these stories are not only about saints or "important" historical figures, people who made a lasting impact. Some of these stories are here simply because they're fun and fascinating, like the tale of the rogue Bulgarian monk who trekked around the United States in the 1870s and 1880s before morphing into a ghost story in Idaho.

My hope is that, once you get to the end of the book, you'll have a good sense of what it was like back then, in the early days of American Orthodoxy. I also hope that you'll have a great time reading this. My mentor Bill James once told me, "When you are writing for the public, finding interesting things to say is the sun and the moon." If you find yourself bored at any point, move on to the next chapter, and please accept my apologies in advance.

This book wouldn't exist without the encouragement of Fr. Andrew Damick, who not only wrote the foreword but had the idea to create my home base, the OrthodoxHistory.org website, back in 2009. My other colleagues on the Orthodox History editorial board—Nicholas Chapman, Sam Noble, and Melissa Kean—have been not only important sounding boards but great friends. Father John Erickson took me under his wing and even let me teach his church history class at St. Vladimir's Seminary about Fr. Ingram Irvine when I was a twenty-one-year-old college dropout. I'm also grateful to my research assistant, Cassidy Irwin, for helping prepare the manuscript. And to my parents, who first transmitted the Orthodox faith to me.

Most of all, thanks again to my wife Catherine, to our children, Jude, Marina, Elijah, Genevieve, Micah, James, and our new daughter (who is due to be born just as this book is going to print), and also to St. Joseph of Volokolamsk, who is like a second patron to me; I'm eternally grateful to all of them.

Introduction[1]

ON OCTOBER 18, 1867, the Russian Empire formally transferred control of Alaska to the United States of America. At this moment, the only Orthodox churches in the Western Hemisphere were in Alaska, the product of seventy-plus years of Russian Orthodox missionary work. The greatest of those missionaries was St. Innocent Veniaminov, who, a month after the sale, was elected metropolitan of Moscow. Shortly after his election, Innocent wrote a remarkable letter to the ober-procurator (the Tsar's official representative) of the Russian Holy Synod:

> Rumor reaching me from Moscow purports that I wrote to someone of my great unhappiness about the sale of our colonies to the Americans. This is utterly false. To the contrary, I see in this event one of the ways of Providence whereby Orthodoxy will penetrate the United States (where even now people have begun to pay serious attention to it). Were I to be asked about this, I would reply:
>
> A. Do not close the American vicariate—even though the number of churches and missions there has been cut in half (i.e., to five).

---

1   In this introduction, I make numerous passing references to stories that are told later in the book. If you run into something like this and want to know more, you'll probably find the answer on the pages that follow.

B. Designate San Francisco rather than New Archangel the residence of the vicar. The climate is incomparably better there, and communications with the colonial churches are just as convenient from there as from New Archangel (if not more so).

C. Subordinate the vicariate to the Bishop of St. Petersburg or some other Baltic diocese, for once the colonies have been sold to the American Government, communications between the Amur and the colonies will end completely and all communications between the headquarters of the Diocese of Kamchatka and the colonies will have to be through St. Petersburg—which is completely unnatural.

D. Return to Russia the current vicar and all clergy in New Archangel . . . and appoint a new vicar from among those who know the English language. Likewise, his retinue ought to be composed of those who know English.

E. Allow the bishop to augment his retinue, transfer its members and ordain to the priesthood for our churches converts to Orthodoxy from among American citizens who accept all its institutions and customs.

F. Allow the vicar bishop and all clerics of the Orthodox Church in America to celebrate the Liturgy and other services in English (for which purpose, obviously, the service books must be translated into English).

G. To use English rather than Russian (which must sooner or later be replaced by English) in all instruction in the schools to be established in San Francisco and elsewhere to prepare people for missionary and clerical positions.[2]

An English-speaking bishop, English church services, books, schools, "converts to Orthodoxy from among American citizens"—the great missionary laid out his blueprint for Orthodoxy to "penetrate the United States."

---

2   Paul D. Garrett, *St. Innocent: Apostle to America* (Crestwood, NY: St. Vladimir's Seminary Press, 1979), 275–277.

Unfortunately, this visionary plan was not fully implemented. It is true that a bishop who knew English—John Mitropolsky—was appointed to America, and the diocesan see was moved from New Archangel (Sitka) to San Francisco. But English did not become the norm, and American converts were practically non-existent. For the next twenty-five years, the diocese added just a single parish in the contiguous United States—the San Francisco cathedral. Apart from this, the only Orthodox churches in what we now call the "Lower 48" were a Greek parish in New Orleans (established at about the same time as the San Francisco cathedral and affiliated with the Church of Greece) and a Russian embassy chapel in New York City (subject to the metropolitan of St. Petersburg and in existence from 1870 to 1883).

By 1890, with the New York chapel closed, there were still only those two parishes in the contiguous United States—New Orleans and San Francisco. The seven largest cities in America had no Orthodox church. The focus of the Russian diocese's efforts was Alaska, where the indigenous Orthodox people were being targeted by American Protestant missionaries. The rest of the United States was something of an afterthought.

ooooo

IN THE LAST decades of the nineteenth century, Byzantine Rite Christians from the Carpathian mountain region began to arrive in America. It is difficult to label these people: they came from an area that today is divided among Poland, Slovakia, Hungary, Moldova, Belarus, and Ukraine, and they were known by a great variety of names, including Carpatho-Russians, Rusyns, Ruthenians, Galicians, and others. Their ancestors were originally Orthodox Christians, but in the sixteenth and seventeenth centuries they submitted to the pope of Rome through a series of "unions," which is why they have long been known to the Orthodox as "Uniates."[3] Despite their subordination to the pope, they retained most of the external forms of Orthodox worship and practice, including allowing married men to become priests.

Upon arriving in America, these Uniates were met by a well-established Roman Catholic church structure, with bishops who generally felt that these new immigrants should be absorbed into the existing Latin Catholic parishes. As Fr. John Erickson writes, "Their thinking ran: If these people really are good Catholics, let them attend the existing Latin Catholic churches of their Slovak, Polish, and Hungarian neighbors!"[4] The Uniates, on the other hand, preferred to start their own parishes and retain their centuries-old liturgy and customs.

All this came to a head in 1889. Father Alexis Toth, a widowed Uniate priest, arrived in Minneapolis to serve the local "Greek Catholic" (Uniate) community. Following protocol, he presented his credentials to the Latin Catholic archbishop, John Ireland. Here is how St. Alexis described the meeting:

> I remember that no sooner did he read that I was a "Greek Catholic," his hands began to shake. It took him fifteen minutes to read to the end after which he asked abruptly—we conversed in Latin:
> "Have you a wife?"
> "No."
> "But you had one?"
> "Yes, I am a widower."
> At this he threw the paper on the table and loudly exclaimed,

---

3   When it began in the sixteenth century, the Unia was centered on what was then the Polish-Lithuanian Commonwealth, which had a Roman Catholic ruler. The newly Uniate parishes were primarily in the Grand Duchy of Lithuania—most of them in the areas that are now Ukraine and Belarus, with some in modern-day Lithuania.

4   John H. Erickson, *Orthodox Christians in America* (New York: Oxford University Press, 1999), 62.

"I have already written to Rome protesting against this kind of priest being sent to me!"

"What kind of priest do you mean?"

"Your kind."

"I am a Catholic priest of the Greek Rite. I am a Uniate and was ordained by a regular Catholic bishop."

"I do not consider that either you or this bishop of yours are Catholic; besides, I do not need any Greek Catholic priests here; a Polish priest in Minneapolis is quite sufficient; the Greeks can also have him for their priest."

"But he belongs to the Latin Rite; besides our people do not understand him and so they will hardly go to him; that was the reason they instituted a church of their own."

"They had no permission from me and I shall grant you no jurisdiction to work here."

Deeply hurt by the fanaticism of this representative of Papal Rome, I replied sharply: "In that case, I know the rights of my church. I know the basis on which the Union was established and I shall act accordingly."

The Archbishop lost his temper. I lost mine just as much. One word brought another, the thing had gone so far that our conversation is not worth putting on record.[5]

The chaos that followed led Fr. Alexis to a momentous conclusion that would have far-reaching consequences: "I made up my mind to do something which I carried in my heart a long time, for which my soul longed: that is, to become Orthodox."

But at that moment—1889—Orthodoxy barely existed in the United States. Apart from the mission in far-off Alaska,

Saint Alexis Toth

---

5   Constance Tarasar, ed., *Orthodox America: 1794–1976* (Syosset, NY: The Orthodox Church in America Department of History and Archives, 1975), 50–51.

there were only two parishes, those of San Francisco and New Orleans (the New York chapel having closed several years earlier). A delegation from Fr. Alexis's parish in Minnesota tracked down Bishop Vladimir in San Francisco, and on the Feast of Annunciation in 1891, the Uniate community of Minneapolis was received into the Orthodox Church. This marked the beginning of a flood of Uniates into Orthodoxy as tens of thousands joined the Russian Orthodox Church in North America over the next several decades. The core of the growing Russian mission—and the core of what we know today as the Orthodox Church in America, or OCA—consisted of these former Uniate parishes. The return of the Unia was one of the two great developments that would shape the future of American Orthodoxy.

ooooo

THE OTHER GREAT development was launched just a few weeks before the Minneapolis parish joined the Orthodox Church. On March 3, 1891, President Benjamin Harrison signed the Immigration Act of 1891 into law. The act paved the way for a flood of new immigrants into the United States. To receive these newcomers, an inspection station was built on Ellis Island in New York Harbor, opening its doors on New Year's Day, 1892. From this point on, for the next three decades, hundreds of thousands of Orthodox Christians streamed into the United States from Eastern Europe and the Mediterranean.

At this pivotal moment, a change occurred at the top of the Russian diocese: the incumbent bishop, Vladimir, unable to run the diocese effectively due to nonstop conflict and scandal (covered in chapter 9), was recalled. His replacement, Bishop Nicholas Ziorov, was the ideal man for this unique situation. Bishop Nicholas was not only a visionary leader but a skilled administrator, pragmatic and flexible. He spent seven years in America, and while he's been overshadowed by his successor, St. Tikhon, much of what St. Tikhon accomplished was, in fact, a continuation of the work of Bishop Nicholas, a further building on his solid foundation.

It was Bishop Nicholas who recruited gifted young men like St. Alexander Hotovitzky, St. John Kochurov, and St. Anatolii Kamenskii (among many others) to serve in America. Bishop Nicholas ordained St. Alexander and St. John to the priesthood, as well as the great American-born Serb, St. Sebastian Dabovich. And it was Bishop Nicholas who first set up special ministries for different ethnic groups, empowering St. Sebastian and importing talented non-Russian clergy, such as St. Raphael Hawaweeny and Fr. Theoclitos Triantafilides. The flood of Uniates into Orthodoxy began with the conversion of St. Alexis Toth shortly before Bishop Nicholas arrived in America, but it was under Nicholas that the return of the Unia really picked up steam, and his welcoming embrace of these former Uniates ensured the success of St. Alexis's mission.

When Bishop Nicholas arrived in 1891, he found a diocese that was reeling from the scandals of Bishop Vladimir, a diocese that had not experienced hierarchical stability since the drowning/suicide of Bishop Nestor Zass in 1883. While not neglecting Alaska (he was a great advocate for the Orthodox natives, as discussed in chapter 19), Bishop Nicholas oversaw dramatic growth in the rest of the United States, with an average of about two new parishes founded every year. Whereas the diocese was tiny and weak in 1891, by the time of Bishop Nicholas's departure in 1898, it was thriving and healthy. Saint Tikhon, his successor, was able to accomplish so much not only because he was a genuinely great man but also because he took the reins of a diocese made strong by Bishop Nicholas.

ooooo

EVEN BEFORE THE Immigration Act of 1891 took effect, Orthodox immigrants had been trickling into the United States. In 1891,
the growing Greek community in New York City began to organize itself. The Society of Athena was formed, composed primarily
of Greeks from Athens. On January 13, 1892, the *Baltimore Sun*
reported that "since the closing of the Russian chapel, they [the
Greeks] have found the lack of spiritual aid and counsel to be a
great drawback to happiness." So in 1891, the New York Greeks
wrote to Archbishop Methodius of Syra, Greece. The *Sun* reported,
"[T]he Archbishop conferred with a dignitary at Athens, and the
dignitary at Athens wrote to the Patriarch of Constantinople, and
the Patriarch said: 'To be sure. They must have a priest. As it is
their souls are in peril.'" Notwithstanding the involvement of the
Ecumenical Patriarchate, the priest who arrived in January 1892,
Archimandrite Paisius Ferentinos, was appointed by the metropolitan of Athens. Thus began Holy Trinity parish.

It was not long before a disagreement arose in the community. A faction appealed to the Ecumenical Patriarchate, which
responded by sending another priest, Archimandrite Kallinikos
Delveis, who started Annunciation parish. This appears to be the
first time the Ecumenical Patriarchate established a parish, and
appointed a priest to serve it, in the Western Hemisphere.

The Russian Archdiocese returned to New York City in
1895, more than a decade after closing its embassy chapel. A
Russian-American journalist explained at the time that the
Russian Orthodox "resident in New York are soon to have
their own house of worship in the place of the Greek Church
organized by the Hellenic colony."[6] New York now had three
Orthodox churches, each under a different bishop. The problem
of overlapping jurisdictions was present from the very beginning of organized Orthodoxy in the United States.

---

6   Valerian Gribayedoff, "A Russian Greek Church," *Outlook* 51:15 (April
     13, 1895), 623.

In Chicago in the late 1880s and early 1890s, a failed attempt was made to form a multiethnic Orthodox parish under Russian jurisdiction. In 1892, the Greeks of the city petitioned the metropolitan of Athens to send them a priest, which he did that spring. A month later, the Russian diocese opened a church. And for several months, there was the beginning of a third parish, with a priest from Serbia. The Serbian community never got off the ground, and the priest returned home later in the year. But Chicago now had two Orthodox parishes, each under a different bishop—the first city in the Western Hemisphere where this happened, two years ahead of New York.

In both New York and Chicago—the two largest cities in America at the time—independent Greek parishes preceded their Russian counterparts. The Greeks in these cities had established a precedent which would be followed by their countrymen throughout the United States. From 1900 to 1917, more than 340,000 Greeks—nearly 19,000 per year—came to America. Bishop George Papaioannou writes that "administratively there was complete chaos."[7] The Greek parishes had virtually no episcopal oversight. Father John Erickson notes, "In practice [the Greek] parishes were independent of any authority beyond the local community."[8]

One of the earliest Greek parishes in America was established

---

7   George Papaioannou, "The Diamond Jubilee of the Greek Orthodox Archdiocese of America, 1922–1997," *The Greek Orthodox Theological Review* 45:1–4 (Spring 2000), 223. This article was written in 1997 and published posthumously.

8   John Erickson, "Organization, Community, Church: Reflections on Orthodox Parish Polity in America," *Greek Orthodox Theological Review* 48:1 (Spring 2003), 72. This does not mean that the Greek parishes were entirely unconnected with each other. In 1893, for instance, the newly formed Greek churches in New York and Chicago provided funds to aid in the establishment of a short-lived parish in Baltimore, Maryland. "Greek Church to Celebrate Christmas," *Baltimore Sun* (January 6, 1894), 8.

in Lowell, Massachusetts. In 1900, the Lowell parish was divided: one portion of the parish wanted to discharge their priest, Fr. Nathaniel Sideris, and "hire" another. "We have the right to tell a priest that he is no longer needed and to engage another priest," one parish leader explained. Other parishioners were appalled at such an approach. "Our complaint," said the leader of the opposition, "is that the people upstairs are conducting the affairs of a Greek church different from anything to which we have been accustomed, and we do not consider it right. The bishop of the Greek church in Athens alone has the power to assign a priest."[9]

Eight years later, virtually the same scenario repeated itself in Lowell: part of the community decided not to retain their priest, and the priest himself appealed to the metropolitan of Athens. "If the Greek Orthodox community here refuses to recognize the authority of the metropolitan of the Greek church in Athens [the priest] will be transferred to some other Greek Orthodox church in this country."[10] The striking fact about both these incidents is that the Russian bishop is not mentioned by either party. One side wanted total independence from all hierarchy; the other acknowledged the authority of the Church of Greece. The Russians were irrelevant.

Both the Church of Greece and the Ecumenical Patriarchate oversaw Greek priests and parishes in America. Greek churches in Norfolk, Salt Lake City, and Washington, DC, were under Athens; those in Lynn, Massachusetts, and Savannah, Georgia, acknowledged the authority of the Ecumenical Patriarchate. The first Orthodox services in Birmingham, Alabama, were celebrated by an Archimandrite Dorotheo, who commemorated both the ecumenical patriarch and the metropolitan of Athens during the Divine Liturgy. When a Greek parish was formed in

---

9   "Lowell Greeks at Odds," *Boston Globe* (April 30, 1900), 6.
10   "Appeals to Athens," *Boston Globe* (April 1, 1908), 8.

Philadelphia, the *Philadelphia Inquirer* noted, "The church is governed from Athens and is not connected with the Russian Greek Church, although the doctrines are essentially the same."[11] Two years later, a black Episcopal deacon who had been attending the Philadelphia parish traveled to Constantinople—not Athens—to be ordained an Orthodox priest. This man, Fr. Raphael Morgan, was then sent back to America by the Ecumenical Patriarchate to "carry the light of the Orthodox faith among his racial brothers."

On occasion, the Russian hierarchy attempted to assert ecclesiastical authority over trustee-governed Greek parishes. The Greeks weren't so keen on this. For example, on Great and Holy Friday in 1904, St. Tikhon, the Russian archbishop of North America, visited Holy Trinity, the uptown Greek church in New York City. "[H]e was barred from entering by its angry trustees," writes Erickson, "who feared a Russian takeover of their parish properties."[12] To understand this reaction of the Greeks, consider that just weeks earlier, Fr. Raphael Hawaweeny, the leader of the Russian-affiliated Syrian contingent, was ordained in Brooklyn by the Russian hierarchs, and it was widely reported that this took place on orders from the Tsar. The Greeks viewed this as a Russian imperial encroachment into the affairs of Orthodox church life in America, and they felt threatened. This tension was exacerbated in 1909, when the New York Greeks protested legislation that would have placed them under the legal authority of the Russian consul.

There are, however, examples of cooperation; for instance, in 1902 Archbishop Tikhon celebrated the Divine Liturgy in a Chicago Greek parish, serving entirely in the Greek language. In the 1910s, Fr. Demetrios Petrides (the Greek priest in Atlanta)

---

11 "Their Christmas Two Weeks Later," *Philadelphia Inquirer* (December 24, 1905), 8. Also see "Christmas is Celebrated by the Greek Christians," *Philadelphia Inquirer* (January 8, 1906).

12 Erickson, *Orthodox Christians in America*, 73.

and Fr. Leonid Turkevich (a leading Russian priest and the future Metropolitan Leonty) were the two Orthodox representatives to an official dialogue group called the Anglican and Eastern Orthodox Churches Union.

In 1900, St. Tikhon wrote:

> There are in America several Greek clergymen. Ecclesiastically they depend either upon the Patriarch of Constantinople or the Archbishop of Athens, but in fact they are dependent upon neither, and remain without any kind of oversight. [. . .] The Greek clergy ought to submit to some sort of diocesan oversight, all the more so because they are now living with the Orthodox North American Diocese; but this issue is beyond my competence.

Five years later, he expressed a similar view:

> [I]t is difficult to trust the Greeks: although they have parishes in America, some are dependent upon the Synod of Athens, some on the Patriarchate of Constantinople, and some on Jerusalem (quite a weak dependence!), and, according to the politics characteristic of Greeks, they would hardly wish to be under any kind of subjection to the Russian hierarchy.[13]

In March 1908, the Ecumenical Patriarchate issued a tomos, ceding to the Church of Greece "the right of oversight of all Greek Orthodox Churches in the diaspora." Fr. Alexander Doumouras explains that this was done in response to pressure from the Ottoman government in Turkey, which was upset about the anti-Turkish stance of many Greek priests in America.[14] The

---

13   Andrew Kostadis, *Pictures of Missionary Life According to the Russian Clerical Press in America and the Ruling American Bishops About the Life of the American Mission in 1900–1917* (unpublished MTh thesis, St. Vladimir's Orthodox Theological Seminary, 1999), 193–194 and 217.

14   Alexander Doumouras, "Greek Orthodox Communities in America Before World War I," *St. Vladimir's Seminary Quarterly* 11:4 (1967), 190.

tomos stipulated that the Church of Greece was supposed to send a bishop to America, but for the next decade, this didn't happen, and chaos continued to reign among the Greek churches.[15]

To summarize, then: the typical Greek parish in America was founded and run by a lay board of trustees without the participation, consent, or even, at times, knowledge of the Russian hierarchy. It was pastored by clergy sent from Greece or Constantinople, again without the participation, consent, or knowledge of the Russian bishops. These parishes were privately incorporated; legally, they were independent entities.

ooooo

THE SERBS HAD a mixed relationship with the Russian hierarchy. The founding members of the Russian cathedral in San Francisco were predominantly Serbian and Greek, with few Russians. The California-born Serb Sebastian Dabovich was the first cradle Orthodox US citizen to be ordained a priest. The first specifically Serbian parish in America—Jackson, California—was founded by St. Sebastian in 1894 as a parish of the Russian diocese. And from then until the Serbian Orthodox Church established a diocese in the United States after World War I, the Serbs were at least nominally subject to the Russian archbishop.

All that said, the Serbs often chafed under Russian authority, and the practical reality of Serbian parish life was not terribly different from that of the Greeks. When St. Sebastian established the Jackson, California, parish, Bishop Nicholas expected it to be chartered as a "Russian church," which provoked frustration among the Serbs. Saint Nicholai Velimirovich, who wasn't in America at the time but later became close to St. Sebastian,

---

15 For background on this tomos, with links to the original Greek and an English translation, see my paper "The Origins of the 'Barbarian Lands' Theory," *Orthodox History* (October 12, 2022), https://orthodoxhistory. org/2022/10/12/the-origins-of-the-barbarian-lands-theory/.

would later write that the Serbs clashed with the Russian hierarchy over this issue numerous times in the years to come.[16]

Of the Serbian priests, writes Fr. Mladen Trbuhovich, "Some were affiliated with their respective church jurisdiction in the Old Country, while others served under the Russian Orthodox Church in America." When the Serbian parish in Kansas City found itself without a priest in 1909, it did not appeal to the Russian archbishop but instead placed advertisements in the Serbian-language American newspapers. When that failed, the parish considered "writing to the Patriarch of Constantinople asking him to secure for them the service of a young priest."[17] When the Serbian parish of Chisholm, Minnesota, was organized in 1910, the local Serbian society president traveled to Europe in search of a priest.[18] When the church building was dedicated two years later, the priest who performed the ceremony did so under the authority of the bishop of Sarajevo.[19]

As early as 1897, both St. Sebastian and Bishop Nicholas wrote to Metropolitan Mihailo of Belgrade to request that the Serbian parishes in America be placed under the care of the Serbian Church. The metropolitan declined, writing, "We could not do this because We could not support so many churches and priests, schools and teachers there."[20] Metropolitan Mihailo also deferred to the Russian hierarchy in America:

---

16   St. Nicholai Velimirovich of Zhicha, "Father Sebastian Dabovich," *The Path of Orthodoxy* 42:10 (October 2007), 5. Originally published in the *Serb National Federation Commemorative Book* (1951).

17   Fr. Mladen Trbuhovich, "St. Vasilije's on the Mesabi," *Serb World USA* (July/August 1994), 57. This article was written in 1953.

18   "Goes to Europe After a Priest," *Duluth News Tribune* (June 3, 1910), 3.

19   Trbuhovich, 57.

20   Hieromonk Damascene Christiansen, "Archimandrite Sebastian Dabovich: Serbian Orthodox Apostle to America," *The Orthodox Word* 43:1-2 (January-April 2007), 28.

I cannot establish and consecrate an independent Orthodox Church in California and America because there is already an Orthodox Church supported by [the] Russian Orthodox Church. Furthermore, we do not have the resources for this. . . . I think you should agree and listen to your Bishop and he will help you and protect the Serbs and Orthodoxy and he will safeguard Serbian national customs. I think you should reconsider all the above [i.e., establishing an "independent Orthodox Church" in America] and refrain from doing anything that would be against the interests of Serbs living there.[21]

In the coming years, the Russian Archdiocese and St. Sebastian in particular would make numerous overtures to the Serbian Church in an effort to obtain a bishop for the Serbs. Yet to many of his fellow Serbs, St. Sebastian was a "Russophile" because of his cooperation with the Russian Archdiocese. The Serbs, writes Fr. Damascene Christiansen, "did not wish to support or be united under the Serbian Orthodox Mission because it was within the jurisdiction of the Russian Church."[22] The 1909 *Catholic Encyclopedia* reports, "The Servian [sic] Orthodox Church is closely affiliated to the Russian Church in this country, except that some of their churches do not recognize the jurisdiction or authority of the Russian archbishop." At a convention held in Chicago in 1913, the Serbian parishes voted to secede from the Russian Archdiocese and asked to be received into the Serbian Church. For various reasons, this did not take place until after World War I; however, at the parish level, most Serbs seem to have had no interest in being part of the Russian jurisdiction.

ooooo

21 Krinka Vidaković Petrov, "An Outline of the Cultural History of the Serbian Community in Chicago," *Serbian Studies* 20:1 (2006), 46.
22 Hieromonk Damascene, "Archimandrite Sebastian Dabovich," 50–51.

THINGS WERE SMOOTHER with the Syrians, at least in the early years. In 1895, the brilliant young archimandrite Raphael Hawaweeny arrived in America, part of Bishop Nicholas Ziorov's remarkable team of saintly priests. Although an Antiochian by birth, by this time St. Raphael was a clergyman of the Russian Church, in a state of de facto exile from the Patriarchate of Antioch because he had protested against the control of Antioch by ethnic Greek patriarchs. His Syrian parishes in America were unquestionably part of the Russian diocese. In 1899, the indigenous Antiochians succeeded in recapturing control of the patriarchate, and after this, Raphael's bond with Antioch became very close.

In 1904, the Holy Synod of Russia elected St. Raphael to the episcopacy to be the vicar of the North American archbishop, St. Tikhon. This was part of Tikhon's visionary plan, drafted the following year in a report to the Holy Synod, to organize American Orthodoxy along ethnic lines: each ethnic group would have its own vicariate, headed by its own bishop. These bishops would sit on a common synod headed by the Russian archbishop. Saint Tikhon pointed out that these different churches have their own peculiarities in canonical structure, liturgical rules, and parish life, and that "these peculiarities are dear to them and are altogether tolerable from the general Orthodox point of view." He said these peculiarities should be accommodated and preserved. Because of this, St. Tikhon said that each group should have "a chance to be governed directly by leaders of the same nationality."

Therefore, St. Tikhon wrote,

> The Syrian Church here received a bishop of its own (the Right Reverend Raphael of Brooklyn), who nominally is the second vicar to the Archbishop of the Aleutian see, but who in his own field of activity is almost independent. . . . The Serbian parishes are directly subject to a separate leader [here he's referring to St.

Sebastian], who at present is an archimandrite, but may be consecrated a bishop in the near future.

Regarding the Greeks, St. Tikhon said that they "have entered into communication with the Synod of Athens" on the subject of getting a bishop for America. Saint Tikhon went on,

> In short, it is possible that there will be formed in America an entire exarchate of national Orthodox Churches with their own bishop, whose exarch is to be the Russian archbishop. In his own field of work each of these bishops is to be independent, but the affairs that concern the American Church in general are to be decided by a general council, presided over by the Russian archbishop. Through him will be preserved the connection of the Orthodox Church of America with the Church of Russia and a degree of dependence of the former on the latter. Also we must keep in view that, compared with life in the old country, life in America has its peculiarities, with which the local Orthodox Church is obliged to count, and that consequently it ought to be allowed to be more autonomous than other metropolitan districts of Russia.

In the original Russian, St. Tikhon even put the word "autocephaly" with a question mark in parentheses, so he was clearly thinking several steps down the road.[23]

This was a remarkable plan—an attempt by a great bishop to

---

23 Archbishop Tikhon, "Projected Unity and Independence for America," *St. Vladimir's Theological Quarterly* 19:1 (1975), 49–50. This is an English translation of a section of a longer document written by Archbishop Tikhon in 1905. A translation of the full 1905 text appears under the title "Views of Questions to be Examined by the Local Council of the Russian Church" in the *Russian Orthodox American Messenger* (English supplement) (March 1906), 68–70. I address the differences between the 1906 and 1975 translations in "St. Tikhon's Vision, 1905," published at http://orthodoxhistory.org/2009/10/st-tikhons-vision-1905 (October 21, 2009).

creatively minister to a complex, diverse flock of Orthodox Christians in an entirely new situation, without helpful precedent. Although his plan was never fully implemented, it continues to this day to be looked to as a model for possible future Orthodox unity in America.

As St. Tikhon readily acknowledged in his 1905 proposal, the various ethnic bishops and leaders were "almost independent." After his ordination to the episcopacy, St. Raphael would simultaneously speak of the body he oversaw as a vicariate of the Russian Church and as a diocese of Antioch. Syrian parish priests were appointed by St. Raphael, who, in some cases, used the Old Country method of having the local community nominate one of their own for the priesthood. He also recruited priests from abroad. The management of the Syrian vicariate/diocese was entirely in Raphael's hands; he was the unquestioned leader. At times, though, he acted as a more typical vicar to the Russian archbishop, such as when he consecrated the grounds of the future St. Tikhon's Monastery or when he chaired a meeting of Russian clergy when the Russian archbishop was not available.

The apparent paradox of the Syrians' status was resolved in the person of St. Raphael, whom everyone accepted. Immediately after his death, though, his parishes were thrown into turmoil, with some priests recognizing the authority of the Russian hierarchy, while others said that of course they had been under Antioch all along. This conflict was exacerbated by the lack of an obvious successor. All of this is discussed in more detail later in the book; for now, suffice it to say that after St. Raphael's death the Antiochians split into "Russy" and "Antacky" factions—a division that would take decades to heal.

CHAPTER ONE

Humanitarian or Fraud?

Agapius Honcharenko

I DON'T KNOW THE true story of Agapius Honcharenko. I don't think anyone does. Honcharenko told the biggest fish stories you've ever heard, and his autobiographical anecdotes need to be taken with a pretty big chunk of salt. Some people, taking his words at face value, have memorialized him as some sort of folk hero. He's been described as a "prominent scholar, humanitarian, and early champion for human rights." The real story is a lot more complicated.

On January 2, 1865, a thirty-two-year-old man going by the name Fr. Agapius Honcharenko arrived by ship in New York City. He claimed to be an Orthodox priest, coming from Greece and affiliated with the Ecumenical Patriarchate but originally hailing from Ukraine, then part of the Russian Empire. Four days later, he served the Divine Liturgy on Christmas Day—Christmas according to the Julian Calendar, which, back then, was the only calendar used in the Orthodox Church. It seems that a handful of Greeks and Slavs in New York attended, but this first liturgy in the United States went unnoticed by the wider world.[1]

---

1   Letter from Agapius Honcharenko to the editor of a newspaper called the *Orthodox Overview*. The letter is undated but was referenced by and

Upon arriving, Honcharenko made contact with Rev. J. Free-man Young, an Episcopal priest involved in the "Russo-Greek Committee," a group newly formed to foster relations between the Episcopalians and the Orthodox Church. Young introduced Honcharenko to his bishop, Horatio Potter, and to Rev. Dr. Morgan Dix, rector of New York's famous Trinity Church. Dix wrote in his diary on January 18, 1865:

> The Revd Mr. Young called in the evening to see me, on import-ant business, connected with the arrival of a Russian priest in this city, who came out to minister to the Greek and Slavonic people here. I promised him a room for their services in one of our buildings. We had much conversation on the Russo-Greek movement wh[ich] is going on favourably to all appearance here & in England.

Honcharenko took Dix up on his offer of a room, and he appears to have held regular services over the coming weeks, attended by a small group of Greeks and Slavs. He baptized several chil-dren and seemed to be settling in as a mission priest for the Orthodox of New York. He also wrote a letter to Bishop Pot-ter, proposing to celebrate a public Divine Liturgy in one of the

---

attached to a letter from St. Philaret, Metropolitan of Moscow, to the ober-procurator of the Holy Synod of the Russian Orthodox Church, dated February 26, 1865. (February 26 was likely the Julian Calendar date; according to the Gregorian Calendar, it would have been March 10.) These documents were found by Nicholas Chapman in the National Archives in London, UK, in 2010, and were translated from Russian into English by Matushka Marie Meyendorff and published at OrthodoxHis-tory.org on August 31, 2010 (https://orthodoxhistory.org/2010/08/31/st-philaret-of-moscow-on-orthodoxy-in-america-in-1865/) and September 7, 2010 (https://orthodoxhistory.org/2010/09/07/aga-pius-honcharenko-in-defense-of-himself/). Nicholas Chapman's introduction to the documents was published at OrthodoxHistory.org on August 24, 2010 (https://orthodoxhistory.org/2010/08/24/the-russian-orthodox-church-in-america-and-its-clergy-1865/).

Episcopal churches in New York. Potter gave his "hearty consent and approbation." This happened in early February, a month before the proposed public liturgy. With Bishop Potter's support, Rev. Young set to work preparing the music, using musical scores he had picked up in Russia and adding English phonetic pronunciation of the Church Slavonic words. He secured an Episcopalian choir and even had vestments prepared.

On March 2, 1865, Honcharenko celebrated the Divine Liturgy in the grand Trinity Chapel (not to be confused with the even grander Trinity Church).[2] The next day, the *New York Times* shouted, "NOVEL RELIGIOUS SERVICE—A Remarkable Event in History—Inauguration of the Russo-Greek Church in America." The *Times* went on:

> The church, both aisles and galleries, was crowded with ladies and gentlemen to its utmost extent, although there had been no advertisement in the papers regarding the celebration. There were present upward of fifty clergymen of the city and neighborhood. The music (only vocal) was very fine. The ceremonies were impressive, solemn, and, to almost everyone present, novel, but exceedingly interesting, and, it might be said, beautiful. We ought to say that there were some sixty Greeks and about twenty Scalvonians [sic] or Russians present, who occupied seats in front of the altar.

---

2   The rest of the story of Trinity Chapel is fascinating: It was built in the 1850s, and despite being called a "chapel," it had a considerable congregation. By the 1940s, though, demographics had changed, and church leaders decided to sell the building. New York City's first full-blown Serbian parish had begun in the late 1930s, and as soon as they heard that the chapel was on the market, they were interested. With help from St. Nicholai Velimirovich, Serbs from across the country, and the Episcopalians themselves, the modest Serbian parish was able to purchase Trinity Chapel in 1942 and transform it into St. Sava Cathedral. On Pascha in 2016, the cathedral was destroyed by fire, leaving only a gutted shell. It was subsequently reconstructed, a process that is still underway.

The *Times* actually reprinted several sections of the liturgy itself.

The Protestants present were especially struck by the absence of the filioque from the Creed. The liturgy was celebrated partly in Church Slavonic, partly in Greek, and, to the delight of the Episcopalians, partly in English—including English renditions of the Creed and the Lord's Prayer, among other things.

Dix was thrilled, writing in his journal:

> This 2nd. day of Lent was a memorable one, because the Liturgy of the Eastern Church was sung in Trinity Chapel, at 11 A.M. This never occurred before so far as I have heard, in any Anglican Church. Bishop Potter was to have been there, but backed out, and went down to S. Paul's instead, to the noon day communion. A full account of this delightful service, will be found at the end of this diary; I cut it out from the *Evening Post*.

But not everyone was happy. The magazine *Evangelical Christendom* commented:

> Some of the religious papers find in it an unbecoming complicity with mischievous superstition and error; since the filioque was omitted from the creed by the Episcopal choir, and the 'sacrifice' 'received' by the priest is claimed to include all the enormities of transubstantiation and the Mass.

Even before that March 2 liturgy, word had begun to spread about Honcharenko—and not all of the news was good. There was a reason Honcharenko, a subject of the Russian tsar, was not serving under the Russian Church. He had a past.

ooooo

WHAT YOU THINK about Agapius Honcharenko's origin story depends on whom you believe—the Russian Orthodox Church of the time or Honcharenko himself. But certain things seem mostly undisputed:

» Honcharenko was born in August 1832 in Ukraine, then part of the Russian Empire. Modern scholars agree that his given name was "Andrii Humnytsky."

» He studied at the Kiev Theological Academy and then became a monk at the Kiev Caves Lavra in 1856.

» The next year, he became a hierodeacon (with the name Agafy) and was assigned to serve at the Russian embassy chapel in Athens, Greece.

» In 1860, he was accused of various things and removed from his post in Athens. Everyone agrees that one of those things was secretly writing anti-tsarist and anti-Church articles for a left-wing Russian journal called *Kolokol*, which was published out of London.

» The Russian government took him into custody and tried to send him back to Russia by way of Constantinople, but (apparently due to intervention by the British government) he escaped and made his way to England, where he collaborated with the publisher of *Kolokol*. It appears to be at this point that he started using the pseudonym "Honcharenko."

» At some point, he went back to Greece, claims to have been ordained a priest, and then sailed for America, arriving in early 1865.

Those are the facts, as best I can tell. The details are where things get a little hazy.

According to Honcharenko himself (in an account by an admiring journalist who visited him in 1911), "From early childhood he had observed the oppression of the serfs and their liberation had become the dominating impulse of his life."[1]

---

1   *San Francisco Call*, April 9, 1911. In Honcharenko's later decades, numerous journalists made the trek to his ranch near Oakland, California. They were uniformly enamored with the intriguing Cossack priest who

We get a different perspective from the former Russian ambassador to Greece, paraphrased in a Russian Church report from 1865:

> The basic idea directing Agafy's life was that all in the world is a convention and that everything can be understood whatever way one wants to. As a result of this, Agafy had a secret opposition to everything legal and generally accepted. He rejected all order and was repulsed by every constraint. This attitude brought him to the deepest and dirtiest amorality.[2]

So—heroic abolitionist or amoral anarchist? Perhaps both. It's hard to tell.

Everyone agrees that the young hierodeacon secretly wrote for the revolutionary journal *Kolokol* until he was found out in February 1860—caught, according to Honcharenko, in the act of mailing a manuscript to *Kolokol*'s editor. He was immediately arrested and shipped off to Russia.

What Honcharenko doesn't say, in any of his accounts, is that he was also accused of inappropriate behavior with a teenage boy. According to the aforementioned 1865 Russian Church report, in January 1860 (a month before then-Hierodeacon Agafy was caught mailing the *Kolokol* manuscript), a boy of about sixteen declared that the hierodeacon had, for a long time, "hounded him

claimed to have fought for liberty and evaded tsarist assassins. For example, see *Washington Post* (April 20, 1890), *Chicago Tribune* (December 4, 1892), *Los Angeles Times* (December 22, 1895), *New York Sun* (April 9, 1899), and *Oakland Tribune* (March 30, 1913).

2   The Russian Church report is undated but appears to have been written in 1865. It was found by Nicholas Chapman in the National Archives in London, along with the previously cited letter from St. Philaret of Moscow to the ober-procurator of the Holy Synod, dated February 26, 1865 (Julian Calendar). The 1865 report was translated by Matushka Marie Meyendorff and published at OrthodoxHistory on September 7, 2010 (https://orthodoxhistory.org/2010/09/07/agapius-honcharenko-in-defense-of-himself/).

with impolite words and at last made an improper proposition." Hierodeacon Agafy didn't deny this but instead claimed that he was actually trying to find out if the embassy church rector had been doing the same thing. It was all part of a trap, Agafy claimed—he wasn't actually propositioning the kid.

Agapius Honcharenko

Then—again, following the Russian Church account—Agafy went on the offensive against the embassy church rector, spreading written slander about him locally and also publishing it in *Kolokol*. Only at that point (says the Russian Church report) was the hierodeacon taken into custody.

Again, which was it—was he arrested for secretly writing revolutionary, anti-serfdom articles? Or for propositioning a teenager and publishing allegations against the rector? Maybe all of it.

So Agafy was arrested, and the tsarist government was taking him back to Russia, presumably to stand trial. But when the ship passed through Constantinople—everyone agrees on this—Agafy slipped out of his clerical attire and fled to London. Honcharenko's own version of the story is amazing: Chained in a Russian dungeon in Constantinople, he was rescued when a Polish Jew, peddling oranges in that city, smuggled Turkish clothing into the prison. From Honcharenko himself:

> I will never forget that day I took off my priest's robes, put on the Turkish costume, and passed out before the faces of the guardians of the prison, and escaped to London. Since then, by Muscovite tyrants, I have been stabbed, shot, drugged, assaulted with brass knuckles, and even clubbed as a dog. I am yet alive, and as a true Cossack, labor to free my people.

In London, he kept writing for *Kolokol* under the pen name Honcharenko. The Holy Synod of Russia defrocked him in August 1861. It wasn't long before the former hierodeacon returned to Greece and continued his vendetta against the Athens Embassy rector. For a time, he resided in a Greek monastery; this appears to be when his purported ordination to the priesthood took place. A modern scholar, Jars Balan, writes that Honcharenko was ordained a priest "in a Greek Orthodox Monastery at Mount Athos" on February 25, 1862.[3] Balan doesn't mention which monastery, and I've never seen hard evidence for an ordination.[4] (In 1866, the journal *Union Chretienne*, a Paris-based Orthodox journal published by the French convert priest Fr. Vladimir Guettee, claimed that Honcharenko's ordination was "irregular"—whatever that means.)

The Russian government kept trying to have him brought back to Russia, with no success. The Russian Ministry of Foreign Affairs explained that they couldn't forcibly return Honcharenko to Russia. According to Balan, at some point Honcharenko visited Jerusalem, "narrowly evading rearrest there by Russian authorities" with help from the holy city's Roman Catholic patriarch, and hid out in a Jesuit monastery in Lebanon. Then he went to Egypt, got a job as a salesman, was noticed by the Russians again, and, according to Balan, "In February 1863 an Ionian Greek in the hire of the Russian consul attacked Honcharenko with a knife as he was working in his kiosk at the Cairo railway station."

I can't confirm that this actually happened, and maybe it

---

3   Jars Balan, "California Dreaming: Agapius Honcharenko's Role in the Formation of the Pioneer Ukrainian-Canadian Intelligentsia," *Journal of Ukrainian Studies* 33–34 (2008–09), 61–92.

4   An 1865 newspaper account from London says that Honcharenko was "a monk of Mount Pentelicus, near Athens." *Guardian*, March 29, 1865, page 303. This appears to be the Monastery of Mendeli. Research should be done to determine Honcharenko's relationship with the monastery and any possible ordination that may have taken place.

didn't. But there's a somewhat ambiguous line in the 1865 Russian Church report saying that the Foreign Ministry "asked our Ambassador in Athens to look for ways to remove Agafy from Greece." What sort of ways? Ways involving a knife-wielding Ionian in Cairo? Or is that just a fish story from Honcharenko, told years after the fact?

The timeline is a little unclear, but this was all happening in the early 1860s. In September 1863, in the middle of the US Civil War, a fleet of Russian ships arrived in the New York harbor. The ships' chaplains were Orthodox priests, and although they didn't serve the Divine Liturgy in America, they did baptize some Greek children. On their return trip to Russia, one of the ships stopped in Athens, where they shared news of Orthodox people in America who needed a priest. It seems this is where Honcharenko got the idea to travel to America, far from the clutches of the Russian government.

For their part, the Russians—church and state—seem to have lost track of Honcharenko. That is, until reports started appearing about a high-profile Orthodox liturgy in New York City. By the mid-nineteenth century, several hundred Orthodox Christians, mostly Greeks and Serbs, were living in New Orleans, making it arguably the largest concentration of Orthodox Christians in the United States at that point. They were there because the city was one of America's major ports, which made it the sixth-largest city in the US in 1860. At about that time, Nicolas Benachi, who was a wealthy cotton merchant and slaveowner (as well as being the Greek consul in the city), decided it was time to establish a parish. But the Civil War put those plans on hold; instead, the Orthodox of New Orleans briefly tried to form a regiment to fight on the Confederate side.

The regiment turned out to be pretty ineffective. On June 1, 1861—just days after the unit's formation—the *Daily True Delta* (a local New Orleans newspaper) reported that there was trouble: the regiment, "for lack of other employment," devolved into factions. Some wanted to limit membership to "pure Greeks," while others wanted to let any Orthodox Christian join, regardless of nationality. "An embittered contest of factions led to personal collisions," the newspaper reported, "in which the sharp logic of steel was used by the opposing parties, as the only argument which would convince obstinate doubters on either side." One man wound up in the hospital, and two were arrested. A few days later, another member of the Greek regiment, Alexandro Philipuso, "was attacked and severely wounded with knives, by some persons [. . .] who from their language are supposed to have been Sicilians" (*Daily True Delta*, 6/12/1861). The regiment's end seems not to have come on the battlefield or even from infighting. On June 20, 1861, the *Daily True Delta* offered its final report on the unit: "There has been some trouble in the Greek company of volunteers, and five of them have been arrested on a charge of larceny, proffered, as we understand, by some of their own officers. This is bad for the Greeks."

New Orleans surrendered to the Union Army early on, in 1862, and it was an occupied city until the official end of the war on April 9, 1865.[5]

ooooo

JUST AS THE war was nearing its formal conclusion, word of Honcharenko's New York liturgy reached Consul Benachi and the Orthodox of New Orleans. Benachi immediately wrote to Honcharenko, asking him to come visit the city and baptize fourteen people. On March 26, 1865, the *New York Times* reported that Honcharenko would leave for New Orleans "in a few days," where he would "make a short stay," baptizing people and visiting the Orthodox of the city, which included a reported three

---

5   On the broader topic of Greeks who fought in the American Civil War, see Steve Frangos, "Greeks Served in Civil War," *The National Herald* (Aug. 25, 2005).

hundred "Sclavonians" (i.e., Slavs, in this case mostly people we'd now call Serbs and Montenegrins).

Upon arriving in New Orleans, Honcharenko wrote a letter to the city's Orthodox Christians. This letter appeared in the *New Orleans Times* on April 11:

Beloved Children of the Orthodox Oriental Church in New Orleans:
Jesus Christ, the head of the Church, is pleased not to leave the members of our branch of the Holy Apostolic Church to remain any longer without the enjoyment of their own ecclesiastical services.

The Divine Mind has sent my humility—His Evangelist—to this New World, to gather together the scattered sheep and invite them again in the privileges of the Church.

I therefore come that I may show you how to so walk in the church militant, and to receive the Holy Sacraments, that you may be the better prepared for the church triumphant.

After spending some time in the Northern States of this great Republic I have just arrived in your city. I intend to remain here only until the 22nd of April—through Passion and Easter weeks.

I earnestly recommend you to prepare yourselves by fasting and prayer for confession and holy communion—yourselves and your dear children.

The divine liturgy, according to the Orthodox Oriental Church, will be celebrated by divine permission on Saturday next, April 15th, at 10 1/2 A.M., in St. Paul's Protestant Episcopal Church, Camp street, corner of Gaiennie. Those desiring to attend will please call at my present residence, No. 7 St. Ann street, Jackson Square, where I may be found every morning, excepting on Saturday next, until 12 o'clock P.M.

Your affectionate brother in Christ and Missionary to America,
AGAPIUS HONCHARENKO
Priest of the Orthodox Oriental Church

Honcharenko is widely reported to have been the first pastor of the New Orleans parish, but really, he was only in New Orleans for a visit (see his above statement, "I intend to remain here only until the 22nd of April"), and he returned to New York soon thereafter.

Incidentally, with regard to St. Paul's Episcopal Church, the site of the first Orthodox liturgy in the American South: The church of Honcharenko's day was built in the mid-1850s, replacing an earlier structure. From 1862 to 1865, St. Paul's was closed, and the church was used to stable Union horses. The Civil War officially ended on April 9, 1865, and Honcharenko served liturgy on April 15. In other words, that Orthodox liturgy must have been one of the first services in the newly restored St. Paul's. Unfortunately, the structure no longer exists; it burned in a fire in 1891.

ooooo

UPON HIS RETURN to New York, Honcharenko found that he was no longer welcome: his past had caught up with him, and even the Episcopalians who had previously been so hospitable were now not interested in helping him.

According to his own testimony, for four months Honcharenko worked with a pickax in the streets of New York for twenty-five cents a day. He then got hired by the American Bible Society to translate the Bible into Slavonic. He began to advertise himself as a linguist, calling for pupils and claiming to teach Greek, Arabic, Romanian, Bulgarian, Slavonic, Russian, and Turkish. He would later assert that during this time, the Russian government made multiple attempts to assassinate him and succeeded in wounding him several times, but there's no evidence that this actually happened.

Honcharenko later claimed that one of his students was Eugene Schuyler, the American diplomat who later became ambassador to Russia. He also supposedly knew such famous figures as Horace Greeley, the New York newspaper editor, and William Seward, the US Secretary of State. In fact, Honcharenko claimed that he was "largely instrumental in securing the purchase of Alaska" from Russia by the United States. He boasted that he had been the first person to discover gold in Alaska and had started the Klondike Gold Rush in 1867. He told one reporter, "It cost me thirty-five cents to discover Alaska." When Seward supposedly offered him a large payment for his help, Honcharenko refused, saying, "All I want is to see Alaska an American State."

By the late 1860s, Honcharenko's story had descended even deeper into the bizarre. Despite being a celibate priest and apparently a tonsured monk, he married an Italian woman in Philadelphia. She was the daughter of a radical Italian immigrant. Years later, newspapers would report that she had come with Honcharenko from Russia after the tsar put a bounty on his head, but that's completely untrue.

Honcharenko and his wife moved to Alameda County in the San Francisco Bay Area. They bought a farm, which Honcharenko named Ukraina. It was an interesting place. Honcharenko supposedly introduced the Attica olive to California, and he experimented with breeding mushrooms and grapes. In fact, there's actually a grape variety named Honcharenko in his honor. He started a Russian-language revolutionary newspaper in 1868, supposedly with the help of Schuyler and Seward. He also published a Russian-English phrase book, marketed for Americans traveling to Alaska. Honcharenko's newspaper was discontinued in 1872, and he blamed the Russian ambassador. He would later resurrect the paper and supposedly sent copies to be secretly distributed in Russia. He founded an organization called the Decembrists, which he hoped would bring about a peaceful revolution in Russia. I don't know if there were any members. He also claimed that hit men hired by the Russian government had been sent to kill him in California on multiple occasions.

Honcharenko had turned into something of a spectacle. In 1872, a newspaper in Maine—on the opposite end of the continent—mentioned that Honcharenko had recently begun wearing a "spring suit of clothes made entirely from white bear skin." Every once in a while, some enterprising reporter would stumble upon Honcharenko and do a big story on the "Apostle of Liberty," the "Nihilist Priest," or whatever. In 1893 he made headlines by telling people that thousands of millionaire Siberian Jews were being exiled to America by the tsar.

The descriptions of Honcharenko match the surviving photos. One reporter, Will Clemens, visited Honcharenko in 1890. He wrote:

> Presently a little old man, slightly stoop shouldered, but vigorous and muscular, and quick in his movements, made his appearance, bearing a pail of milk warm from the udder. He was a singular looking man, and the visorless cap of an Arctic fox skin which he wore heightened the picturesque effect of his long, gray beard, his broad, high forehead furrowed deep with wrinkles of concentrated thought, and the twinkling, restless black eyes. . . . When Father Honcharenko afterward removed his cap it was observed that his hair was thin on top of his head and that he combed it back to cover the bald spot. Closer acquaintance revealed traits of character—a nervous enthusiasm, a keen sense of humor, a persistent purpose, and a lack of system.

The facts of Honcharenko's life gradually began to fade, replaced by ridiculous exaggerations. He had been a modest deacon at the Russian embassy in Athens, but by 1913 he was referred to as the former Russian ambassador to Greece. He claimed that Leo Tolstoy was his "spiritual child," because, according to Honcharenko, he had heard Tolstoy's confession once years before in

Egypt. He began to be known as Tolstoy's confessor, despite the fact that Tolstoy probably had no idea who he was.

Honcharenko had long since cut himself off from the Orthodox Church. Just months after his 1865 visit to New York, one newspaper reported that he had been excommunicated "for countenancing a church outside of the Apostolic succession." In response, said the paper, Honcharenko would become a Presbyterian.

A couple years later, a Boston paper called him "a swindler and a cheat" and reported that he had started a "Russo-Greek Methodist Episcopal Church" in San Francisco. The paper commented, "We hope there is no irreverence in the suggestion; but wouldn't it be well to have Trinity Chapel disinfected?"

The Orthodox weren't too thrilled with Honcharenko, either. In 1896 the *Russian Orthodox American Messenger*, the official newsletter of the Russian Church in America, ran a story on Honcharenko:

A certain runaway, monk Agapius Honcharenko, residing not far from the city of Alameda in California, on a farm of his own, which he has named "Ukraina," occasionally makes the local population aware of his existence by volunteering most preposterous items of information concerning Russia and the Russian Government. . . . At one time he was very busy intriguing against our Orthodox Mission in San Francisco, especially during the episcopate of Bishop Ioannes [John], and, now, at the close of his days, he apparently is at his old tricks again. Thus he recently stated in the "Examiner," that Russian agents are persecuting him, that his life is in danger, that a price is set on his head, and other absurdities. Persons unfamiliar with our country might believe him; therefore we think it necessary to declare that not a soul in Russia takes the least interest in Honcharenko, and that all that he tells about the persecution he suffers from Russian agents, is unmitigated nonsense—the driveling of a half crazy old man. Russia will always be glad to make a present of such specimens to anybody that wants them, so as to be rid of the bother of dealing with them at home.

The locals in the nearby town of Hayward weren't so harsh. They found the Honcharenkos to be pleasant people—quirky, yes, but also kind and hospitable. On New Year's Eve in 1909, the seventy-seven-year-old Honcharenko was gored by a cow, and a local doctor rushed to his aid. Hayward high school girls made day trips to visit the Honcharenkos. In 1912, the Honcharenkos were behind on their mortgage payments and nearly lost their ranch, but some charitable townsfolk pitched in and saved them. A couple years later, the Hayward community gave Honcharenko a surprise birthday party. When Mrs. Honcharenko died in 1915, numerous locals trekked out to the Honcharenko ranch for the burial service, which was conducted by a local Methodist clergyman.

After his wife's death, Honcharenko's health noticeably declined. He died a little over a year later, in 1916, at the age of eighty-three. Neighbors found his body, and a group of local ranchers conducted a simple funeral service. He was buried on his ranch, next to his wife.

Honcharenko hasn't been totally forgotten. In 1963 and 1970, a Ukrainian-American named Theodore Luciw published a pair of books about Honcharenko that portrayed him as a Ukrainian patriot and a champion of liberty. In 1999, through the efforts of Luciw and other Ukrainian-American activists, Honcharenko's Ukraina ranch was declared a registered landmark by the State of California. Hundreds of admirers, including a number of Ukrainian Orthodox and Catholic priests, converged on the ranch for the dedication. A joint memorial service was held for Honcharenko and his wife, and some called for the US Post Office to issue a commemorative stamp in Honcharenko's honor.

Earlier I quoted a recent description of Honcharenko which referred to him as a "prominent scholar, humanitarian, and early champion for human rights." That's actually a quotation from the plaque at Ukraina, placed there by the California Department of Parks and Recreation. Of course, you could just as easily refer to him as an apostate, a liar, and a fraud. But whatever your view on Agapius Honcharenko, you've got to admit one thing: he was anything but boring.

CHAPTER TWO

The First Orthodox Parishes in the United States

THE QUESTION, "WHAT was the first Orthodox parish in the United States?" is surprisingly difficult to answer.[1] A big part of the problem comes from the word "parish." What is a parish? When does a collection of Orthodox people become a parish? There's no canonical definition, and different American Orthodox jurisdictions today have their own standards for when a community becomes a parish. It's a matter of interpretation, and particularly in the early years of Orthodoxy in America, the lines were quite fuzzy.

Many sources claim that Holy Trinity, the Greek church in New Orleans, was the first parish in America (outside of Alaska). Nicolas Benachi, wealthy cotton merchant and the city's Greek consul, began efforts to build a church in 1860. This bore no immediate fruit, and the Civil War put everything on hold. In 1865, just as the war ended, Agapius Honcharenko appeared on the scene and spent Holy Week and Pascha in New Orleans. He's

---

1   To be clear: I am speaking about the first Orthodox parish in the states that were then part of the Union. Alaska, home to Orthodox parishes beginning in 1794, was part of the Russian Empire until 1867 and did not become a US state until 1959.

often reported to be the community's first priest, but this is inaccurate—he was only there for a visit.

It seems that, from 1864 to 1867, some sort of lay services were held in various locations, including on Benachi's property. In 1866, Benachi sold part of his land to the Orthodox community. The following year, a church was built, and in late 1867, the first priest arrived: Fr. Stephen Andreades, the first resident Orthodox priest in the contiguous United States.

Very little is known about Andreades, and most of what we know comes from a short homily he gave on his arrival. The homily was published in the March 15, 1868, issue of the *Alaska Herald* (vol. 1, issue 2), a periodical published by Honcharenko. Andreades gave his homily in Greek on Christmas Day, December 25, 1867/January 6, 1868.[2] He expressed joy at "the establishment of the first Orthodox Church in the New World," and he commended the faithful for building it: "You, coming here from so far away for trading business and for improving your fate, did not forget your motherland and your protectress Orthodox Church."

Andreades was not in America simply on a visit; he viewed his assignment to New Orleans as permanent:

Blessed and glorified [be] the name of God, who granted me to conduct a spiritual service in this new church, and I beg Him for help in my task. The permanent duty of my service in this church will be: to keep the commandments of God and to comply with church bylaws. To conscientiously perform the

---

2 In the nineteenth century, the gap between the Julian and Gregorian calendars was only twelve days, meaning that December 25 according to the Julian Calendar corresponded to January 6 on the Gregorian. In 1900, the gap expanded to thirteen days, giving us the January 7 Christmas that has become so familiar. The gap will become fourteen days in 2100, which will result in Julian Calendar Christmas falling on the Gregorian Calendar's January 8. This will undoubtedly cause no small amount of confusion.

holy mysteries, as the source of immortality, so as our life is not deprived of God's grace.

As it turned out, Andreades remained in New Orleans for about five years. By 1872, a new priest, Fr. Gregory Yiayias, was there, and Andreades vanishes from the historical record.

So when was Holy Trinity Church established? Was it in 1864, when lay services began to be held on the Benachi property? Or in 1865, when Honcharenko visited and served the first Divine Liturgy? Or in 1867, when the first resident priest arrived?

There is another contender for the title of first Orthodox parish in the United States—the community now known as Holy Trinity, the OCA cathedral in San Francisco. It's gone through many name changes over the years, but this San Francisco parish was established around the same time that the New Orleans community was organizing itself.

The Holy Trinity Cathedral website explains the parish history in this way:

> Holy Trinity Cathedral Parish traces its history to December 2, 1857, when the first Orthodox Society was founded in San Francisco. Ten years later, on September 2, 1867, it was incorporated as the Greek Russian Slavonian Orthodox Eastern Church and Benevolent Society. During these years, the Orthodox population of the Bay Area was spiritually and sacramentally served by chaplains from Russian Navy ships that frequented San Francisco Bay. During the Holy Week of 1868, an Orthodox Priest was sent to the City from Alaska to conduct the Paschal services here. That priest, Father Nicholas Kovrigin, became the first permanent Orthodox minister in San Francisco.

Again, there's the question: When did this parish begin? In 1857, when the first Orthodox benevolent society was founded? In 1867, when the society was incorporated and, late in the year, requested a priest and a church building? Or in 1868, when the first parish priest arrived?

It all depends on your premises—on how you define "parish." And it might depend on specific facts we don't necessarily have, such as what exactly that Orthodox Society in San Francisco was doing, as a practical matter, in the years 1857 to 1867. Were they holding regular services? Or was this more of a typical benevolent society, wherein individuals with a common background (say, being Orthodox) would contribute to the organization, which would then give aid to members in need?

One small bit of evidence to consider, in this case: At the General Convention of the Episcopal Church in 1862, an Episcopalian priest from San Francisco reported that "some" of the three to four hundred Orthodox people in San Francisco were "under his charge" (although not receiving communion) and "were about to build a church of their own and become organized into a parish." It's just one source, but this suggests that, at least in 1862, the Orthodox in San Francisco weren't yet a parish, although they were definitely moving in that direction.

In the end, I think the race between New Orleans and San Francisco for the title of first Orthodox parish in the United States is too close to call.

CHAPTER THREE

The First American Convert Priest

James Chrystal

JAMES CHRYSTAL WAS the first convert priest in American Orthodox history. Born in 1831, he was ordained a deacon in the Episcopal Church at twenty-eight and a priest shortly thereafter. In 1861, he published a book called *A History of the Modes of Christian Baptism*. In the preface, Chrystal himself described the book as "an apology for the belief of the early Church, that Christ enjoined triune immersion." Chrystal argued that sprinkling—the form of baptism practiced by both Roman Catholics and Anglicans/Episcopalians—was insufficient and contrary to Christ's teaching. The Orthodox Church, he concluded, had alone preserved the correct practice.

Naturally, Chrystal wanted to get one of these authentic baptisms for himself. So at the end of 1868 he traveled to Greece, where he sought out Archbishop Alexander of Syra, on the island of Tenos. Chrystal probably went to that particular hierarch because Archbishop Alexander was a fairly well-known figure among Anglicans: he had visited England and had a good relationship with the Anglican Church. Archbishop Alexander met with Chrystal and was impressed with his learning and his sincerity. A local Greek newspaper commented, "He has acquired such accuracy concerning the theoretical parts of theology, as few of the clergy and theologians among us possess."

After this brief examination, satisfied with Chrystal's Orthodoxy, the archbishop baptized him on the eve of Theophany, just after Vespers. Chrystal, being unmarried, had to obtain permission from the Holy Synod of Greece to be ordained. The Synod gave it, and within a few months Chrystal was ordained and then elevated to archimandrite.

So here we have a Greek precursor to the Russian story of Bjerring, which we'll cover in the next chapter: An intelligent visitor from America, desiring to be "correct," comes to an Orthodox country, impresses everyone with his knowledge, and is immediately received into the Church, ordained, elevated to a high rank, and sent home. These two incidents occurred within the span of about a year and a half.

The English Orthodox journal *Orthodox Catholic Review* noted that Chrystal

> had for six years studied the Orthodox faith, and was fully convinced that it was the only true Catholic religion. The neophyte recited the Creed both in Greek and English. He intends entering the ministry of the Church, and will in due time become Bishop in Alaska, lately ceded by Russia to the United States. He is anxious to become a lawful medium between the Reunionist party of the Anglo-American Church and the Orthodox Church; and the Greek ecclesiastical authorities hailed his scheme. He is now busy in translating the necessary service-books into English.

The Greek newspaper quoted earlier said, "We shall in a short time see formed there [in America] an Orthodox Church of many thousands, and the light of the East shining bright and clear even in that new world." It then exclaimed, "What glory then will it be for the Greek Church and for our nation, if by means of this her learned priest she should send out first the shining lamp of Orthodoxy."

Jonas King, a Protestant missionary in Greece, translated that Greek newspaper article for a Protestant journal in the United States, and in conclusion King commented sarcastically, "It may be well, perhaps, to give publicity to this novel transaction, so that the people beyond the wide Atlantic may be prepared to see the light, which, it is supposed, will soon break in upon them from the East."[1]

No such light would come from the East, at least not as a result of Chrystal's conversion. James Chrystal had his own interpretation of Christianity. Father David Abramtsov explains, "The erratic Chrystal soon repudiated his ties with the Orthodox Church and, upon his return to America, formed his own Baptist-type sect." Insofar as the Orthodox Church agreed with him—namely, in regard to baptism—he wanted to be a part of it. But that fact was soon superseded by another. Just a year later, we find the following report: "Mr. Christal [sic] [. . .] could not subscribe to the articles of the Seventh Synod of the Greek church, relating to the images and creature worship."[2]

So James Chrystal could not accept the veneration of icons. He was hardly alone among Protestants in the conviction that it was wrong. What escapes me is how he could have failed to notice the icons covering the walls of the cathedral in which he was baptized and ordained. Did he simply not look up? Was he—clearly a learned man, who had studied Orthodoxy for half a dozen years—unaware of the Seventh Ecumenical Council or the Protestant objections to icons? Or did his views toward icons change in a matter of months?

---

1 *New York Evangelist* (April 8, 1869), 2.
2 David F. Abramtsov, "The Western Rite and the Eastern Church: Dr. J. J. Overbeck and His Scheme for the Re-Establishment of the Orthodox Church in the West," University of Pittsburgh MA thesis (1961), 21, 27.

What's more likely is that Chrystal, like so many Episcopalians, was focused on the question of "validity." He likely viewed the Orthodox as having valid apostolic succession and sacraments—hence, his desire for a properly performed baptism. But while the Church may have been "valid" in his eyes, he probably still viewed her as heretical, perhaps even as he was accepting Orthodox baptism and ordination.

In any event, it took the Orthodox some time to figure out that Chrystal had left the Church. In 1870, there were various reports that the Russian government planned to assign a bishop to New York and had even offered the job to Chrystal. He reportedly declined, citing his opposition to icons. Only a few months later, Fr. Nicholas Bjerring opened the doors of Holy Trinity Chapel in New York City (about which, see chapter 4).

As for Chrystal, he initially rejoined the Episcopal Church, but it wasn't long before he was on the move again. In his own words, he left the Episcopal Church "on account of unchecked and unpunished idolatry and service of creatures in it contrary to the faith of its reformers of blessed memory." He continued his opposition to icons for the rest of his life. In a February 12, 1899, letter to the *New York Times*, Chrystal argued against the practice of kissing the Bible. He went on to publish a series of books on the Third Ecumenical Council, which he claimed supported his iconoclastic position. His argument, which he also made in his letter to the *Times*, was basically that, because the Council condemned the division of Christ into two Persons, divine and human, and thus condemned the worship of Christ's humanity alone (rather than the single divine-human Person of Christ), it implicitly forbade the veneration of any and all matter. Of this book series, titled The Third World Council, Chrystal dedicated the second volume to the "Greek race" and the third to the "Russian people," in both cases exhorting them to reject the Seventh Ecumenical Council and return, in his words, to true orthodoxy.

James Chrystal died in 1908 in Jersey City, New Jersey, at the age of seventy-seven. His death appears to have gone unnoticed by the Orthodox in America, who by that point were becoming quite numerous.

CHAPTER FOUR

The Second American Convert Priest

Nicholas Bjerring

NICHOLAS BJERRING WAS one of the first Orthodox priests in American history. He was born in Denmark in 1831, the son of a local city official. He studied philosophy and theology at the University of Breslau and then became a missionary to Lapland. In 1868, he immigrated to America and became an instructor at a Roman Catholic school in Baltimore.

Two years later, the Roman Catholic Church declared papal infallibility to be a dogma of the faith. Bjerring couldn't accept this. He wrote a letter to Pope Pius IX objecting to the doctrine. This letter was published in various newspapers and magazines.

"It is impossible," wrote Bjerring, "that the duty of being a good Christian involves the necessity to cease being a citizen, to abstain from all progress, to shut out all light, and to go back, groping in the dark, to the middle ages, with all their concomitant evils and pernicious abuses." He continued,

Holy Father, in my name and in that of many thousands of laymen, who are laboring under the same impressions as myself, I protest against the doctrines which you seem determined to promulgate, and which openly conflict with all divine and human laws. I protest against the fatal contest which you have originated between Church and society. I protest against the sacrilegious sentence you have pronounced against all progress, and against every department of science. I protest against the principle of Papal infallibility, which you aim to establish as a dogma, in papal contradiction with the text of the Gospel and with ecclesiastical traditions.

Having given up on Roman Catholicism, Bjerring wondered what to do next. He said to the pope:

In the face of such a serious and irretrievable wrong, what consolation remains then for the souls of the faithful and believing? Must they, in abandoning that Church of Rome, to which their convictions urge them no longer to belong, embark with rationalism as their only compassion on the troubled waters of Protestantism, at the risk of perishing among the breakers of pantheism?

Bjerring then answered his own question. "I have found the true Catholic and Apostolic Church. It is the Orthodox Church of the East. . . . That Church has maintained, uncontaminated, the holy ark of the evangelical doctrines." Finally, he said, "The Orthodox Church will deign, I trust to extend to me her maternal arms."

Then he wrote another letter, this time to the Holy Synod of Russia, asking to join the Orthodox Church. The Holy Synod wrote back and asked Bjerring to come to St. Petersburg. He did, and what happened next never ceases to amaze me: he was not only received into the Church but was immediately ordained an Orthodox priest. He served his first liturgy in German, since he didn't know Church Slavonic. And then, very soon after this, he was elevated to archpriest and sent to New York to found a mission! As they say, the chrism wasn't even dry yet.

Bjerring founded Holy Trinity Chapel in New York City in

October of 1870. The chapel was located on the parlor floor of his home at 651 Second Avenue. It was a modest place, though the *New York Times* (5/15/1871) called it a "tasty little Greek chapel." The iconostasis in the chapel had only Royal Doors—it didn't have deacon's doors—so Bjerring would have to do the Little and Great Entrances directly from the Royal Doors, which must have been awkward. For years, there would be talk of building a proper Orthodox temple in New York, but it would be decades before that dream became a reality. The Orthodox community in the city was small, numbering around a hundred.

One of the odd things about Bjerring—a brand-new convert, who became Orthodox due to ideological opposition to Roman Catholicism—is that he expressly discouraged conversions. In 1871, less than a year after his ordination, the *New York Times* (5/15/1871) wrote, "It is Father Bjerring's wish that it be generally known that the Greek Chapel is a private chapel of the Russian and Greek Legations, and is not open for public worship." Bjerring welcomed "orderly and respectable" ladies and gentlemen to visit if they were curious to see what the Orthodox Church looked like, but he was not interested in evangelism.

This attitude stemmed partly from a view, held by many at the time, that the Orthodox and Anglican/Episcopal Churches would soon unite, at which point, presumably, the Episcopal Church in the United States would become the Orthodox Church in the United States. So there was little point in converting Americans to Orthodoxy. One article in 1870 said,

> It must not be supposed . . . that Father Bjerring contemplates introducing a fresh element of discord into the religious world of America. For a long time the union of the Greek and Episcopal Churches has been advocated by many members of both and the good Father hoped that the opening of a Greek church in New York may do much towards consummating this movement.

Bjerring saw himself as a sort of religious ambassador to America, serving the Russian and Greek embassies, ministering to the very small Orthodox flock in New York, and engaging in what we would today consider to be "ecumenical relations." He was an ecclesiastical ambassador, not a missionary.

One of Bjerring's main tasks was publishing. He couldn't read Russian or Church Slavonic, but he did translate some Orthodox texts from German into English. He started a periodical, *Oriental Church Magazine*, in which translations and other articles were published. The magazine's subtitle was "Devoted to Religion, Science, Literature, and Art." According to Fr. Oliver Herbel, Bjerring saw the journal's purpose as twofold. First of all, it was supposed to educate non-Orthodox people about anything and everything related to Orthodoxy. Bjerring was particularly interested in "progress," that is, Orthodoxy's engagement with society and its moral development. He also wanted to talk about traditionally Orthodox cultures, such as Russian culture. The other purpose of the *Oriental Church Magazine* was ecumenical—to promote relations between the Orthodox and other Christian bodies.

One of the big moments in the early years of Bjerring's Orthodox career was the 1871–72 visit of the Russian Grand Duke Alexei to America. On his visit, the grand duke was a huge celebrity. He was received as an honored dignitary in every city he visited, and famous Americans were eager to meet him. President Ulysses S. Grant

Bjerring's chapel with Grand Duke Alexei

and most of his cabinet were there to meet the grand duke in Washington. Alexei went on a widely reported buffalo hunt with Buffalo Bill Cody; he went underneath the Niagara Falls; he attended Mardi Gras in New Orleans (and met with Orthodox representatives in the city, about which more later). And also, in November of 1871, the grand duke visited Bjerring's little chapel in New York City, which of course was the only Russian Orthodox place of worship east of California at the time.

The grand duke's visit was a very big deal. Bjerring had the chapel renovated for the occasion, and suddenly, he had to deal with a crush of visitors trying to catch a glimpse of the grand duke. Most of those unwanted visitors were young American girls who were crazy about this handsome young Russian prince. According to one account, "The house of the priest of the Greek Church, has been besieged by the sex, we are told, begging the privilege of attending service in the chapel (which would not hold a tithe of them) that they might get a single glimpse of his Royal Highness."[1]

The visit went well; a lot of dignitaries were in attendance, and Bjerring gave a little speech in which he said that God had granted Russia the divine mission of uniting all Orthodox Christians.

Bjerring wasn't focused only on being a priest; he was fairly active in New York society. He was a member of the American Geographical Society and later (after leaving Orthodoxy) he joined a Masonic lodge. He was very public about his political views. For a time he was vice president of the German Republican Central Committee. When he switched allegiance from the Republican to the Democratic Party in 1892, the news made it into the *New York Times*.

---

1   *Christian Union* 4:22 (November 29, 1871), 345. For much more on the Grand Duke's visit, see Lee A. Farrow, *Alexis in America: A Russian Grand Duke's Tour 1871–1872* (LSU Press, 2014).

Bjerring was a big believer in the "betterment of humanity," what's been called the "social gospel." He tried to help new immigrants and the poor. In 1881, he cofounded a Russian Benevolent Society, which helped needy Russians get money, find work, or receive help when they were sick. According to Fr. Oliver Herbel, Bjerring "maintained a dogmatic commitment to an understanding of Christianity that necessitated involvement in social ministry."[2] This was the common thread in Bjerring's life, throughout all his religious changes.

As an Orthodox priest, Bjerring had a lot of issues. In 1879, Bishop Nestor, who was based in San Francisco, paid a visit to the New York chapel, and after that visit, he sent a report back to Russia. It was bad. The bishop said that Bjerring was "completely ignorant of Slavic," and that he "pronounced and spoke so badly, that it was understood only because the content of the Liturgy is known by everyone. [. . .] Fr. Bjerring did not have the courage to read the Gospel in Slavic, and read it in English, but here too words 'Jesus Christ' he pronounced in Slavic, not in English, therefore it became a mixture of Slavic and English, which produced an unpleasant impression on the Russians and on others, Greeks and English, who were present. In addition, Fr. Bjerring has bad pronunciation because he is of a non-English heritage, pronouncing English with an unpleasant accent."[3]

Bishop Nestor went on to talk about various errors Bjerring made while serving the liturgy—mistakes that a properly trained priest simply would not make. Of course, Bjerring wasn't a properly trained priest. Bishop Nestor said that "in spite of years of

---

2   D. Oliver Herbel, "A Catholic, Presbyterian, and Orthodox Journey: The Changing Church Affiliation and Enduring Social Vision of Nicholas Bjerring," *Zeitschrift für Neuere Theologiegeschichte (Journal for the History of Modern Theology)* 14:1 (June 2007), 49–80.

3   Bishop Nestor's letter is published in George Soldatow, trans., *The Right Reverend Nestor, Bishop of the Aleutians and Alaska 1879–1882: correspondence, reports, diary* (AARDM Press, 1993), 33–36.

service in the Church, Fr. Bjerring showed himself completely inexperienced." He also didn't know many services. He knew how to serve the Liturgy of St. John Chrysostom, and also Great Vespers, but on Great and Holy Friday, which is the one day of the year when you're not allowed to serve the Divine Liturgy, Bjerring would still serve the Liturgy, because he didn't know the services of Holy Week.

Bjerring's own flock had grown tired of him. He couldn't speak their language, he didn't know the services, and they asked that he be transferred somewhere else. But, as Bishop Nestor asked, where could you send him? In the end, the bishop suggested that Bjerring be transferred to St. Petersburg, Russia, where he could be an assistant priest at some large parish.

In 1883, the Russian government, which funded Bjerring's ministry, decided to close the New York chapel. Bjerring was offered a very nice teaching position back in St. Petersburg, but he declined and decided instead to leave the Orthodox Church and become a Presbyterian minister. It was an unfortunate end to an ill-conceived ministry. Really, Bjerring never had any business becoming an Orthodox priest—at least, not until he'd been an Orthodox layman for a while and received proper training and education.

As a Presbyterian, Bjerring continued his social action work. He stayed in New York, where his parish consisted of German immigrants. I have to think that Bjerring, who spoke German, must have been more comfortable among Germans than among Russians. He did relief work with immigrants who lived in New York's tenement houses, continuing to live out that social gospel.

Not long after leaving the Orthodox Church, Bjerring published a book of Orthodox church services in English. In the introduction, he talked about how ignorant most Russians were—he said they needed a "moral influence"—and he hoped for the day when the Orthodox would accept the Bible as the "only source of salvation." Further on, he would lament that the Orthodox had condemned the seventeenth-century Ecumenical Patriarch Cyril Lucaris, who was believed to hold a Calvinist theology. Bjerring thought it was a tragedy that this "tendency to Protestantism had been conquered," as he put it, and that "together with it the better scientific and literary life, which Cyril had begun, has ceased to exist."[4] So in Bjerring's mind, Orthodoxy, in condemning Protestant theology and not adhering to the doctrine of sola scriptura, was essentially cutting itself off from life.

Remarkably, at the very end of Bjerring's life, he made yet another change in religious affiliation, coming full circle back to the Roman Catholic Church. As a married man, he couldn't be a priest, so he was received as a layman. He ended up arguing for exactly that thing that he had once argued against—the infallibility of the pope. He said, "The infallibility of the pope, when he speaks ex cathedra, has become dear to me in all its depth, in its whole significance, and in its absolute necessity." He went on to say that the Roman Catholic Church is "the living current through which God's grace flows into human life."[5]

At this point, it was 1899—Bjerring was nearly seventy years old. And it would be his last conversion—he died on September 10, 1900. As Herbel writes, "throughout his journey from Roman Catholicism to Orthodoxy to Presbyterianism and to Roman Catholicism again, Bjerring held firmly to the conviction, however imperfectly discerned, that where the One, Holy, Catholic, and Apostolic Church exists, there the advancement of humanity and social ministries exist." Unfortunately, this view may have influenced Bjerring to jump ship every time he was disappointed with his religious superiors.

---

4   Nicholas Bjerring, *The Offices of the Oriental Church with an Historical Introduction* (Anson D.F. Randolph & Co., 1884).

5   Quoted in Herbel, 73.

Looking back at his Orthodox career, some have tried to overlook Bjerring's abandonment of Orthodoxy and view him as someone almost like St. Innocent, the champion of American Orthodoxy. In reality, though, Bjerring was a tragic, conflicted man, a religious chameleon who unfortunately was received and ordained into the Orthodox Church without the necessary preparation.

CHAPTER FIVE

The Strange Tale of the Bulgarian Monk

Father Experidon

His appearance, dressed in a coarse black cassock, red Turkish fez, with tassel and shoes, without stockings, long hair and oriental appearance, caused him to be much remarked on the streets. He says he came from China to San Francisco, and has traveled through the South preaching, where he was often taken for a ku-klux, though he was never so much annoyed in any part of the world as by the ill-mannered boys in Baltimore, who followed him on the street, calling him "Dom Pedro."

—*Baltimore Sun*, May 22, 1876

IN APRIL OF 1875, almost a full decade after the end of the Civil War, a strange man appeared in the American South. He claimed to be a Bulgarian monk from Jerusalem, and he was touring the United States, giving lectures. He had previously been a missionary to China—so he said—and had then traveled across the Pacific Ocean to San Francisco. He spoke in Vicksburg, Mississippi, where one newspaper commented, "There is undoubtedly room for another church in the South, and the Greeks might as well occupy it." Two weeks later, he was in Georgia, where he told an audience that he had met a couple of old Confederate generals in Egypt, where they were serving under the Egyptian khedive. The next year, also in Georgia, this man—going by the name Rev. A. N. Experidon—lectured about the Holy Land. "His appearance created quite a sensation in Covington," wrote a reporter. "Some negroes took him for King Rex, and thought he had come to re-establish slavery; others took him for a fool-killer. . . . He occasionally quoted Mark Twain, and it is the opinion of your reporter that it is from this history, [that] he obtained most of his information."[1]

The writer here is referring to Mark Twain's book *Innocents Abroad*, in which Twain talks about his visit to the Holy Land. Years later, Fr. Experidon said that he was "like Mark Twain, 'An Innocent Abroad.'"[2] And later still, he began to claim that he had actually been Twain's tour guide in Jerusalem.

Mark Twain wasn't the only famous person Fr. Experidon claimed to have known. He told people that he had traveled through Utah and met Brigham Young, the Mormon leader. When they were introduced, Brigham Young reportedly said, "What kind of an Injun are you?" Fr. Experidon attempted to convert Brigham to Orthodoxy and convince him to give up polygamy, but Brigham wasn't interested.[3]

On travels that took him all over the United States, Fr. Experidon was viewed as a sensational, almost comical figure. Not everyone liked him. One reporter mocked him in this way:

You have seen and heard the musical talent of Italy upon your streets, you have witnessed the wonderful feats of the Japanese, and the dexterity of the Chinese juggler, and heard the red man whoop and observed his green corn dance in your operas, but when this wonderful man makes his appearance upon your

---

1   H.H.P., "A Bulgarian Priest in Town," *Atlanta Constitution*, Jan 8, 1876, 1.
2   "A Bulgarian Monk in Nebraska," *St. Louis Daily Globe-Democrat*, May 24, 1882, 11 (originally published in the *Omaha Bee*).
3   *Baltimore Sun*, May 22, 1876.

streets, you need not be surprised if children have recourse to the ringing of bells, beating of brazen instruments, and that your street loafers will at once begin to speak in unknown tongues, as a salutatory introduction to this eighth wonder of the world.[4]

In West Virginia, people thought Fr. Experidon was a fraud and chased him out of the state. In Arkansas, people were more amused than anything. Here's a story from 1882:

> A queer specimen of the genus homo has been wandering aimlessly about our streets for several days past, clad in a long flowing black robe, wearing a small red skull cap, and armed with an iron rod about thirty inches long. In answer to inquiries he says he is Christ No. 2, come here to save, to heal and to perform miracles. One of the latter, he said, he would do yesterday afternoon at 3 o'clock. At this time he would walk across the raging Arkansas as Christ before him had walked across the waters of Galilee. About two hundred of the curious assembled to see the performance, but as might have been expected, were sorely disappointed. The crank was wanting.

Yet the same reporter continued, "Persons who have conversed with him describe [him] as being quite intelligent, a fine linguist and a great traveler, but withal somewhat cranky."[5] Father Experidon's linguistic ability was, by all accounts, prodigious. "He speaks now thirty-two languages and dialects," reported the *San Jose Daily Evening News* on March 28, 1889, "and if he has the same command of the others as he exhibits in English he may be said to be fluent in all." Fr. Experidon claimed to have studied at Oxford University and afterwards in Paris, St. Petersburg, Berlin, and Constantinople. He said that, before becoming a monk, he had been an attorney. By his own account, he was born sometime

---

4   *Atlanta Constitution*, Jan 8, 1876.
5   "Fort Smith Notes," *Daily Arkansas Gazette*, Feb 26, 1882.

around 1829 and began to travel and preach when he was about thirty. That would put him in his middle forties when he came to America.

He somehow became acquainted with politicians from all over the United States. The man who introduced him to Brigham Young was George Woods, former governor of Oregon and then governor of the Utah Territory. Father Experidon took sides in the various American political debates of the time. He told the *Milwaukee Journal* (7/8/1885) that "the people of northwestern Wisconsin were the profanest and most sacrilegious that he has yet encountered in his circuit of the world, and that Congressman Price was a good representative of them." In 1884 he supported James G. Blaine's presidential campaign. That same year, a former Kansas governor named John St. John had run for president on the Prohibition Party ticket. The next year, in 1885, Governor St. John was speaking in favor of prohibition in Wisconsin. Father Experidon happened to be in the crowd. The *Milwaukee Sentinel* (7/7/1885) reported, "The Bulgarian monk, who had spent some time in Kansas, was invited to the platform to tell what he knew of prohibition there. He told St. John he was a fraud, and that there was as much whisky drank there as ever."

He may have disliked Governor St. John, but Fr. Experidon got along with other politicians. In Texas, Governor Ross actually gave him a pet dog as a gift. The dog would be Fr. Experidon's constant companion. Here's the first mention of the dog, in 1881:

> Rev. A.N. Experidon, of Bulgaria, a monk of the Greek Church, has been for several days encamped in the limits of our town. He is a rare bird. He seldom indulges in the luxury of a bath. . . . He sleeps in his small tent with his dog and his gun as his only companions, and does his own cooking. He speaks more languages than you can number on the fingers of your two hands.[6]

---

6   "State News," *News and Observer* (Raleigh, NC), Mar 26, 1881, 1

Here's another fantastic description, with the dog playing a prominent role:

> His costume is a cross between the latest style of "Mother Hubbard" and a baptismal robe, while his unshorn locks are partially covered by a red flannel cap. His only companion is a bay dog with a hungry look and so poor he would not cast a shadow unless standing sideways with a bone in his mouth. The poor dog eats and sleeps with the Monk, and yet seems happy. That the Monk is intelligent cannot be denied, but when you think that "cleanliness is next to Godliness" you are impressed with the thought that he is way out of rifle shot of that characteristic.[7]

Father Experidon and his dog lived a rugged life. This is from the *Omaha Bee* in 1882:

> Experidon, in accordance with the vows of his order, never sleeps in a house unless he is sick, but carries about with him a small "dog tent," a kettle and frying pan, and is an exemplification of the motto, "Every man his own boarding-house." Although rather thinly clad, wearing only the calico gown described, winter and summer, he sleeps on the ground, does his own cooking, and enjoys life to its fullest extent. His only companion is a fine dog. He had seventeen, but on account of the expense of transportation for them, sent all but one to a friend in Boston to keep until his return."[8]

Speaking of transportation, Fr. Experidon apparently visited every state in the Union. From local newspapers, I've verified his presence in about half of the states and territories of his day, and I'm inclined to believe him when he claims to have set foot in the rest. Here is one description of his travels, from the

---

(originally published in the *Fayetteville Examiner*).

7   "The Bulgarian Monk," *Wisconsin State Journal*, Jul 11, 1885.

8   Quoted in the *St. Louis Daily Globe-Democrat*, May 24, 1882.

August 28, 1885, edition of the *Milwaukee Sentinel*:

> The 18th of the present month he finished his tour of the United States, having visited every county and spoken in every state capital of the United States. He will make a pilgrimage through South America similar to the one made in this country and from his observations will furnish material for an encyclopaedia, which is being edited by the Greek Church. . . . During his thirteen years' travels in this country his expenses have been $9,863, which have been more than paid by his lecture revenues.

The total of $9,863 in 1885 works out to roughly $330,000 in today's money. In other words, Fr. Experidon was spending the equivalent of $25,000 per year in travel expenses.

The above quotation mentioned an encyclopedia. It seems that Fr. Experidon's purpose in coming to America was to write a book about "the moral and social condition of the United States." He never bothered to finish his research and complete the book. He just stayed in America, traveling from state to state camping, fishing, and giving speeches. People referred to him as "the Bulgarian Monk," and he eventually adopted this as his stage name. When he would go to a new town, there would inevitably be some newspaper article announcing that the Bulgarian Monk would "hold forth" at some opera house or street corner at a certain time.

Until the mid-1880s, he talked mainly about the Holy Land and his own travels. But about 1885 or so, he shifted from lecturer to preacher. His new speeches were entitled, "To Convert All American Preachers, Priests, and Christians." It's not clear what he was trying to convert them to. I don't think it was Orthodoxy. The *San Francisco Evening Bulletin* (10/20/1888) actually claimed that he was preaching a new religion and calling for the abolishment of all churches. I don't think it was that extreme, though. The *San Jose Evening News* (3/28/1889) said that Experidon "preaches the Gospel of Christ, love and charity, regardless of any sect, and recognizing no arbitrary teachings, no traditions, and no canonical laws." It continued, "the monk seems to delight in demonstrating from the Bible the inconsistency of the teachings of each of the Christian sects. He quotes Timothy to prove that women are forbidden to preach until after they are 60 years of age, and offers it as an indication of the absurdity of any divine inspiration being received by the Salvation Army or the Methodist female revivalist."

Whereas in years past he had hit the southern and eastern parts of the United States, by the late 1880s Fr. Experidon was spending most of his time in the West, in places like Idaho, Oregon, and Northern California. The people of Sonoma, California, did not want him around; they threw wads of paper at him along with small shot (the little lead bullets used in shotguns). He was once preaching while standing on a chair, and someone pulled the chair out from under him. But that didn't deter the Bulgarian Monk from speaking. The next day, he preached without any trouble, thanks to a double-barreled shotgun he kept under his arm.

As you can see, he was getting more radical in his approach. One Idaho newspaper warned its readers that the Bulgarian Monk was an anarchist. An Episcopal bishop in Idaho by the name of Ethelbert Talbot happened to run into the Bulgarian Monk in the late 1880s. He said he tried to ask him about his life, but the Bulgarian Monk "repelled all attempts to draw him into conversation, nor would he accept hospitality or kindness from any one." "His movements," said Talbot, "were shrouded in mystery."[9] He became less an object of amusement than of

---

9   Ethelbert Talbot, *My People of the Plains* (New York: Harper & Bros., 1906), 56–57. Years later, Talbot would clash with his former classmate, the Episcopal priest Ingram Irvine, which eventually led to Irvine's high-profile conversion to Orthodoxy (discussed in detail in another chapter). Even later still, Talbot was elected presiding bishop of the Episcopal Church, a position he held from 1924–26.

mystery and even fear. His identity as Fr. Experidon was gone, replaced entirely with the strange Bulgarian Monk. Mothers in Idaho would warn their children, "You'd better behave; don't make me get the Bulgarian Monk!"

And then one day, he was gone. He disappeared sometime around 1890 or 1891. Ethelbert Talbot, the Episcopal bishop, said he didn't know what happened to him. But the people of Bayhorse, Idaho (which is now a ghost town), began to develop their own theories. Reports began to circulate that the Bulgarian Monk had fallen into the Salmon River and drowned. Some people even said that pieces of his clothing had been found on the riverbank.

But then more stories began to come out. As the years passed, there were reports in Bayhorse of a shadowy figure in black robes pacing along the river bank and chasing any children who came near him. He was, they said, the ghost of the Bulgarian Monk, and he was haunting little towns in the middle of Idaho.

And that is how Rev. A. N. Experidon has been memorialized to this day. The book *Historic Haunted America* has a whole chapter about the Bulgarian Monk. Other haunted-house and ghost-story books and websites talk about him as well. They don't know anything about his life, his travels, or anything else. As far as the ghost stories are concerned, he was a weird character in Idaho, not a well-traveled monk from Jerusalem. But it's clear, if you read the stories, that they're talking about the same person.

We may assume Fr. Experidon did not actually become a ghost, and he is not haunting places in Idaho. But how did this ghost story develop? I have a theory. We know from Bishop Ethelbert Talbot that parents would frighten their children with stories about the Bulgarian Monk. And I think we can be pretty confident that he did drown, or die of some similar accident, sometime in the early 1890s. It would be perfectly natural for these kids who had been afraid of the Bulgarian Monk to make up a campfire tale about his becoming a ghost and haunting their town. They would probably tell their younger siblings about this, and gradually, the details of Fr. Experidon's life would fade, and the caricature of the Bulgarian Monk's ghost would be all that would remain.

CHAPTER SIX

The Mysterious Death of Fr. Paul Kedrolivansky

FATHER PAUL KEDROLIVANSKY died on the evening of June 18, 1878, in the prison hospital in San Francisco, the victim of an apparent blow to the head.

Since December 1870, Kedrolivansky had been the dean of St. Alexander Nevsky Cathedral in San Francisco. In what must have been an awkward arrangement, his predecessor, Fr. Nicholas Kovrigin, became his assistant. Years later, a certain V. K. (possibly Deacon Basil—or Vasily—Kashevarov) said of Kedrolivansky,

> Father Archpriest was continually occupied with keeping peace and quiet in the community with which he was involved. He was straight forward and even tempered, honest and not malicious. He was a benefactor to those in need, a true friend to his friends, reliable and trustworthy in his relations towards those with whom he served in particular and to all in general.[1]

---

1   Fr. Sebastian Dabovich, "The Orthodox Church in California," *Russian Orthodox American Messenger* 15 (April 1–13, 1898), 455–460 and 16 (April 15–27, 1898), 479–482.

This near-saintly portrait of Kedrolivansky stands in contrast to the general picture painted of him during his lifetime. On May 27, 1877, the ober-procurator of the Holy Synod wrote this in an imperial edict to the Alaska Spiritual Consistory:

> A member of the Spiritual Consistory in San Francisco and district dean, Archpriest Paul Kedrolivansky, can not be left in America any further since he has not cleared himself from the accusation of transporting contraband, brought upon him by the Alaskan Trade Company, as a result of which our Ambassador in Washington and our Consul in San Francisco declare it extremely necessary to remove him from America; and now he is being accused of incorrectly reporting the expenditure of sums allocated for the diocese.

Incidentally, if Kedrolivansky was recalled to Russia in May 1877, why was he still in San Francisco in June 1878?

In regard to his death: On the night of June 17—a Monday—Kedrolivansky went drinking with his "roommate," a fellow named Mindeleff, at the Tivoli Garden saloon. (Kedrolivansky was married and had a number of children, so it's not clear why he had a roommate. Mindeleff could have been a boarder, I suppose, though later the claim surfaced that Kedrolivansky and his wife were separated. Years later, the *San Francisco Examiner* referred to Mindeleff and said, "he was a boarder of his," but I'm not sure who they mean when they say "he" and "his." Was Mindeleff a boarder of Kedrolivansky, or the other way around?)

At any rate, around ten o'clock at night, Kedrolivansky was seen at Rosenthal's tobacco shop, where he showed off a fancy-looking document and boasted that Fr. Nicholas Kovrigin would pay ten thousand dollars to get hold of it. Apparently the document contained some incriminating evidence against Kovrigin, and Kedrolivansky was going to send it to the authorities in Russia. It would, so the story goes, spell ruin for Kovrigin's career.

Kedrolivansky—who had a problem with alcohol—then moved on to another saloon, this one belonging to Joseph Blumberg. All these saloons and shops were in the same general vicinity, in what is today San Francisco's financial district. He left the Blumberg establishment around a quarter to one in the morning. He was never seen conscious again.

Sometime between 12:45 and 2:00 AM, Kedrolivansky received a sharp blow to the head.

Fr. Paul Kedrolivansky (L) in 1868. The bishop in the center is Bp. Paul Popov.

A little before two in the morning, Special Officer Stivers found Kedrolivansky unconscious outside Eggers' saloon at the corner of California and Spring streets. Stivers went off to get Kedrolivansky some black coffee in an effort to rouse him. The offices of the *San Francisco Chronicle* were located at this same intersection. While Stivers was away, a *Chronicle* reporter noticed Kedrolivansky on the ground and notified two other policemen, Brinkley and Hill, who deposited the priest in a hack and sent him to the city jail. He was wearing a hat; nobody noticed the head wound.

This wasn't the first time that Kedrolivansky had been arrested for public drunkenness, and he was considered a "respectable drunk." After being booked and searched, he was handed over to a "trusty" and locked in a cell. These trusties were actually prisoners themselves, serving out their sentences, and they were given various responsibilities in the prison. Around four thirty or five in the morning, Kedrolivansky was dragged out of his cell so that it could be cleaned. He was then returned; the whole time, he remained unconscious. At eight or nine AM—the reports conflict on this point—his assigned trusty figured that something must be wrong; drunk men don't remain unconscious that long. So he called the hospital steward, who was just another trusty (and, as the *Chronicle* said, "knows as much about illness as the man in the moon"). The steward did feel Kedrolivansky's head and noticed a "dent" in it, but he thought nothing of it and diagnosed him with mere intoxication.

At ten o'clock, the police surgeon visited the hospital. He left at noon; nobody told him about Kedrolivansky. Just after this, there was a shift change, and a new prison keeper assumed duty. He was apparently a bit more perceptive than his predecessor, and he took Kedrolivansky to the prison hospital and called for the surgeon to return. The surgeon, a Dr. Stivers (no apparent relation to Special Officer Stivers), bled Kedrolivansky, but it was too late. He never regained consciousness, and around seven thirty in the evening, he was pronounced dead.

Four days later, a coroner's jury concluded that Kedrolivansky had been murdered by "person or persons unknown." The newspapers immediately zeroed in on Kovrigin, for obvious reasons. The two men were rivals, and neither had a particularly good reputation. Kovrigin was apparently a scoundrel. In the same imperial edict that detailed the accusations against Kedrolivansky, there was this item on Kovrigin:

> Sailor Wilson's statement about a blameworthy liaison between a member of the Spiritual Consistory in San Francisco, Priest Kovrigin, and the wife of a certain Philip Kashevarov, must be investigated because of the gravity of the accusations detailed in this statement.

About a year later, in May 1879, Bishop Nestor wrote, "Right after beginning my administration of the Aleutian diocese I found myself forced to remove Priest Nikolai Kovrigin, who had become known, sadly, all over Russia for his deeds." In a report to Metropolitan Isidor of St. Petersburg the next day, Bishop Nestor said,

> Upon my arrival in San Francisco, I heard verbal statements from many people and also from the clergy about all kinds of unseemly actions by the priest Nikolai Kovrigin. To protect the honor of Orthodoxy and to prevent all kinds of squabbles that badly reflect on the Orthodox Faith in foreign lands, I was, by necessity, put into the situation of relieving Kovrigin from his duty. [. . .] Considering all circumstances, the future tenure of Priest Nikolai Kovrigin in America, because of many matters existing against him, will cast a shadow on Orthodoxy.

Kovrigin seems to have had the most obvious motive to kill Kedrolivansky. More than the rivalry, there is the ten-thousand-dollar document that Kedrolivansky displayed at Rosenthal's tobacco shop. What was in that document? From the *Chronicle*:

> Mr. Rosenthal, a tobacco dealer on Washington street, related that deceased had talked with him previous to the night on which he died, and had communicated the fact that he was afraid to be out late at nights. He had an important paper on his person which he was going to send to D.V. Petersburg [presumably the church or government authorities in St. Petersburg], and "that priest," referring to his clerical assistant [Kovrigin], would give $10,000 to have it from him. The witness remembered that the dead priest had exhibited the document exteriorly. It was an impressive-looking document, long, and folded peculiarly in the center. The priest was somewhat under the influence of liquor at that time, as indeed, it appeared he was most of the time. Prison-keeper Lindheimer remembered that when the man was brought

into the Prison he had, among other papers, some document of that description, but there all account of it ceases. It appears to have vanished immediately, and a search among the Prison records failed to discover it.

The document wasn't the only thing missing from Kedrolivansky's property. Apparently, a released prisoner was allowed to walk off with his silk hat.

The Russian consul in San Francisco, Vladimir Welitsky, told the *Daily Alta California* that the paper was related "to a divorce case, in which two subordinate priests were alleged to be concerned; the paper was written in English and translated into Russian, [to] be forwarded to St. Petersburg; the translation was placed in the hands of one of the priests, who failed to send it; a demand was made upon him, and he surrendered it to deceased." Later in the same article, they report that Welitsky said that the paper "was only a translated copy of an affidavit, made by a lady in a suit for divorce. . . . The affidavit contains charges against the moral character of a priest of the Greek Church."

From the *Chronicle* we learn that it was Welitsky himself who translated the document from English into Russian and then "returned it to deceased for transmission to Russia." Welitsky said

that some time ago an American gentleman had been divorced from his wife, who was a Russian lady and a follower of the Russian Church in this city, on the ground of adultery. It appeared that she had visited the deceased [Kedrolivansky] and his deacon [possibly Basil Kashevarov], and had written out a long explanation in English to the Home Government explaining the matter, and reflecting on Father Kovrigin, whom she accused of giving her pernicious advice in reference to married life. The matter was brought to the Consul for translation and it was translated. He endeavored to induce the priests not to send the document home and to refrain from indulging in such gossip, but they refused, and the paper was given to the deceased. The Consul retains the

English copy. He stated that there was nothing in the document which could injure Mr. Kovrigin in the estimation of the home Government. He admitted that there had been some ill-feeling between the priests. He could conceive of no motive for murder.

Welitsky was adamant that the document was not damaging to Kovrigin. This is difficult to understand. Kedrolivansky, Kovrigin's enemy, certainly considered it damaging. And anyway, how do we know the "ten-thousand-dollar document" is the same as the document Welitsky referred to? We only have Welitsky's word for it. It's possible that Kedrolivansky was boasting to Rosenthal about another document entirely, one which was even more damaging to Kovrigin.

As noted above, Bishop Nestor sent Kovrigin back to Russia as soon as he (Nestor) arrived in America in 1879. The reasons for this, however, seem to have more to do with Kovrigin's reputation as a philanderer than with any suspicion that he was a murderer. Only a few days after the coroner's jury gave their verdict, the following note appeared in the *San Francisco Daily Evening Bulletin*:

> Detective Jehu, who has been making inquiries into the cause of the death of the late Paul J. Kedvolivansky [sic], the arch-priest of the Greek Church in San Francisco, reported to have been murdered, reports that he has found several persons who saw the deceased fall on the sidewalk at the corner of Spring and California streets, a few minutes before he was discovered by the arresting officer. It is deemed certain that his death was caused by injuries received in the fall.

Jehu's findings are detailed in a letter written by Police Chief John Kirkpatrick to Welitsky on June 25. Three witnesses swore that they had seen Kedrolivansky fall, and that he had "violently struck the back of his head against the stone curbing."

That seemed to close the case, and what had looked like a

sensational murder just days before was now transformed into a run-of-the-mill drunken, accidental death. I'm not entirely convinced, though, and neither were the Russians in San Francisco. After the June 22 inquest, one newspaper reported, "The Police Surgeon, Dr. Stivers [. . .] thought that the fracture might have resulted from a fall, but deceased would have had to fall upon his side in a peculiar manner; the fracture might have been caused by a blow; it could not have been caused by a slung-shot or sandbag." While the coroner's report has not survived (it was burned in the fire that followed the 1906 earthquake in San Francisco), sections from it were reprinted in the newspapers.[2]

Leaving aside the three witnesses found by Detective Jehu, this looks like an obvious murder. Kedrolivansky had a known enemy, Kovrigin, who had, among other motives, the immediate concern of the "ten-thousand-dollar document." But Kovrigin isn't the only suspect. Years later, the name of an otherwise unknown man named Amosov came to the surface. One newspaper, in 1891, reported the rumor that this Amosov had been hired by Kovrigin to kill Kedrolivansky. Around the same time,

---

2   "The autopsy disclosed the fact that the scalp of deceased was very thick and strongly adherent, and on the whole of the left side there was a large amount of suffused blood. On the left side was found a fracture of the skull, commencing in the temporal bone, running upward and slightly backward into the parietal bone, being three inches in length; thence at right angles backward half an inch; thence downward and slightly backward two inches; thence at right angles forward one and three-fourth inches intersecting the first line described, leaving a detached piece pressing upon the brain. This portion of the skull was quite thin. From the point of intersection there was a fracture running across the temporal bone and ending in the median line of the frontal bone at a distance of about four and a half inches. There was also a fracture from the lower corner of the detached piece running backward across the parietal bone a distance of about half an inch. The brain directly under the fracture was lacerated and a brain clot weighing four ounces was found. The brain was in a healthy condition." This comes from the *San Francisco Examiner* article "The Russian Church," cited above.

Bishop Vladimir (the Russian bishop in San Francisco from 1888 to 1891) also mentioned Amosov (calling him a "nihilist"), saying that he had been hired by "the Jews" of the "notorious Alaska Company" and had killed Kedrolivansky with a sandbag.

Again the Alaska Company. This organization, the Alaska Commercial Company (ACC), is the same one that accused Kedrolivansky of "transporting contraband" a year before his death. The ACC was headed by Gustave Niebaum, a native of Finland, which at the time was a part of the Russian Empire. At sixteen, Niebaum became a cabin boy for a ship of the Russian American Company. By twenty-one, he was captain of his own ship for the Company, and he became an expert sailor and trader in Alaska. After the sale of Alaska in 1867, the Russian American Company was divided between two US companies, one of which included Niebaum.

In 1868, Niebaum arrived in San Francisco with half a million dollars' worth of furs. The same year, the two US companies merged to form the ACC, of which Niebaum was a partner. He eventually became the head of the company. He married into an elite San Francisco family, and just after Kedrolivansky's death, he started a winery in Napa Valley. This winery was extremely successful; it produced Inglenook wines, and many decades later it was purchased by Francis Ford Coppola.

A year after Kedrolivansky's death, Niebaum became Welitsky's vice-consul. Welitsky promptly returned to Russia, leaving Niebaum as the acting Russian consul in San Francisco. In the late 1880s, during Bishop Vladimir's tenure in America, Niebaum again served as acting consul. Given that he was the head of the ACC and was close to the Russian authorities in San Francisco, it's reasonable to assume that Gustave Niebaum was involved in the 1877 accusation made by the ACC against Kedrolivansky.

Kedrolivansky left a family. His wife, Alexandra, was pregnant with their sixth child at the time of his death, and the child was born in September 1878. As Kedrolivansky was a Russian subject, his widow was entitled to a pension from the Russian government. A certain Mrs. Goodall, who worked for the Ladies' Protective and Relief Association, appealed to acting consul Niebaum on behalf of Mrs. Kedrolivansky. Niebaum apparently told Mrs. Goodall that Mrs. Kedrolivansky was "a bad woman," and he "advised Mrs. Goodall to have nothing to do with her, and further asserted that [she] had not lived with her husband for two years previous to his death, and that it was owing to her action that her husband took to drink, and while in a state of intoxication fell and was killed." The clear implication was that Mrs. Kedrolivansky "had deserted her husband and had, previous to his death, led a dissolute and unchaste life, and became enceinte [pregnant] while living apart from him."

Alexandra Kedrolivansky denied all of this, and in 1881 she sued Niebaum, charging defamation of character. Five years later, the Supreme Court of California ruled in her favor.

Niebaum certainly didn't get along well with Fr. Paul or Alexandra Kedrolivansky. His predecessor and colleague, Welitsky, seemed particularly anxious to deny that Kedrolivansky's death was a murder, even before any witnesses surfaced. I don't think one could go so far as to call the two Russian officials suspects, but they did at least behave suspiciously. Two points:

1. The surgeon who examined Kedrolivansky said that he was probably struck by another person with a blunt object. He said that a fall was unlikely, as it would have to have been at an awkward angle. The surviving description of the wound seems to support this. Basing their decision on the surgeon's testimony, the coroner's jury declared the death to be murder.

2. By June 25, the police found three witnesses who testified to seeing Kedrolivansky fall and hit his head on the ground

at California and Spring Streets. Basing their decision on this testimony, the police declared the cause of death to be an accidental fall.

These are two apparently contradictory sets of facts. Since the fact of the doctor's testimony and the fact that the police found three witnesses are both equally true, we must find some way to reconcile them. How could they both be true?

1. The surgeon could have been mistaken. This seems unlikely.
2. The witnesses could have been lying. How could this be the case? They could have been induced to lie by either the actual killer or some other powerful agent. I'm thinking of either the Russian Consulate or the Alaska Commercial Company.
3. Then again, what if both the surgeon and the witnesses were correct? It could be that, however unlikely, Kedrolivansky actually did fall in a very awkward way. After all, the surgeon did say that it was possibly a fall.
4. There's another way they could both be correct: Kedrolivansky could have been struck by a murderer, regained consciousness, stumbled about, and finally fallen at California and Spring. Thus he would have been murdered, but the witnesses would still have seen him fall.
5. It's possible that he was pushed to the ground and that somehow the witnesses only saw the fall and not the push. Along the same lines, he could have been hit and then fell, but the witnesses only saw the fall.
6. Finally, it could be that the witnesses did see Kedrolivansky lying on the ground at California and Spring. Perhaps they were drunks, and their memory of the night was not entirely clear. A detective came around to the saloon to question them, and they had already heard about the death in the papers. They convinced themselves that they had seen him fall, when in fact they had only seen him fallen.

If you ask me, the best possibility is number four: Kedrolivansky was murdered, but the witnesses only saw him stumble about and fall.

Some other considerations: One thing that confused me was the question of the "ten-thousand-dollar document." There's reason to believe (from the prison keeper's testimony) that Kedrolivansky had the document on him when he was taken to prison, and that sometime after that the document disappeared. Another prisoner took his silk hat, so it's entirely possible that the document was misplaced in a similar way. Assuming he did have the document when he was taken into custody, and assuming he was murdered, one immediately wonders why the murderer didn't take the document with him. It could be that the murderer didn't care about the Kovrigin document—that Kedrolivansky was killed not because he was agitating against Kovrigin but because he was a threat to the Alaska Commercial Company. It seems likely, though, that the killer didn't know that Kedrolivansky had the document on his person. All he had to know was that Kedrolivansky was a threat. He was probably a hired hand, and he was told to kill Kedrolivansky. He never would have thought to search his person for papers.

As with many mysterious deaths, we must leave this one ultimately unsolved. There is no smoking gun, so to speak, no solid evidence one way or the other. All we can say for certain is that Kedrolivansky was a man with enemies, and his death smells like murder. Alas, it was just one in a series of scandals that would rock the San Francisco parish in the years to come.

CHAPTER SEVEN

Bishop Nestor Dies at Sea

IT MUST HAVE been awful to be an Orthodox parishioner in San Francisco in the late 1800s. There was one scandal after another, and even an apparent murder in 1878. Another tragedy came in 1882, when Bishop Nestor mysteriously drowned at sea.

Bishop Nestor had been traveling on the St. Paul, a steamship of the Alaska Commercial Company. He was on his way back to California from Alaska, where he had just made his annual pastoral visit. Actually, he was coming back early: at first, his plan had been to return in late autumn, but while he was in Alaska, he decided to stay there for another whole year. However, suffering from headaches, he abruptly changed his plans again and left in midsummer.

Prior to the trip, said St. Sebastian Dabovich, Bishop Nestor "frequently complained of headaches and suffered from general malaise." The headaches remained a problem while he was in Alaska. The *San Francisco Chronicle* (8/15/1882) reported, "Nothing unusual was noticed in the Bishop's behavior during this pastoral visit, except that he complained at times of a rush of blood to the head, a malady to which he had been subject for some years." The *San Francisco Morning Call* (8/15/1882) wrote, "For years he had at times suffered intensely from severe attacks of neuralgia, the pains of which he experienced while aboard the steamer at

St. Michael's, and for which he could find no relief. So intense was his suffering that he began to act in a strange manner, which led his friends to believe that he was somewhat out of his head." The fact that the *Call* explicitly referred to the bishop's ailment as "neuralgia" is significant.

At eight in the morning on July 12, the ship's captain stopped by the bishop's room to wish him a good morning. Nestor was there, and everything seemed fine. Fifteen minutes later, though, a doctor aboard the ship asked the captain if he had seen the bishop. The captain had just seen him; what was wrong? The bishop was missing, said the doctor; he was nowhere to be found. His room was neat and orderly; his papers were carefully arranged, but, oddly, his watch, jewelry, and part of his robes were in the room (as opposed to on his person). Someone suggested "that he had committed suicide while in a fit of dementia brought on by acute pain." A thorough search of the ship turned up nothing. The captain stopped the ship immediately and sent a search party out in a lifeboat. They searched for hours but found no trace of the bishop. Bishop Nestor was gone.

Today, such an event would become public knowledge almost instantly. But this was the 1880s, and it wasn't until the St. Paul reached San Francisco on August 14—over a month later—that the Orthodox of the city learned of the bishop's death. Consul General Olarovsky immediately ordered Bishop Nestor's rooms to be sealed, and he boarded the ship to investigate. Among those joining him were the local priest, Fr. Vladimir Vechtomov, and the vice-consul, Gustave Niebaum.

Olarovsky saw Bishop Nestor's room exactly as he had left it:

When the door was opened we saw that the belongings of the bishop consisted of several large and small hand traveling bags and small trunks, that were locked by key and all of them were standing in order on the upper bunk. There was also laying a carefully rolled downy blanket for travel and the bishop's hood, where inside there was a pearl panagia, then there was his pocket watch and fishing rod, a silver snuffbox, silk handkerchief, purse with keys for the traveling bags and several prayer books. A rolled gutta-percha cassock was laying on the lower bunk."

The consul then collected the testimonies of various people from the ship, including the captain and the doctor. They had all noticed the bishop's odd behavior in the days before his death, but they had thought nothing of it. Everyone present apparently agreed that the death was suicide; there was no suggestion of an accident or foul play. But Olarovsky was certain that Bishop Nestor had not been in his right mind:

> [I]t is enough to know the personality of the departed Nestor and his strong religious convictions to state without doubt, that naturally, the bishop could not decide on a conscious suicide, and the misfortune happened to him only under the influence of a severe moment of such mental disorder or influence of such effect, when he acted completely unconsciously.[1]

Not everyone thought it was suicide. "The natives here assert that God wanted the Bishop," wrote a *Los Angeles Times* correspondent in Alaska, "and took him up bodily from the deck of the steamer, as Elijah was translated in the fiery chariot." The same correspondent continued,

> I have never read of an instance, since the time of Jonah, where sailors did not have a strong prejudice against preachers; and the Bishop ought not to have gone among them. [. . .] So, the

---

1   Consul General A. E. Olarovsky, report to the Ober-Procurator of the Holy Synod (Aug. 20, 1882), reprinted in George Soldatow, *The Right Reverend Nestor, Bishop of the Aleutians and Alaska 1879–1882: Selected Letters, Documents & Diary, Volume Two* (Minneapolis: AARDM Press, 1993). In this volume, Soldatow published many primary sources related to Bishop Nestor's death.

question now stands for future disputants to decide, whether: (1) the Bishop jumped overboard and committed suicide; or, (2) whether he flew up to heaven; or, (3) whether the superstitious sailors drowned him.[2]

Bishop Nestor's body was found a couple weeks later, putting to rest the Elijah theory. The suspicion of murder would resurface in the years to come. Nine years later, the *San Francisco Examiner* (6/13/1891) claimed that Nestor's death had been one in a series of killings, part of a grand conspiracy. He had, so said the *Examiner*, discovered that "certain of the church officials were dishonest" and had taken money from the cathedral. "He worried very much, but being a man of kind heart did not report his discoveries to the Synod." Then, the *Examiner* went on, Nestor learned that some of the priests in Alaska were robbing the natives.

"One night, just as the vessel lay to off Unalaska," the newspaper continued, "Bishop Nestor went on deck. The next day his dead body was found on the beach. He had either jumped over or been pushed overboard."

This is all wrong. Nestor was last seen at eight in the morning—in his room—and disappeared shortly afterwards. And his body was found seventeen days later, not "the next day."

Anyway, the paper went on,

> It was openly asserted that he had been murdered, but no proof of this could be gathered. Many of his warmest friends contended that there was no reason for him to put an end to his life, being in the highest position in the gift of the Synod, with a glorious future before him. They intimated that there were, on the other hand, potent reasons for his being put out of the way.

The *Examiner* did acknowledge that some thought the death was suicide. "The higher class of Russians believed that he had

---

2   *Los Angeles Daily Times* (Aug. 18, 1882).

become disgusted with the condition of the church, and to save himself the pain of writing a report that would bring many persons to disgrace, committed suicide in a fit of despondency."

The newspaper neglects to mention anything about the bishop's neuralgia and odd behavior; in fact, it's clear that the paper is reporting based on 1891 gossip, not 1882 facts (or even 1882 speculation). The one person on record as suggesting murder in 1882—the unnamed *Los Angeles Times* correspondent—suspected the sailors, with the assumed motive being superstition. And even that suggestion appears to have been tongue-in-cheek, paired as it was with the theory that Nestor was translated into heaven like Elijah.

The *Examiner* concludes, "The mystery surrounding his tragic end has never been pierced." Perhaps not. But the *Examiner* was trying to sell papers with sensationalism, taking advantage of a volatile situation in 1891. Nestor's eventual successor, Bishop Vladimir, didn't think his predecessor was murdered. "There was much talk about his murder but no proof," Vladimir said.

Neuralgia is an awful, debilitating condition. It is a disorder of the nervous system that can cause (among other things) excruciating pain in the face and head. It has been described as the worst pain a human being can experience. Its nickname is "the suicide disease"—too often, people with neuralgia are driven to suicide by the extreme pain. If Bishop Nestor indeed had neuralgia—and there is every reason to believe that he did—then the simplest explanation for his death is the original one: that, in his great suffering, he threw himself overboard.

Years later, St. Sebastian Dabovich wrote, "It is difficult to imagine the horror and sadness with which all were overcome. [. . .] And thus was our Church widowed once more."[3]

---

3   Fr. Sebastian Dabovich, "The Orthodox Church in California," *Russian Orthodox American Messenger* 15 (April 1–13, 1898), 455–460 and 16 (April 15–27, 1898), 479–482.

CHAPTER EIGHT

Early Orthodox Unity in Chicago

THE STORY OF Orthodoxy in Chicago begins in the 1880s. In 1885, a Greek couple, Peter and Georgia Pooley, moved to Chicago from Corfu. Georgia immediately organized a benevolent society of the Orthodox Christians in Chicago, regardless of ethnicity. The purpose of this society was to establish an Orthodox parish in the city. This marks the beginning of Orthodoxy in Chicago, in any organized way.

The following year, 1886, the first documented Orthodox liturgy was celebrated in Chicago. The priest was Fr. Misael Karydis, who was the pastor of the Orthodox church in New Orleans. The service was held in a place called Berry's Hall, where the Orthodox had improvised an altar table out of two dry goods boxes covered with a sheet. The music was performed antiphonally by Greeks and Serbs, with five Greeks on one side of the room and twenty Serbs on the other. About a hundred people were present, and the *Chicago Herald* was particularly impressed with the size of the collection—he said that the Orthodox had donated "far more liberal[ly] than those in English-speaking churches."[1]

---

1   *Chicago Herald*, May 31, 1886, reprinted in the *New Orleans Daily Picayune* (June 7, 1886), 3.

Around the time of that first liturgy in 1886, a Montenegrin saloonkeeper named Krsto Gopcevic wrote a letter to the Russian ambassador in Washington, asking the Russian government to establish an Orthodox church in Chicago. The ambassador forwarded his letter to the Russian Holy Synod, and in 1888, it reached Bishop Vladimir, the new bishop in San Francisco.

In May of 1888, Bishop Vladimir replied to the letter, asking Gopcevic to organize a meeting of all the Orthodox in Chicago to see how many people were interested in starting a church. Vladimir planned to visit the city later in the year, and he wanted to know what to expect.

The meeting was held on May 13. The *Chicago Tribune* sent a reporter to the event, and the next day, he published one of my favorite newspaper articles on early American Orthodoxy. It's so good, in fact, that I'm going to reprint almost the entire thing here.

Mr. K.M. Gopchevich, a Montenegrin, with black hair and a light mustache, called the Greek Catholic meeting to order last night. All the Greek Catholics of Chicago were represented in the assembly. There were Athenians and Spartans, islanders of the Archipelago, sailors from the seaports of Asia Minor. And there were Slavs of all nationalities—Dalmatians from Ragusa and the Bocca al Cattaro; Servians from Prisrend and Belgrade; Bulgarians from Rustchuck. Only one Russian was in the hall, which was at No. 118 Fifth avenue; and he, feeling out of place, retired before the meeting was over.

A small Greek in a pea-jacket, who might have been a pirate, but was really a dealer in coffee and spice, mounted the platform and discoursed with another Greek in hexameters and pentameters. He was so rapid in utterance, so excited in gesture, that a Servian at the end of the hall called him to order. The small Greek, who seemed to be on the point of drawing a knife to give point to his remarks, subsided in an instant, and his Servian conqueror demanded that hereafter the language of Thucydides should be discarded and that of Robert G. Ingersoll should be adopted. The Servian youths—the lads who had witnessed Prince Alexander's overthrow—understood not a word of either speaker, but they mildly applauded their compatriot.

Mr. Gobchevitch then drew from his pocket the letter which had occasioned the meeting. Time was when Mr. Gobchevitch had worn a yataghan at his side and a fez upon his head. Time was when Mr. Gobchevitch had looked along the barrel of a long rifle and had picked off Turks as they clambered over his native rocks. Time was when Mr. Gobchevitch, under the leadership of a soldier-priest, had scaled hills, had burnt villages, had hidden in caves, had rolled huge bowlders down upon the enemy. Mr. Gobchevitch went through every recent Montenegrin revolution; he has fought invaders like the sturdy mountaineer that he was; and today he keeps a saloon on West Twenty-second street, and is a modest, self-contained man, with a record that many an American General might envy.

But before Mr. Gobchevitch could read the letter Mr. George Brown, a veteran of our own war [presumably the Civil War], was called to the chair. He was quite a boy when he came from Samos, and he was somewhat misty in his recollections of "the Isles of Greece, the Isles of Greece, where burning Sappho loved and sung." Still there was the old Greek spirit in the vigor with which he rapped the table with his walking stick and bade Servians and Greeks to give ear to the following Homeric speech:

"Gentlemans," [he said] "Union is the strength. Let everybody make his mind and have no jealousy. I have no jealousy. I am married to a Catholic woman but I hold my own. Let us stick like a brothers. If our language is two, our religion is one. The priest he make the performance in both language. We have our flags built. It is the first Greek flags raised in Chicago. We will surprise the Americans. Let us stick like a brothers. And now gentlemen, if you will please sit down; sit down, will you; sit down, you Servian gentlemans (rap, rap, rap, with the walking stick); we shall like to hear something from you."

Mr. J. Vuchetitch, the President of the Servian Society, rose to reply. He is as handsome a Slav as ever rowed a boat on the

Adriatic. Tall, erect, graceful as a Greek god, he had served in Dalmatian regiments against the Turks, and on many a war vessel that sailed at midnight from Boccadi Cattaro. He glowed with enthusiasm when Montenegro's battle for freedom was mentioned, and vowed that if his countrymen needed his dagger or his gun he would go back in the mountains tomorrow. Having, however, no immediate occasion to depart, he delivered the following reply.

"Gentlemans—It is important we shall all put in our shoulder. I hope there will be one meeting in the June and one in the July to prescribe the money for our purpose. I have nothing to say for present. I see everybody satisfied with business as we translate tonight."

Mr. Gobchevitch then read the letter. It was written by Bishop Vladimir, who had lately arrived in San Francisco from Russia. The Bishop had conceived the project of establishing a Greek church in Chicago; and he suggested to Mr. Gobchevitch that all the Greeks, Servians, Bulgarians, and Russians in this city should sign a petition, which he would forward to the Holy Synod, and should raise funds to establish a church and pay a preacher.

This was the purpose for which Mr. Brown advised his hearers to "stick like a brothers" and Mr. Vuchevitch counseled them to "prescribe the money."

The signing of the petition was a task of much difficulty. Some of the Greeks had names like Nicolaos Kristolambros and Dimitri Korphiatis, and they spent as much time in spelling them out as though they were writing a book of the Iliad. Others signed for the whole family, as Pietros Poulos, George Poulos, Jans Poulos. Others could not sign at all and their names were affixed by the zealous Mr. Gobchevitch.

Among the latter was a handsome but diminutive youth with a rose at his button-hole and thick black hair plastered over his forehead. He was the latest arrival from Athens, where he was considered quite an Adonis. What had he to tell of Athens? He knew many pretty women there. Had he ever been to Marathon?

He had never heard of Marathon. What did he think of the Parthenon? He had never heard of the Parthenon. Had he read Sophocles or Euripides? He could not read or write. But he was quite a fashionable youth in modern Athens.

So the petition was signed at last, and then the older men gathered round the platform and told of old Greek liberty.

From other newspapers, we know that there were roughly a thousand Orthodox living in Chicago at the time—about six hundred Greeks and four hundred Slavs, which total included Serbs, Montenegrins, Bulgarians, Russians, and so forth. About a hundred men attended the meeting—and it would have been nearly all men, because there were hardly any Orthodox women in Chicago at the time. George Brown, the Greek veteran of the Civil War, was elected chairman, and the Montenegrin Gopcevic was chosen as secretary. One newspaper, the *Inter Ocean*, reported that the assembly discussed the issue of language: with Orthodox of different ethnicities, what language would they use in the services? They decided that they'd leave the final decision to the Russian authorities, since, presumably, they would be the ones footing the bill for a building and a priest, although there was discussion of alternating Greek on one Sunday and Slavonic on the next.

In October of 1888, Bishop Vladimir visited Chicago; unfortunately, though, this didn't lead to the establishment of a parish. I've seen this early Chicago community described as a sort of "proto-parish," and that's a pretty good description. In 1891 there was another meeting, led by three Greeks, three Russians, and three Serbs. Their hope was to start a parish in time for the 1893 Chicago World's Fair. A Greek priest from San Francisco came for a visit and celebrated the Divine Liturgy. This priest, Fr. Kallinikos Kanellas, had come to America from India, where he had been the priest of the Greek church in Calcutta. Although he was Greek, he was affiliated with the Russian cathedral in San Francisco.

George Brown, the Greek veteran of the Civil War, told a newspaper that the Chicago Orthodox were working with the Russian Church and had been promised their own priest as soon as they built a church. This seems like an odd approach, requiring the laity to build a church before sending a priest. But no building was ever erected, and no priest was sent.

At exactly this time—1888 to 1891—Bishop Vladimir was embroiled in a series of horrible scandals at his cathedral in San Francisco. Early on, his cathedral was burned to the ground (and some whispered that it was arson). Rumors swirled that funds had been embezzled. The accusations against Vladimir himself were the worst—he was charged by his detractors with sexually assaulting numerous young boys. To this day, it's not clear whether these accusations were true or false—whether Vladimir was a monster or an innocent victim of slander. I mentioned a moment ago that one of the leaders of the early Chicago community was a Montenegrin named Krsto Gopcevic. Gopcevic had relatives in San Francisco, and one of them was a sworn enemy of Bishop Vladimir. The Chicago Orthodox heard regular reports of the trouble in San Francisco, and they decided that they wanted nothing more to do with the Russian bishop.

So they started looking at other options. Gopcevic wrote to Serbia, and others wrote to Constantinople and Athens. The Russian Church finally replaced Bishop Vladimir in early 1892, and in March of that year, the new Russian bishop, Nicholas, passed through Chicago on his way to San Francisco. He met with some of the leading Greeks and Montenegrins, and there was again talk of starting a multiethnic parish. But it didn't happen. Just a month later, in April 1892, a priest arrived from the Church of Greece in response to an earlier appeal to the archbishop of Athens. The priest's name was Fr. Panagiotis Phiambolis, and he established Annunciation, the second exclusively Greek parish in America (lagging slightly behind Annunciation in New York City, which had been formed two months earlier).

Also in April 1892, Bishop Nicholas sent Fr. Ambrose Vretta to Chicago to start a church under the Russians. For the first time in American history, two Orthodox churches answering to different bishops coexisted in the same city. The Greek church was, as I said, exclusively Greek. The Russian church didn't have a great many Russians to begin with; there were Slavs from the Austro-Hungarian Empire, plus lots of Serbs and Montenegrins, and a handful of prominent Russians. The first priest of that Russian church, Fr. Ambrose Vretta, was not a Russian himself. Contemporary sources refer to him as being from Macedonia. He went to medical school in Constantinople, then studied in Rome, and ended up in Russia because he wanted to avoid the Turks. In Russia, he became a priest, and he was sent to America with Bishop Nicholas in 1892.

So in a span of about a month, Chicago went from having no Orthodox parishes to having two. And for a short time that year, they had a third. In response to a request from the Montenegrin Gopcevic, the metropolitan of Belgrade sent Fr. Firmilian Drazic to Chicago to start a Serbian church. Father Firmilian arrived just in time for the Fourth of July. To celebrate, he took the thanksgiving service for Serbian independence and replaced all the references to Serbia with "America." Basically, he improvised hymns and prayers in commemoration of American independence.

The Serbian community wasn't ready to support its own parish, and after about six months, Fr. Firmilian returned to Serbia, where he went on to become the metropolitan of Skopje. When he left the country, Fr. Firmilian gave the Chicago Serbs a set of vestments and holy vessels. The Serbs attended the Russian church until 1905, when they founded their own parish and were able to use the items given to them by Fr. Firmilian back in 1892.

Unfortunately, the Russian priest, Fr. Vretta, had a drinking problem, and in 1895 he was replaced by the newly ordained, twenty-four-year-old Fr. John Kochurov, the future hieromartyr. This ushered in an era of great progress for the Russian church in Chicago. Hundreds of former Eastern Rite Catholics converted to Orthodoxy during St. John's Chicago career, and in 1903, construction was completed on Holy Trinity Cathedral, which remains one of the most distinctive Orthodox temples in America. Saint John was also one of the best examples of the circuit-riding American Orthodox priest, responsible not only for his own parish, but for large parts of the country that didn't have an Orthodox church.

During St. John's tenure in Chicago, the ties between the Greek and Russian communities remained strong, with continued joint services. Another example of cooperation is the search for the Russian church bell in 1902.

It's a story interesting enough to retell here. The quarter-ton bell of Chicago's Russian church was originally a part of the Russian exhibit at the World's Fair. At the time, the church building was too small to house the bell, so it sat in storage for nearly a decade. By 1902, construction on Holy Trinity Cathedral was underway, and a special belfry was designed for the bell. But on an early May morning, three men broke into the storage area, rolled the bell into an alley, hoisted it onto a wagon, and took off. The Russian congregation was up in arms, and the next day, a huge general meeting was held, with seventy percent of the Orthodox of Chicago in attendance. Father John begged everyone for their help, and all went off in search of the bell. I don't know what the outcome was—whether they ever found the bell or caught the thieves—but this incident shows that the Orthodox community of Chicago remained cohesive a decade after dividing into ethnic parishes.

CHAPTER NINE

Three Years of Scandal

IN 1868, FOLLOWING the sale of Alaska to America the previous year, and also following a petition by the local Orthodox of San Francisco, a Russian Orthodox priest came from Alaska to California to establish a parish. This was the beginning of what is now Holy Trinity Cathedral (OCA), although both the name and the location have changed over the years.

From 1870 to 1877, Bishop John Mitropolsky governed the Diocese of the Aleutian Islands and Alaska. Despite the fact that San Francisco was neither in the Aleutian Islands nor Alaska proper, Holy Trinity became his diocesan cathedral. He was succeeded by Bishop Nestor, who took up his post in 1879. As we've seen, in between these dates, the leading clergyman of the diocese, cathedral dean Fr. Paul Kedrolivansky, was (most likely) murdered. Bishop Nestor himself died under somewhat mysterious circumstances a few years later, in 1882. From Bishop Nestor's death in 1882 until the arrival of Bishop Vladimir Sokolovsky in 1888, the diocese had no resident bishop.

For years, I've gone out of my way to avoid writing about the complete dumpster fire that was the San Francisco cathedral situation during the era of Bishop Vladimir, 1888 to 1891. It's gross and unpleasant and such a tangled mess that I really am not sure

whom to believe. But I can't write a book like this and not at least mention the story.

Bishop Vladimir arrived to find a pretty bleak situation at the cathedral: despite the Russian government subsidizing the diocese and its nine parishes to the tune of a reported $53,000 ($1.8 million in today's terms), the *San Francisco Chronicle* (6/11/1888) reported, "Practically there is no congregation in this

Bishop Vladimir

city. Not infrequently the services at the cathedral are conducted in the empty church, the only persons present being the priests and members of the choir. At the Christmas and Easter services there were perhaps 100 people in the cathedral."

But Vladimir, it was said, was a man on a mission. The *Chronicle* repeated complaints that he had ignored the needs of the Alaskans in favor of a push to convert Americans to Orthodoxy. He announced that church services in San Francisco would now be held in English (this being the common language of the Greek and Serbian parishioners of the cathedral), and he brought a throng of young students from Russia to attend he cathedral's school. He began a project to enlarge and renovate the cathedral. Many of the community's old guard weren't on board with any of this.

The parish was divided into two factions, with different Serbian family clans staking out their own interests. Bishop Vladimir called a meeting to try to build consensus, but it devolved into a shouting match. Here is how a local newspaper, the *Daily Alta California* (6/15/1888), describes it:

> Trouble was brewing, however, and Bishop Vladimir, seated on a raised chair in the rear of the little hall, and attired in the robes of office, had scarcely called the meeting to order when the trouble began.
>
> When B. M. Gopchivitch arose and flourished a set of

resolutions which he had carefully prepared for presentation, there was an angry roar and cries of "Shut up" and "Sit down."

Gopchivitch did not sit down, but waited until order had been partially restored. Then he began relating how certain members of the society had mismanaged affairs, and particularly the cemetery. He declared that if the advice of the Bishop was taken, all the differences might be satisfactorily settled. "There are some members here," he continued, "who want to make trouble and run the society to suit themselves."

"You're a liar," yelled Bozo Radovitch. "You control the Bishop, and think you are going to run this society."

"You are a liar yourself," retorted Gopchivitch, as he sprang forward with clenched fists.

This was the signal for a general uprising, and an all-round hubbub ensued.

A. Chilovitch could contain his wrath no longer. He dropped a huge umbrella and rushed at Gopchivitch, who dodged behind a stalwart member of his faction, and Chilovitch ran into the arms of his nephew, Radovitch.

Everyone wanted to talk at the same time, and during the general confusion the lie was given and fists shaken in all directions. Excited members soon began rushing out on the sidewalk, and soon only a band of about fifteen, all faithful to the Bishop, remained in the room.

[These supporters then spoke as follows.]

"WHEREAS, Some evil inclined person has circulated the rumor that the course of His Eminence Archbishop Vladimir, since assuming charge of the Russian-Greek Church in this jurisdiction, has been arbitrary, and subject to criticism, and has secured the publication in the press of this city of such rumor; now, therefore, we, the members of the Orthodox Eastern Church, in meeting assembled hereby condemn such charge as false and unfounded. And we further desire to give expression to our utmost confidence in the Christian worth and ability of His Eminence, feeling assured that he is exerting his best endeavors to heal the dissensions which existed in our church prior to his advent among us, and that if he is not hampered by senseless opposition his presence and labors will be productive of much good among our brethren of this Coast. This faith and confidence which we have expressed are warranted by his course since he commenced ministry among us, and it is with the greatest pleasure that we avail ourselves of this opportunity to record our commendation of his every act and to assure him our fullest support to the end that he may fulfill his divinely-appointed mission."

Bishop Vladimir then made a sorrowful little speech in broken English. He said that he was very much grieved indeed that his children could not settle their little quarrels and again be united. He hoped that some time in the near future this might be accomplished, and dismissed those who remained in the room with his blessing.

On the sidewalk, just around the corner from the church, Bozo Radovitch, who was one of the first to bolt from the hall, held a little meeting of his own. He claimed that the Bishop had no business to call a meeting to settle grievances in the church. As head of the American Diocese his word was law, and he had only to command to be obeyed. Radovitch concluded by expressing his opinion of Gopchivitch, in terms by no means complimentary to that gentleman. Later in the evening, Gopchivitch, speaking to an ALTA reporter, was equally severe in his references to Radovitch. He says that another meeting will soon be held, at which the Radovitch faction will not be admitted.

That early meeting set the tone for Vladimir's entire brief episcopate in America. Another thing that happened right after Vladimir's arrival was his excommunication of a physician named Nicholas Russel. Despite his American-sounding surname, Russel was from Russia—his real name was Nikolai Sudzilovskii, a socialist revolutionary who'd fled the Russian Empire with the tsarist police on his heels. He changed his name to Russel, eventually ended up in San Francisco, and opened a medical practice.

(We have no word on whether he ever linked up with Agapius Honcharenko, another on-the-run Orthodox socialist with an assumed name living in the Bay Area.) From the moment Bishop Vladimir arrived, Russel was a thorn in his side. It seems that Vladimir excommunicated Russel for having allegedly abandoned his wife and moved in with another woman.

The cathedral community was full of tension for the better part of a year. Then, in May 1889, the cathedral burned to the ground. Bishop Vladimir told the newspapers that he thought it was arson but couldn't imagine who the culprit might be. Saint Sebastian Dabovich, at the time a hierodeacon a month shy of his twenty-sixth birthday, told a reporter, "I am so unnerved by the fire, that I hardly know what to say or what to think. I cannot give you any opinion as to whether the fire was the work of an incendiary or an accident. I must take time to consider the matter." Others suggested that the fire was set to cover up evidence of embezzlement. The newspapers dredged up the story of Fr. Kedrolivansky's death, but Bishop Vladimir claimed that he had no fear for his life and slept with his door unlocked every night.

A couple months later, in a memo to clergy at the cathedral in Sitka, Alaska, Vladimir changed his tune, saying, "All the newspaper rumors that someone set fire to our church in order to kill someone are absolute lies. The fire probably occurred because the student-altar boy lost the iron insert and placed coal directly into the silver censer." He also claimed that "there is now peace in our church in San Francisco." This, unfortunately, was not true.

Less than five months after the fire, reconstruction was complete, and Vladimir dedicated the new cathedral to St. Basil the Great. But the bishop's troubles were far from over. Nicholas Russel declared war on Vladimir, sending a remarkable letter to the diocesan office:

Gentlemen,
In reply to your letter of December 12th inst. summoning me

to appear before your ecclesiastical Court on charges of bearing false name, those of calumny and revolting parishioners against you as well as bigamy, I beg to inform you:

that I do not acknowledge your jurisdiction in this country.

that I deny all above charges as absolutely groundless.

that I protest against the motives, which have guided you in sending me this offensive letter.

Yours obediently

Nicholas Russel, M.D.

San Francisco, December 19th 1889

Russel filed a civil lawsuit against Vladimir for slander, seeking an incredible fifty thousand dollars (equivalent to $1.7 million today). Then criminal libel charges were filed against the bishop. If found guilty, he could face prison.

But this was only one part of Bishop Vladimir's problems. He'd brought over a bunch of Russian boys to live at the school connected with the parish. Accusations began circulating that conditions at the school were abysmal and that the bishop himself had abused the boys. There was, it was said, a dungeon, and slavery, and torture. The local Society for the Prevention of Cruelty to Children got involved, and one of the boys sued Vladimir for back pay, claiming that he'd been basically enslaved for two years. I won't repeat every charge against the bishop except to say that the allegations included the worst things you can imagine short of murder. There's a whole book about this mess, with the very descriptive title *Alleged Sex and Threatened Violence*. The author, retired Stanford professor Terrence Emmons, doesn't have a favorable view of Bishop Vladimir, and the book itself is well-written but absolutely gut-wrenching to read and not in any way edifying. I cite it here only to say that books could be written about the Bishop Vladimir crisis, and one has been.

In the middle of all this, in the spring of 1891, a delegation from St. Alexis Toth's Uniate parish in Minneapolis arrived in

San Francisco, seeking to join the Orthodox Church. It's remarkable that, just as utter chaos and scandal reigned in the San Francisco Orthodox community, the great "return of the Unia" began.

Finally, in June 1891, the Holy Synod of Russia mercifully
recalled Vladimir from America, reassigning him to be an auxiliary bishop in the Diocese of Voronezh. He eventually got another
chance to be a ruling bishop in Russia. He retired in 1910, at the
age of fifty-seven, but eleven years later the newly reestablished
Moscow Patriarchate—led by St. Tikhon—appointed Vladimir as an archbishop in what is now Ukraine. Conditions never
allowed him to reach his new diocese, and he died in 1931, a
month shy of his seventy-eighth birthday.

Vladimir died in communion with the Church and, at least
according to some sources, with the reputation of being a holy
ascetic. I'm not aware of any allegations against him apart from
those leveled in San Francisco. Most accounts about him that
you'll find, online or in print, gloss over the whole San Francisco
controversy, presenting him as a forward-thinking hierarch who
happened to have a short tenure in America. The real question—
which I cannot answer—is, was he a monster or was he a victim
of slander?

CHAPTER TEN

A Greek Priest in the Russian Mission

Father Kallinikos Kanellas

FATHER KALLINIKOS KANELLAS was one of a handful of Greek priests who served under the Russian hierarchy in America, and he later joined the newly established Greek Orthodox Archdiocese. But before that, in 1880, he was invited to become the priest of the Greek church in Calcutta, India. At this point he was forty-three years old and a simple monk. His bishop quickly ordained him a deacon and then a priest, elevated him to archimandrite, and sent him off to India.[1]

The Calcutta parish gave Fr. Kallinikos a five-year contract; at the end of it, he signed on for another five years and was given a raise. But before the first year of the new contract was out, Fr. Kallinikos fell ill and went to Europe to recuperate. Then he traveled to America, simply as a tourist. But again, he got sick, and by now he was out of money. So he attached himself to the Russian Orthodox cathedral in San Francisco, quickly earning the

---

1   I wish I knew how the Greek expats in Calcutta got the idea to request Fr. Kallinikos, an unordained monk, as their priest. Presumably one of them had a personal connection to him.

trust of the new bishop, Vladimir. This would have been in about 1888, and it was rather useful to have a Greek-speaking priest on staff—the parish may have been under a Russian bishop, but its parishioners were mostly Greeks and Serbs. Father Kallinikos was appointed to serve on the Alaskan Spiritual Consistory, which ran the day-to-day affairs of the diocese.

In 1891, Fr. Kallinikos made a cross-country missionary trip. He stopped in Savannah, Georgia, and baptized a Greek child. A local newspaper reported that the child's father spent six hundred fifty dollars to bring Fr. Kallinikos to town, but that amount seems outrageous: when you factor in inflation, it works out to over twenty thousand dollars in modern terms. From Savannah, Fr. Kallinikos went to New York City (which didn't yet have a parish), where he baptized the daughter of a wealthy Greek merchant, Anthony Ralli. The *New York Sun* (6/26/1891) described Fr. Kallinikos as having a "patriarchal beard and jewelled gown." According to one account, he had to bring his own baptismal font—can you imagine taking one of those on a train?

Next, Fr. Kallinikos almost certainly went to Chicago. On July 11, 1891, the *Chicago Inter Ocean* reported that a certain "Archimandrite Lininas," "who presides over a temple in San Francisco," was visiting Chicago and holding services for the Orthodox there. This must have been Fr. Kallinikos. But the newspaper described the priest as "a finely educated gentleman, speaking German, Russian, and French fluently, but his English is best understood through an interpreter." No mention of Greek, which was Fr. Kallinikos's first language. However, there are no other traces of any Archimandrite Lininas, and given the timing of Fr. Kallinikos's cross-country trip, it's likely that he was the man.

In 1892, as we have seen, Bishop Vladimir was recalled to Russia and replaced by Bishop Nicholas Ziorov. On July 1 (June 19 according to the Old Calendar), the members of the Spiritual Consistory (of which Kanellas was apparently no longer a member) wrote to the new bishop, "Today, the Archimandrite Kallinikos was informed that he has to leave the Mission as of July 1. He replied that he has nowhere to go. In accordance with Your Grace's will, we deemed it was better to say nothing in reply: Your Grace has ordered not to drive him out."[2]

At this point, Fr. Kallinikos was fifty-five. He did eventually leave San Francisco, traveling to New York City, where he offered his services as a Greek tutor. He visited Birmingham, Alabama, in 1900, and two years later, the Birmingham Greeks hired him to be their first parish priest, under the jurisdiction of the Church of Greece. He was one of only a few Orthodox priests in the entire American South, and he remained in Birmingham for eight years. He resigned in 1911 because of cataract in his right eye. After his surgery, the Greek Holy Synod sent Fr. Kallinikos—by now seventy-four years old—to Tarpon Springs, Florida, but health problems soon forced him to move to Hot Springs, Arkansas, which was renowned for its healing thermal springs.

In 1913, in the book *Greeks in America*, Thomas Burgess quoted the *Greek American Guide* as saying, "The Rev. Arch. Kallinikos Kanellas is a very sympathetic and reverend old man of whom it is possible to say that of the Greek clergy in America he is the most—shall we say 'disinterested'? The Greek word is a dandy, (literally, 'not loving of riches'). Plutarch used to use that word."

The same year, Fr. Kallinikos was hired to be the first priest of the Greek church in Little Rock, Arkansas. It was a rough situation. Five years into his pastorate—when he was past eighty— he wrote to the Athens Metropolitan Meletios Metaxakis, who was visiting America, complaining that he had been ordered by the Little Rock parishioners to celebrate the Divine Liturgy very quickly, because they didn't want long services. The parish board

---

2   The text of this report has been printed on the website of Holy Trinity Cathedral (OCA), San Francisco: https://www.holy-trinity.org/history/1892/07.01.Consistory_Nicholas.html.

forbade him to take an active role in the parish. As far as the parishioners were concerned, he was a hired employee whose job was to perform services—nothing more.[3]

But he stuck it out, remaining in Little Rock until his death in 1921, at the age of eighty-four. He'd kind of seen it all.

---

3   Letter from Fr. Kallinikos to Archbishop Meletios (September 16, 1918), printed in Greek in Paul Manolis, *The History of the Greek Church in America in Acts and Documents, Vol. I*, page 333, and translated into English by Ioannis Fortomas.

CHAPTER ELEVEN

The Lost Convert Parish of 1891

IN THE LATTER half of the nineteenth century, and especially after the first Vatican Council in 1870, which promulgated the dogma of papal infallibility, a number of Roman Catholics broke away from their church.

Joseph Rene Vilatte was born in Paris in 1854. Originally he was a Roman Catholic, but as an adult he became the quintessential religious chameleon. In the 1880s he came to the United States, where he served as a Presbyterian missionary in a Belgian Old Catholic community in Green Bay, Wisconsin. While there, he made contact with local Episcopal Bishop John Brown of Fond du Lac, who in turn recommended to the Old Catholic Bishop Edward Herzog of Bern, Switzerland, that Vilatte be ordained a priest. This took place in 1886.

Soon, Bishop Brown died, and the new Episcopal bishop of Fond du Lac, Charles Grafton (the future friend of St. Tikhon), did not see eye to eye with Vilatte. Forced to make a choice between Episcopalianism and Old Catholicism, Vilatte chose the latter, and he tried to have himself consecrated a bishop in the Old Catholic Church. The church authorities in Europe declined. This is where our story begins.

Vilatte wanted to be consecrated a bishop, and he wanted as much autonomy as possible. That is the first thing to understand.

Theodore Natsoulas says that the Old Catholics turned down Vilatte because he was "unpredictable," and they did not want him to be their sole representative in America. Here is how Natsoulas describes what happened next:

> [Vilatte's] attempts to be raised to the episcopate included approaches to the Bishop of the Russian Orthodox Church in America and to the Roman Catholic Bishop of Green Bay. Both turned him down, although Vladimir, the Russian Bishop, in order to incorporate the Old Catholics within his fold, did extend some form of recognition and protection to Vilatte and the Old Catholic Church. Vladimir and Vilatte, however, could not arrive at a mutually satisfactory agreement.[1]

It all began when Vilatte traveled to San Francisco to meet with Bishop Vladimir, sometime in 1890 or early 1891. Interestingly, this coincided almost precisely with the visit of a delegation of Uniates from St. Alexis Toth's parish in Minneapolis. It must have been amazing for Bishop Vladimir, sitting there in San Francisco, to receive near-simultaneous unsolicited visits from two Upper Midwest groups connected to Roman Catholicism and seeking reception into the Orthodox Church.

Bishop Vladimir traveled to Minneapolis in March of 1891 and formally received the Minneapolis parish into Orthodoxy. After that historic visit, Vladimir passed through Chicago, which had a sizeable Orthodox community that was determined to remain independent of the controversial Bishop Vladimir. He left Chicago on April 10, and by April 11 he was in Green Bay. The *Milwaukee Sentinel* reported the next day that Vladimir came for the purpose of visiting Vilatte and his Old Catholic parish in

---

1   Theodore Natsoulas, "Patriarch McGuire and the Spread of the African Orthodox Church to Africa, *Journal of Religion in Africa* 12:2 (1981), 81–104. This is one of the few scholarly sources that discusses Vilatte at any length.

nearby Dyckesville. The Russian bishop "expressed great sympathy with [Vilatte's] work, and it is stated that he was agreeably surprised to find that the doctrinal basis of the Old Catholics at this place, and that of his own large church of 100,000,000 souls were precisely identical."

But what, exactly, was the relationship between the Russian Diocese and the Old Catholics in Wisconsin? According to a web-published biography of Vilatte by Bertil Persson (the reliability of which is unclear, and which appears to be no longer accessible), Vilatte had originally visited Bishop Vladimir in San Francisco in January 1891, at which time Vladimir "approached The Holy Synod of The Russian Orthodox Church suggesting that Vilatte should be consecrated." I don't doubt that Bishop Vladimir notified the Holy Synod of Vilatte's visit, but I cannot believe that he actually suggested that the Russian Church consecrate the man.

Also according to the Persson biography, after visiting Vilatte's parish in April, Bishop Vladimir issued the following certificate:

CERTIFICATE.
The Russian Ecclesiastical Consistory of Alaska, San Francisco, Cal: May 9, 1891.
By the Grace of God and the Authority bestowed on me by the Apostolic Succession, I, VLADIMIR, Bishop of the Orthodox Catholic Church, announce to all clergymen of the different Christian denominations and to all Old Catholics that The Reverend Joseph René Vilatte, Superior of the Old Catholic Parish in Dyckesville, Wisc:, is now a true Old Catholic Orthodox Christian, under the patronage of our Church, and no Bishop or Priest of any denomination has the right to interdict him or to suspend his religious duties, except the Holy Synod of the Russian Church, and myself. Any action contrary to this declaration, is null and void on the basis of liberty of conscience and the law of this country.
‡VLADIMIR, Bishop of the Greco-Russian Orthodox Ch.

I have no idea whether this document is authentic or not, and unfortunately, Persson only reprinted the text, so we can't examine the letterhead or Bishop Vladimir's signature. I will say the wording is quite strange for a decree by a Russian Orthodox bishop, so if Vladimir did in fact issue it, it's possible that Vilatte himself was the drafter.

Anyway, Bishop Vladimir was recalled to Russia soon after all this. His replacement, Bishop Nicholas Ziorov, visited the Wisconsin Old Catholics in May 1892. According to Dom Augustine de Angelis in the *Fond Du Lac Reporter*, "Bishop Nicholas, head of the Greek church in America, visited the Old Catholic mission at Dyckesville, last Monday. He has been in America only a month and a half, but has already made his episcopal visitation of the Orthodox and Old Catholic churches, preparatory to his annual visitation of the vast region of Alaska and the Aleutian Islands. [. . .] His first impressions of America and Americans are very favorable, and he sympathizes with us in our hopes of seeing an Orthodox American church, in which mass shall be said in English, French, German, etc., until all have become so American that English shall be the common tongue of all."[2]

But the parish priest, Vilatte, wasn't there. He was in Sri Lanka (Ceylon), awaiting his long-sought consecration to the episcopate. He had found a taker in the ancient Malankara Orthodox Syrian Church, the non-Chalcedonian church in India. Vilatte never seems to have considered himself to be a Malankara Syrian Orthodox; he was interested in their apostolic succession, not their actual church. (As Theodore Natsoulas puts it, "Vilatte's commitment to the [Malankara] Church of Antioch, or, in fact, to any other religious organization, never was very deep.") Vilatte returned to Dyckesville in August, and on September 11, the *New York Times* reported that he had created the American Catholic Church. Needless to say, any connection he might have had

2 Quoted in the *Milwaukee Sentinel* (May 16, 1892), 5.

with the Russian Diocese of the Aleutian Islands was dead by this point.

Vilatte went on to have an exceedingly colorful career as a vagante bishop, and many little Old Catholic and pseudo-Orthodox groups have websites claiming "apostolic succession" through him. More importantly for our purposes, Vilatte remained in occasional contact with Orthodoxy. Robert Josias Morgan—soon to become Fr. Raphael, the first black Orthodox priest in America—was briefly a deacon in Vilatte's church in the early 1900s. (See chapter 28 on Morgan.) Many years later, in 1921, Vilatte consecrated George Alexander McGuire, who immediately formed the African Orthodox Church.

Was Vilatte's Old Catholic parish once a part of the Russian Orthodox Church? Even if we assume that the purported certificate from Bishop Vladimir is authentic, I don't think we can be sure. Bishop Vladimir may have viewed St. Alexis Toth and Joseph Rene Vilatte as parallel church leaders, and he may have imagined that, just as St. Alexis began a flood of Uniate conversions to Orthodoxy, so too Vilatte would be the first of thousands of Old Catholics to join the Russian Mission. But from Vilatte's perspective, this whole idea would have been laughable. He was, it seems, utterly committed to becoming a vagante bishop. He wanted a mechanical, legalistic "apostolic succession," and then he wanted to be left to his own devices. There is simply no way that he or his Wisconsin parish could have been effectively incorporated into the Russian Mission.

CHAPTER TWELVE

The Most Powerful Woman in Early American Orthodoxy

Barbara MacGahan

FROM 1870 TO 1883, as related in a previous chapter, Fr. Nicholas Bjerring operated a Russian chapel in New York City. At the time, there were very few Orthodox Christians in New York, and Bjerring's parish was always small. In 1883, the Russian government decided to pull its funding and close the chapel. Bjerring responded by leaving the Orthodox Church and becoming a Presbyterian minister. The next year, Fr. Stephen Hatherly, a convert priest of the Ecumenical Patriarchate, traveled from England to America and attempted to start a new Orthodox church in New York City. His efforts failed, mainly due to lack of interest from the tiny Orthodox community.

Thus, for the rest of the 1880s, New York—in common with all of the Eastern United States—did not have even one Orthodox parish. But things were about to change. As the Greek community in New York grew in the early Ellis Island years, two Greek Orthodox churches were established, one in 1892 and another in 1894. Finally, in 1895, Russian Orthodoxy returned to the city with the founding of St. Nicholas Church. Saint Nicholas began in the former home of one of the parish trustees, at 207 East 18th Street. The main floor housed the chapel; the priest, Fr. Evtikhy Balanovitch, lived upstairs with his family; and a Sunday school and reading room occupied the basement. (Before long, the parish moved around the corner, to 233 2nd Ave.)

But despite these modest beginnings, from the start, the parish had some impressive characteristics. Its iconostasis had previously been owned by the Russian army and was used in the field during battles in the Balkans. A twelve-person choir was led by Eugenie Lineff, a former opera singer. The church trustees included some notable people—the Russian ambassador and consul general and, most significantly, Barbara MacGahan.

Barbara MacGahan was perhaps the most influential Orthodox woman in early American Orthodox history. Despite her surname, MacGahan was a native Russian—she had married a famous American war correspondent and had taken his last name, and after he died, she became a journalist herself. By 1895, she was in her prime, in her early- to mid-forties, with bylines in the leading newspapers in both New York and Russia. She was a strong, independent woman, and it was principally due to her efforts that the leading Russians of the city petitioned the Holy Synod to establish a parish.

The first priest of St. Nicholas, Fr. Evtikhy Balanovitch, was likely an ex-Uniate who had recently converted to Orthodoxy: sources indicate that he was originally from the Austrian Empire and had only recently become associated with the Russian Orthodox Church. The *New York Times* (1/11/1896) describes him as "a man of striking appearance. Of immense frame, clear complexion, and with locks hanging far down his back, he had the appearance of a prophet of old." He was well educated, with a doctorate of divinity from the Theological Academy in St. Petersburg. He must not have been terribly practical, though, as he quickly made an enemy of the founder of the parish, Mrs. MacGahan.

During a meeting of the church trustees on November 17, 1895, Balanovitch called MacGahan some sort of name—a name which, according to the *New York Times*, "meant that Mrs. MacGahan's pen is at the disposal of the highest bidder, and that consequently no value could be placed on her statements as a newspaper correspondent and magazine writer." St. Raphael Hawaweeny, the newly arrived Syrian priest, was present at the meeting and didn't know what the word meant. Confused, he asked somebody. That person told MacGahan, and MacGahan promptly filed a lawsuit against Balanovitch.

MacGahan soon dropped the suit. On December 1, Balanovitch had agreed to resign as pastor and leave the country. Mac-Gahan determined that Balanovitch himself wasn't entirely to blame—"the whole trouble had been brought on him by outside parties," MacGahan's lawyer said, explaining that others within the new parish had incited the priest to make an enemy of Mac-Gahan. Mrs. MacGahan herself told the *Times* that, while Balanovitch "is a man of good intentions, he is easily led by others." Things ended up working out for the best, at least for MacGahan and St. Nicholas parish, as the next priest was St. Alexander Hotovitzky.

MacGahan remained a leading figure in the parish and in the Russian Mission in the years that followed. In 1903, she visited her home country of Russia. The same year, she made a statement on behalf of the mission to the *Washington Post* (1/26/1903), clarifying that the Greek priests in America were not under the Russian bishop:

> The Greek priests in this country are not under the rule of the Russian Bishop of America, the Right Rev. Tichon [sic]. There is no Greek bishop in this country at all. The direction extended over the Greek clergy here from far-off Athens (Greece) is exceedingly lax, in consequence of which the Greek priests here struggle along without any ecclesiastical guidance or supervision, and are

apt to indulge in grievous irregularities as to church observances, for which the Russian Church clergy, under the steady guidance of Bishop Tikhon, should not be held responsible.

A year later, in 1904, Barbara MacGahan died, aged just fifty-two or fifty-four, depending on the source, and since then she's been entirely forgotten.

CHAPTER THIRTEEN

The World's Parliament of Religions

THE STORY OF Fr. Christopher Jabara has weird connections to St. Raphael Hawaweeny, although it's not certain whether the two men ever met. For years, Jabara was head of the Antiochian *metochion* (representation church) in Moscow. During this period, he happened to meet with the ecumenical patriarch, and he helped arrange for an Antiochian student to attend the patriarchal seminary at Halki. That student was a young monk named Raphael Hawaweeny.

A decade later, Jabara started preaching that all religions were the same and that Christianity should merge with Islam. This understandably caused a scandal—the official representative of the Patriarchate of Antioch to Russia teaching heresy—and Jabara was run out of the Russian Empire. His replacement as head of the metochion was Hierodeacon Raphael Hawaweeny.

It's unknown where Jabara went after that, but by the end of 1892, he was in New York, carrying credentials from the patriarch of Antioch. The local Arab Orthodox, at this point a small but growing community, were thrilled to see an Antiochian priest. They had been worshipping in the new Greek parish in town, but now they could have a church of their own. They set up a temporary chapel, and in June 1893, Jabara dedicated it with the help of two Russian priests who served as chaplains on a visiting Russian warship.

The chapel didn't last, though, as Jabara's new parishioners appear to have soured quickly on their priest, who kept going on about his basically Unitarian theological ideas. He wrote a book, *The Unity of Faith and the Harmony of Religions*, laying all of this out.

Jabara had come to America at the perfect time for someone interested in creating a One World Religion: the legendary Chicago World's Fair was happening, and in conjunction with the Fair, the World's Parliament of Religions was organized. The Parliament featured not only all the flavors of Protestants but also Muslims, Hindus, and Buddhists. Although Orthodoxy in America was barely getting off the ground, several Orthodox figures played prominent roles. Jabara came, of course—how could he miss it?—but the most notable Orthodox clergyman at the event was Archbishop Dionysius Latas of Zakynthos (or Zante), the first Greek Orthodox bishop to set foot on American soil.

ooooo

ARCHBISHOP DIONYSIUS HAD been born on Zakynthos in 1836, went to seminary in Jerusalem, and then studied at the University of Athens. While in Athens, he was helping out at the city's cathedral when he began to stand out as an unusually talented young man. Here's an account from a few years later:

This young priest was originally one of the candle-snuffers, a lad of no education, and with no apparent gifts, except a fine rich voice. Promoted because of this to assist in the chorals, he somehow obtained leave to talk or preach, and astonished every one, and greatly captivated the people by his eloquence. He speedily acquired a wide notoriety, and won many friends. Among them was a rich Athenian, who proposed to him to spend three years in the schools of Germany and France, at his expense. He accepted the offer, spent time in diligent application, and has just returned, and is creating the highest enthusiasm.[1]

Dionysius returned to Athens in 1870, by now one of the most educated and cultured men in Greece. The metropolitan appointed him to be the city's main preacher at a time when most priests in Greece weren't allowed to give homilies. Dionysius was an immediate sensation. This is from an American visitor to Athens in the years when Dionysius started preaching:

> I went on Friday morning to hear him preach, and found the church literally packed. And the Greek churches having no seats, admit of such a crowding as is entirely unknown to American audiences. There was no getting near the main entrance, the throng extending into the street. I found a side door, however, to the women's gallery, and there at last succeeded, by climbing upon a pile of boards, in getting a view of the preacher and his congregation. Below me was a sea of men's faces, all upturned toward a man of fine intellectual features, and searching dark eyes, and who in the black gown and round brimless hat or high stiff fez of a Greek priest, stood in a pulpit projecting from one of the columns near the middle of the church.[2]

Dionysius preached for an hour and a half, and the whole congregation stood in rapt attention the whole time.

He continued preaching in Athens for fourteen years, until 1884, when he was elected archbishop of his home island of Zakynthos. He went on to make some waves by fighting against Freemasonry, which was growing in popularity. In 1886, he published the text of the Liturgy of St. James, reinstituting this ancient liturgy, which had long since fallen out of use. At

---

1   *New York Evangelist* (July 21, 1870), 6.
2   Ibid.

Zakynthos, the Liturgy of St. James was celebrated once a year, on the feast of St. James the Brother of the Lord (October 23). In 1900, the patriarch of Jerusalem began to celebrate it each year on December 31.

Archbishop Dionysius Latas of Zante

Dionysius was fifty-seven when he came to the United States, accompanied by his deacon, Homer. He visited specifically to attend the Parliament of Religions. One of their first stops was the new Greek church in New York City; Dionysius told the *New York Times* (8/1/1893), "It reminded me of the little churches I preached in years ago when I was an Archimandrite."

Dionysius was invited to Saratoga Springs—at the time a wildly popular resort town—to be the guest of the Episcopalian bishop Henry Potter. Dionysius arrived in Saratoga Springs just as another international visitor, a Sikh maharajah, was leaving the resort town. "Since the Maharajah's departure the reigning foreign favorite has been the Archbishop of Greece," the *New York Times* (8/6/1893) reported. The paper went on, "The distinguished prelate is as approachable as his recent predecessor in Saratoga, and all who meet him find him most companionable. He is a man of fine physique, with a strong, intellectual face. He speaks excellent English and fluent French, which latter language he likes to use."

By all accounts, the archbishop had a great time. "He has a keen eye," the *Times* said, "which twinkles with humor." Next, he was off to Washington, DC. He hoped to meet President Grover Cleveland, but the president was out of town. On August 12, a

Washington Post reporter wrote that Dionysius had "a jolly face, a hearty laugh, and although he cannot always understand questions in English, he is quite communicative." He delighted the reporter with his humor:

> "Americans and Englishmen are different," he said. "The Englishman is like this," and then he drew in his head and put on a stiff, gloomy, and morose expression, which was comical in the extreme. "But the American," he continued, changing his mood, "is always this way," and the archbishop burst into a hearty laugh to illustrate what he meant.

But he couldn't stay in Washington long; he needed to get to Chicago to attend the Parliament of Religions.

ooooo

AT THE PARLIAMENT, Archbishop Dionysius gave a talk on the history of religion in Greece, but his actual words made less of an impact than his physical presence at the event. Another Orthodox hierarch made a brief appearance: Nicholas Ziorov, the Russian Orthodox bishop in America, attended the Parliament on its opening day, but he was conspicuously absent from the meetings themselves, citing "church duties" that prevented his further participation.

The Orthodox figure who made a real splash was Fr. Christopher Jabara, who saw in the Parliament a golden opportunity to create a single world religion. Here's an excerpt from one of his speeches:

> My brothers and sisters in the worship of God! All the religions now in this general and religious congress are parallel to each other in the sight of the whole world. Every one of these religions has supporters who prefer their own to other religions, and they might bring some arguments or reasons to convince

others of the value and truth of their own form of religion.

Therefore, I think that a committee should be selected from the great religions to investigate the dogmas and to make a full and perfect comparison, and, approving the true one, to announce it to the people. This is easy to do in America, and especially in Chicago, as here the means for realization may be found.

First, there is full religious liberty; second, there is great progress in all branches of science; third, there is presence of great learning; fourth, wealth and benevolence; fifth, the piety of the American people in general and their energy in so many things useful to humanity, making this country a refuge to all nations.

Columbus discovered America for the whole world and discovered a home for the oppressed of all nations. As Columbus discovered America, so must Americans show the people of all nations a new religion in which all hearts may find rest.

That wasn't all. Jabara told a reporter:

I think and believe that when the gospels and the Koran, which are really one, are reconciled and the two great peoples, Christians and Mahometans, are also reconciled, the whole world will come into unity and all differences fade away. All the human kind will become brethren in worshipping the true God and following Christ, the savior of the world, and I, as a servant of religion during all my life, have come from far away Damascus on my own account and in my poverty pray, in the name of God the omnipresent, that the people may consider my ideas on the unity of religion, especially between the sacred books.[3]

There was one other Orthodox clergyman at the Parliament, and he was pretty much the opposite of Jabara: Fr. Panagiotis Phiambolis, pastor of Chicago's brand-new Greek parish. Phiambolis was staunchly Orthodox; he opened his talk with, "Believing is not the question—believing rightly is the question." After

---

3   *Boston Globe* (March 18, 1894), 7.

referring to Rome's schism from Orthodoxy, Phiambolis took aim at Islam:

> This division resulted in the prevention of Christianism and the progress of Mohammedanism, whose motto is, "Kill the Infidels," because every one who is not a Mohammedan, according to the Koran of the prophet, is an infidel, is a dog. [. . .] The people of the orient suffered, and still suffer; the Christian virgins are dishonored by the followers of the moral prophet, and the life of a Christian is not considered as precious as that of a dog.

In stark contrast with Jabara, Phiambolis saw no need for some kind of melding of world religions; Orthodoxy alone was the true Church, lacking nothing:

> Regarding the church, the Orthodox Church, we are true to the examples of the apostles and the paradigma of the synods, we follow the same road in religious questions, and after discussion do not accept new dogma without the agreement of the whole ecumenical council; neither do we adopt any dogma other than that of the one united and undivided church whose doctrine has been followed until to-day. The Orthodox Apostolic Catholic Church contains many different nations, and every one of them uses its own language in the mass and litany and governs its church independently, but all these nations have the same faith.

ooooo

ARCHBISHOP DIONYSIUS HUNG around the United States for a while after the Parliament, mostly hanging out with Episcopalians. He attended an Episcopalian bishop's consecration in Boston, stayed as a houseguest with another Episcopalian bishop in St. Louis, and gave a speech at an Episcopal Church convention in Chicago. Dionysius was rather enamored with the Episcopalians, declaring publicly, in both Boston and Chicago, that

the Episcopal Church "is the center toward which all the emi-
nent persons of the distinctive churches will cast their eyes in the
future, when, by the grace of God, they will decide to take steps
for the union of all the Christian world into one flock, under one
shepherd."[4]

From Chicago, Dionysius traveled westward, stopping in
San Francisco. It's unclear whether he visited the city's Russian
Orthodox cathedral or met with Bishop Nicholas Ziorov. And
finally, he departed America, going west rather than east, across
the Pacific Ocean. On a train ride from Singapore to Calcutta,
he happened to run into a Methodist bishop, who invited him to
attend a Methodist conference in Calcutta. Dionysius accepted.
According to one American periodical, "Although he remarked
privately that Bishop Thoburn was not a real bishop, he bestowed
upon him when taking leave the apostolic kiss."[5] At his host's
request, Dionysius delighted the Methodists by delivering St.
Paul's Mars Hill sermon in its original Greek.

The Archbishop finally made it back home to Zakynthos
in the middle of 1894, but soon after his return, he died, aged
fifty-eight.

ooooo

AS FOR FR. Christopher Jabara, after the Parliament, unwanted
among the Syrians in New York, he went to Boston. But he
wasn't there to minister to the Orthodox of the city; according
to the *Boston Globe*, he "came to Boston especially as a center of
Unitarianism where the tenets of religion and the principles of
his mission can be sifted and appreciated."

Eventually, Jabara left the United States and traveled to Egypt.
An American Protestant named John Henry Barrows ran into

---

4   *Dallas Morning News* (Nov. 14, 1893).
5   *Congregationalist* (April 26, 1894), 601.

him there in 1896–97. Barrows wrote the following account in his travelogue *A World-Pilgrimage* (1897):

> Two other men, who were present at the Parliament, I unexpectedly met at the Sunday services in the American Mission. One of them is Christophora Jibara, formerly Archimandrite of Damascus. He is still very active and earnest in what he deems his chief mission, persuading Christians to give up the doctrine of the Trinity, which prevents, as it seems to him, their coming into any union with Mohammedans and Jews. He believes that Christ is the Son of God and wrought a gospel of redemption. Jibara is a master of several languages, and I tried in vain to persuade him to employ his powers of speech in preaching a positive gospel, instead of smiting all his life at a dogma which has worn out many hammers.

In Cairo, Jabara started a short-lived journal, trying to push his idea that Christianity and Islam should merge. This idea offended both Christians and Muslims, leaving Jabara, the ultimate ecumenist, rejected by everyone. He died in 1901, and no religious community in Cairo would allow his body to be buried in their cemetery. Finally, a witness came forward claiming that Jabara had renounced heresy and returned to Orthodoxy, and so the Orthodox agreed to let him be buried as an Orthodox Christian.

CHAPTER FOURTEEN

Constantinople's First Priest in America?

Archimandrite Kallinikos Delveis

THE FIRST GREEK Orthodox parish in New York City, Holy Trinity, was founded in January 1892. By the end of 1893, a sizeable minority of the parishioners had decided they needed their own separate church. At the time, the local newspapers reported that Holy Trinity was "attended chiefly by the up-town colony of Greeks, and did not fully meet the wants of those who live at the lower end of the city." This led Solon Vlasto, the president of the Greek Society of Athena, to make direct contact with the Ecumenical Patriarchate and request a priest. Father John Erickson has written that a "dissatisfied group wrote to the Patriarchate of Constantinople, rather than to the Holy Synod of Greece, asking for 'an educated priest.'" But Holy Trinity's priest, Fr. Paisios Ferentinos, was actually quite well educated, so it's not clear what was going on.[1]

---

1   Erickson, *Orthodox Christians in America*, 72. On Ferentinos's education: After becoming a monk on the island of Patmos, he studied at the theological school at Halki, near Constantinople. He then returned to his monastery and taught Greek to the youth of Patmos. Then, for two years, he was a deacon to the patriarch of Alexandria, after which he

In any event, the Ecumenical Patriarchate responded by sending Archimandrite Kallinikos Delveis to New York. (This is not the same Fr. Kallinikos covered in chapter 10.) This appears to be the first time Constantinople directly sent a priest to serve in America—or, possibly, the entire Western Hemisphere. The Greek priests in America before Fr. Kallinikos were either sent by the Church of Greece or came on their own initiative. Father Kallinikos arrived in January 1894, and he was described as "a man of striking personality. He is thirty-two years old, of medium height, olive complexion, and long black hair and beard. He was born in Constantinople, and was educated in the theological seminary of Halki, in that city. His voice is resonant, and he is reputed to be a preacher of great eloquence."[2] Just after Fr. Kallinikos arrived in New York City, Solon Vlasto founded the Greek newspaper *Atlantis*, and Fr. Kallinikos worked as one of the first editors.

The new parish, called Annunciation, began worshipping in the basement of a Baptist church—a space normally used by a Baptist kindergarten class. While Annunciation was predominantly Greek, Fr. Kallinikos was open to cooperating with other Orthodox ethnic groups. Shortly after his arrival, Fr. Alexis Toth of the Russian Mission visited New York and concelebrated the Divine Liturgy with Fr. Kallinikos. The *New York Herald* (3/19/1894) explained, "This service in Russian was an experiment which will probably be repeated. It was part of an endeavor to bring together all those who are members of the Greek Orthodox Church, with the hope of building one large church in this city where all of that faith can assemble." When the Russian Tsar Alexander III died later in 1894, both Greek churches held

---

was ordained a priest. In the years immediately prior to his arrival in America, he served as librarian and assistant chaplain at the Pisarian Theological School in Athens. Such a biography suggests that Ferentinos was in fact quite educated. *Baltimore Sun* (January 13, 1892).

2   *New York Times* (January 8, 1894), 9.

memorial services. Holy Trinity drew a crowd of three hundred to the memorial, while one hundred attended Annunciation.

Father Kallinikos didn't last long in New York. When he came to Annunciation, he was given a one-year contract that called for a thousand-dollar annual salary (roughly thirty-five thousand today). According to Fr. Kallinikos, the contract was renewed for 1895; according to Solon Vlasto, the lay leader of the parish, the contract was never renewed. In any event, Fr. Kallinikos was paid for half the year, but on July 1, Vlasto refused to pay the other half, and Fr. Kallinikos was dismissed. He sued the parish, and in June 1896, a jury awarded him five hundred dollars (six months' pay). Vlasto and the parish trustees refused to pay up, and eventually, the sheriff seized a valuable oil painting from Vlasto's Society of Athena to cover the amount due.

By that point, however, Fr. Kallinikos was already gone: in August 1895, he had moved to Lowell, Massachusetts, and founded St. George Greek Orthodox Church. As in New York, the fledgling parish rented space from an established Protestant church. And as in New York, Fr. Kallinikos ran into trouble with one of the lay leaders of the parish. In this case, the parish president was voted out of office, and—in an unusual move—Fr. Kallinikos was elected to replace him. I've only heard of one other instance where a Greek priest also served as president of his parish board. The outgoing president turned over the books to Fr. Kallinikos, who soon discovered a discrepancy. The parish launched an investigation, concluding that the old president had embezzled thirty-two dollars (around eleven hundred dollars today).

In June 1896—the same month Fr. Kallinikos won his case against Annunciation—he reportedly received word that he had been elected a bishop of the Ecumenical Patriarchate, and he left America for Constantinople. However, he doesn't appear in Demetrius Kiminas's indispensable *The Ecumenical Patriarchate:*

A History of Its Metropolitanates with Annotated Hierarch Catalogs, which catalogs the bishops of the Ecumenical Patriarchate in recent centuries. Thus it's uncertain whether he was ever consecrated or what became of him.

CHAPTER FIFTEEN

P. T. Barnum's Widow Marries in a Greek Orthodox Church

P. T. BARNUM was the greatest showman of the nineteenth century. Today, he's most closely associated with the circus that bears his name, but in his own day, he was much more than a circus organizer. In an era before blockbuster movies, Barnum was the closest you could get to a larger-than-life Hollywood producer. He was impossibly famous and impossibly rich.

By 1874, the fifty-four-year-old Barnum was a household name. He'd only been in the circus business for a few years, but before that, he had owned the Barnum Museum, the biggest attraction in New York City. He was, in short, at the height of his powers when the widowed Barnum married twenty-four-year-old Nancy Fish, an English girl and the daughter of one of Barnum's longtime friends. Here's how the *New York Times* tells the story twenty-odd years later (8/8/1895):

She was the daughter of a Lancashire, England, cotton miller named Fish. In 1858 Mr. Barnum lectured in Manchester, England, and after the lecture Mr. Fish called on the great showman to tell him that his success in life was due to his reading of Mr. Barnum's autobiography, which fired his ambition to make money. When Mr. Fish built a new mill, his daughter christened the engine "Barnum."

After the death of the first Mrs. Barnum, Mr. Fish visited America. His daughter's letters so delighted Mr. Barnum that, as he put it, he fell in love with her before he saw her. They were married in 1874. The bride was half the age of her husband.

The couple remained together until Barnum's death in 1891. Four years later, in 1895, Nancy Barnum remarried. She had been engaged in a very discreet courtship with Demetrius Callias Bey, a Greek from Turkey. Callias had supposedly made millions in the olive business, but there were rumors that he actually had no money at all. In any event, he was handsome, and according to one story (which may or may not be true), the pair met when Nancy was visiting Egypt and happened to fall off the Great Pyramid, whereupon Callias caught her. The couple were married on August 7, 1895, at Annunciation Greek Orthodox Church in New York City, with Fr. Agatheodoro Papageorgopoulos officiating.

At least, that's according to the *New York Times* the following day. I'm inclined to believe the report, although the *Boston Globe* passed this along (by way of the *Knoxville Daily Journal*, 8/13/1895):

> The minister who married Mrs. P.T. Barnum to her wealthy Greek lover Wednesday is named Rev. Agathedorus Papageorge-pouto, according to the *New York Journal*, Priest Archimandrite Paisius Ferentinos, according to the *New York World*, and Agathodoros Papageorgopoulus according to the *New York Herald*. It would have delighted Mrs. Barnum's late husband to get either of those names to put among his curiosities.

Father Paisius Ferentinos, mentioned above, was the former priest of Holy Trinity, New York's other Greek church.

The name of the officiating priest notwithstanding, the marriage between Nancy Barnum and Demetrius Callias Bey didn't last long. A little over a year later—September 22, 1896—Callias died of liver disease in Constantinople. His wife was on a brief visit to America at the time, and after learning of her husband's death, she left the United States for good. Two years later, in Paris, she was married for a third time, to a French nobleman. The marriage was apparently pure business—the baron got some of Nancy's money to pay his debts, and Nancy got to call herself a baroness. Nancy's real love, it seems, was her departed Greek husband. When she died in 1927, she was cremated and then buried, not next to P. T. Barnum, but next to Demetrius Callias Bey.

In the grand scheme of things, the story of Nancy Barnum and Demetrius Callias Bey isn't all that significant. It is, however, an early example of an Orthodox-related story that made its way into newspapers across the United States. And the marriage of Barnum and Callias has always struck me as a sort of distant forerunner to the union of another famous American widow to a wealthy Greek man—that of Jacqueline Kennedy to Aristotle Onassis.[1]

---

1   Just a little postscript here: A version of this chapter originally appeared as an article on my website, OrthodoxHistory.org, in 2010. Seven years later, the movie *The Greatest Showman* came out, based (somewhat loosely) on the life of P. T. Barnum, and my article got a massive surge of hits from people searching for information about Barnum's (first) wife. So, weirdly, this very minor story from American Orthodox history remains the most widely read thing I've written on the subject.

CHAPTER SIXTEEN

From the Tsar's Court to Galveston, Texas

Father Theoklitos Triantafilides

FATHER THEOKLITOS TRIANTAFILIDES'S father was from Athens—not the Athens of ancient Greece or the bustling Greek capital of today, but the backwater Athens, a small village situated amidst the ruins of a once-great civilization. It was the same city, and yet it was a very different city. The elder Trianta-filides fought in the Greek Revolution and then settled on the Peloponnese Peninsula. He named his son, born in November 1833, after the man he had fought under, the renowned general Theodoros Kolokotronis.

Just months before the future Fr. Theoklitos was born, the Church of Greece declared its independence from the Ecumenical Patriarchate. The EP initially rejected this, and for the next seventeen years, the status of the Church of Greece was up in the air. The church was also subjugated to the Greek government, which was run, not by Orthodox Christians, but by the Roman Catholic King Otho and his German Protestant and Catholic advisors. Protestant missionaries converged on Greece, hoping to convert the Orthodox people, whom they saw as backward idolaters. This was the environment in which Fr. Theoklitos grew up.

Father Theeoklitos Triantafilides

As a young adult, he was tonsured a monk and moved to Mount Athos, joining St. Panteleimon's Monastery. In centuries past, St. Panteleimon's had been a Russian monastery, but over the years it came to be dominated by Greeks. By the time Fr. Theoklitos was born, the monastery had fallen on hard times, and in 1835 (two years after Fr. Theoklitos's birth), they invited Russian monks to come and inhabit the monastery once again. In the decades that followed, the Russian monks came to outnumber the Greeks. This was a hard transition for a lot of the Greeks. In 1866, the monastery switched from reading only Greek texts in the refectory; the Greek monks protested, boycotting the refectory for a while.

Father Theoklitos seems not to have had any issues, though. He had a knack for languages, learning Russian, Church Slavonic, and Serbian (the latter of which he picked up thanks to frequent visits to Hilandar Monastery). He most likely left the Holy Mountain before the refectory language problem came up—he was invited to study at the Moscow Theological Academy. After a few years, he was asked to return to Greece to become the tutor to Prince George, son of the new Greek King George I, who had assumed the throne in 1863. King George's wife was Olga, the sister of Tsar Alexander III of Russia. The tsar then asked Fr. Theoklitos to come back to Russia and tutor his own children, including the future Tsar-Martyr Nicholas II. When Nicholas married Alexandra in 1894, Fr. Theoklitos was one of about thirty priests invited to officiate.

The following year, the tsar received a petition from the fledgling Orthodox community in Galveston, Texas, asking the

Russian Church to send them a priest. Tsar Nicholas responded by sending them his old tutor, Fr. Theoklitos, who by now was past sixty years old. He traveled to America in the fall of 1895; his traveling companions included Bishop Nicholas Ziorov and the young Syrian Archimandrite Raphael Hawaweeny.

Orthodoxy in America was in its infancy. The great immigration had begun only a few years earlier—so, too, the conversion of the Uniates, led by St. Alexis Toth. From his base in the boom town of Galveston (population 23,000 in 1890 and 37,000 by 1900), Fr. Theoklitos traveled throughout the Gulf region and beyond, one of the earliest circuit-riding American Orthodox clergy. His linguistic skill was particularly valuable: he now served in the Russian Mission but with a congregation of mostly Greeks and Serbs, with a handful of Syrians. Conveniently, Fr. Theoklitos had picked up a good deal of Arabic, along with Bulgarian and at least a bit of Spanish, English, French, German, and Romanian. He proved to be perhaps the most pan-Orthodox figure in early American Orthodoxy. His original deacon was Romanian; he liturgized in Greek, Slavonic, and Arabic; and he actively worked to evangelize Americans—possibly the first Orthodox priest to do this.

On September 8, 1900, a devastating hurricane struck Galveston, killing about a quarter of the city's population. Throughout the storm, Fr. Theoklitos and his assistant priest were in the church praying, and many parishioners and other residents of the city joined them. The flood waters moved the church ten feet to the west, but the building was intact and everyone inside was safe. Fifteen years later, the same pattern repeated itself: another terrible hurricane; the church moved by the waters, this time fifty feet; Fr. Theoklitos inside praying with the people, unharmed.

He became a beloved figure in Galveston, regularly visiting the sick in local hospitals. Children were particularly drawn to him. His biographer, Mimo Milosevich, writes, "On weekly trips to the business district, the neighborhood children would gather on the church steps and wait for his return. He would always have a large bag full of fruit and the latest sweets for them, saving a large portion for his parish children."

On October 22, 1916, Fr. Theoklitos died just shy of his eighty-third birthday. He was not buried, but instead, his body was interred in the church altar, where it remains to this day.

A text of Fr. Theoklitos's 1914 Christmas sermon has survived, published in the *Galveston Daily News* on January 8, 1914. It's a short sermon, but it reveals a lot about the kind of pastor Fr. Theoklitos was. According to the newspaper, Fr. Theoklitos began by recounting the story of the star, the wise men, their gifts, and King Herod. Then, said the paper, "Father Theoklitos took off his spectacles and used them to gesticulate with, as he preached a fatherly sermon on charity and its relation to happiness."

My children: Before Jesus came into our world the earth lacked the attributes of sympathetic understanding, which we find necessary to our happiness in this era. The Lord gave us his son, Jesus, to soften us, to give us understanding of human wants, to give us a sense of forgiveness, to teach us that to forgive is our duty, and to teach us charity.

My children, be charitable, open your hearts, for only in charity is there happiness. Make life brighter for your brother and your sister and the candle you light for them will make your light brighter.

God gave us Jesus, and Jesus gave us his all, even his life. We can do no more than emulate him, and in doing that we do all.

Think today of the poor whom he loved, lighten their burdens, even as he did. Open your hearts, oh, my children, even as did Jesus of Bethlehem.

My children, when he came among us he did not ask, "Of what nationality art thou? What is thy belief?" No! He came down among us and was one of us and he ministered to us. Open thy hearts, likewise, my children, and go among the poor and succor them; all the poor, for they are thy brothers and sisters, my children, and they are his people.

My children, many of you are not native to this land and it is well to treasure memories of thine own country, but think that this is a good land, and its people are good to thy people, and you all are his people. Learn to love, be honest, tolerant, forgiving, and charitable.

I pray you Merry Christmas, my children, and many, many years of happiness.

After the sermon, Fr. Theoklitos passed a plate to collect alms for the poor. "The plate was heaped high with bills and coins," reported the *Daily News*, "the merry chink-clink-chink of the contributions accenting like tiny cymbals the smooth melody of a beautiful hymn."

CHAPTER SEVENTEEN

Saint Alexander Hotovitzky

SAINT ALEXANDER HOTOVITZKY was the son of a priest in Russia—the rector of a seminary, no less—and so Alexander's future as a priest was almost automatic. But early on, he showed himself to be the cream of the crop, moving on from seminary (which was more like high school/college in Russia at that time) to the prestigious St. Petersburg Theological Academy, where only the best and brightest were admitted. After graduation, he was recruited by Bishop Nicholas Ziorov to come to the nascent Russian mission in America. This was 1895, the same year that Bishop Nicholas brought over an almost unbelievable haul of great priests, including St. Raphael Hawaweeny, Fr. Theoklitos Triantafilides, and Hotovtizky's friend St. John Kochurov, among others.

Saint Alexander was only twenty-three years old and not yet married, so his initial job was serving as a reader at the newly established St. Nicholas Church in New York. After his wedding, he was ordained to the diaconate and then to the priesthood—his priestly ordination was in 1896 in San Francisco. It's easy to forget, but this was one of the first ordinations to take place in the United States. He was appointed pastor of St. Nicholas in New York, replacing the ousted Fr. Evtikhy Balanovitch (see chapter 12 for more on that story).

Saint Alexander Hotovitsky

From 1896 to 1914, St. Alexander was the leading priest in North America. His church became a cathedral, and in addition to his duties as cathedral dean, he had extensive responsibilities in the Russian mission/diocese/archdiocese. After Bishop Nicholas came St. Tikhon, who quickly came to rely on St. Alexander as his most trusted lieutenant. He worked closely with a host of saints, including his longtime friend St. John Kochurov, St. Raphael Hawaweeny, St. Sebastian Dabovich, and St. Alexis Toth (with whom he helped bring thousands of Uniates into the Orthodox Church).

By 1914 St. Alexander had been in America for nineteen years but was still only forty-two years old. The Holy Synod of Russia transferred him, initially to Berlin and Helsinki. In 1917, he was appointed dean of Christ the Savior Cathedral in Moscow, where he was reunited with St. Tikhon, who became patriarch. Saint Alexander worked closely with St. Tikhon during the hard years that followed. He was imprisoned and exiled multiple times before finally being sentenced to death in 1937. He was executed in August 1937 at the age of sixty-five.

Here are some interesting stories and nuggets from St. Alexander's time in America.

Saint Alexander and the Jewish Convert

LEAVING ASIDE NATIVE Alaskans and Uniates, conversions to Orthodoxy in America were quite rare at the turn of the last century. Yes, American women occasionally converted when they married cradle Orthodox men, and there was the odd Episcopalian convert, but even taking those into consideration, conversions were very uncommon. And if Protestants joining the Orthodox Church were rare, a Jewish convert was rarer still. In fact, I've found only one solid example of a Jewish convert to Orthodoxy in America in the early years of our history.

We don't know his name or his story, but the event was sufficiently notable that the New York newspapers reported on it. The convert—baptized with the name Vladimir—was received on Sunday, February 14, 1897, at St. Nicholas Russian Church in New York City. Described by the *New York Times* two days later as "young," Vladimir renounced the "false doctrines of the Hebrews," including the teachings of the Talmud. He swore that he was joining the Church only out of genuine conviction of faith and love for Christ, and not because of fear, coercion, the hope of personal gain, or any other reason. While the Hours were read, a wooden baptismal font was filled with water. The font was behind a low screen, which blocked the baptism from the view of the congregation. From the *New York Sun* (2/16/1897):

> The priest, the convert and the male sponsor went behind the screen. The woman sponsor staid [sic] outside. The screen was not high and the congregation could some times see garments that were raised in the convert's complete disrobing. They could hear the solemn words of the service by those within. They could hear the splashing and gurgling of the water as the convert was immersed for the first, second and third time. They saw the symbolical white robe and the cross as they were raised above his head. Meanwhile they joined in singing the hymn of baptism.

The ceremony coincided with the Feast of the Entrance of Christ into the Temple, and the officiating priest was St. Alexander Hotovitzky. Presumably, St. Alexander played a major role in bringing this young Jewish man to Christ. But how exactly did a young New York Jew come to join the Russian Orthodox Church in 1897, just two years after St. Nicholas parish was founded? What effect did this conversion have on his life? Was he unique, or were there other Jews who converted around the same time? I don't know the answers, but they may yet be discovered in the records of St. Nicholas Cathedral.

Saint Alexander on Liturgical Language

ON NOVEMBER 4, 1905, a religious and literary journal entitled *The Friend* published a letter from St. Alexander Hotovitzky in response to an article in the same publication that claimed, "In this Russian service, of course, no one understood what was said, not even the Russians themselves, as the whole of it was in the ancient ecclesiastical Slavonic tongue. As the Romish Church addresses the Lord in Latin, so do the Greeks use this Slavonic language." Here is St. Alexander's reply:

This is not true.

Our ecclesiastical Slavonic tongue is the original of modern Russian, Servian, Slavonian, and of other branches of the Slavic world.

Every Russian, even children (of school age) understands well the real text and meaning of all prayers in Slavonic, excluding, perhaps, not many expressions which are lost for living use and are not fitting for ordinary practice.

Easy to be understood, this Slavonic language has, besides, immense dignity of words, and is sanctified as proper church language by long ecclesiastical usage.

To compare the use of the Latin tongue in the Roman Church and of Slavonic in the Russian is, then, far from consistency and knowledge of true conditions of things, because the chief rule of the Eastern Church (which combines Russia, Greece, Jerusalem, Antiochia, etc.) is to say the divine services in the language of the people for whom the services are intended; in Japan we celebrate and preach in Japanese, in China in Chinese, in Alaska in the native tongue of the Aleutians, and in some churches of America in English, always according to the needs and understanding of the congregation.

Russians do not understand Greek, and Greeks do not understand the Russian; so in a Greek church you never hear one word of the Slavonic tongue, and vice versa; yet both are of the same Eastern Catholic confession.

A. Hotovitzky, Dean of the Russian St. Nicholas Cathedral.

New York, Ninth Month 24, 1905.

Saint Alexander on Saint John of Kronstadt

IN 1903, ST. ALEXANDER visited Russia, where he paid a visit to Fr. John Sergiev—better known today as St. John of Kronstadt, who was famous even in his lifetime as a wonderworker. After his return to America, St. Alexander talked with a reporter from the *Wilkes-Barre Times* (4/7/1904) about his experience with St. John:

In the study of Rev. Alexander A. Hotovitzky, Archpriest of the church of St. Nicholas, the chief adornment is a large picture of Father John bearing his autograph. This was presented to Father Hotovitzky last Summer when, during a visit to Russia, he called upon Father John to thank him for the interest he had taken in his little flock. A portion of the funds necessary for the erection of the handsome new church edifice was collected in Russia, and Father John both by personal donations and by enlisting the interest of others in the cause became a substantial contributor.

The visit of Father Hotovitzky to Cronstadt [sic] occurred on July 19 (old style). It so happened that this was Father John's name day. Faithful to a custom of many years, the Russian divine on that day celebrated a solemn mass in the cathedral and then entertained at dinner the many friends who had come to extend their good wishes. The Rev. Father Hotovitzky was one of the guests.

"Vice Admiral Marakoff was toast-master at the dinner," said Father Hotovitzky yesterday. "It was only natural that he should be, for he and Father John are bound together by ties of warm personal friendship. There were present at that dinner many dignitaries of Church and State, but, nevertheless, it was a most democratic affair. Father John has some quaint notions, and even in a land of such marked class distinction as Russia, rich terms of equality. It was a good dinner, and good things to drink went with it, for Father John, though ordinarily he lives as frugally and abstemiously as a monk, believes that God put the good things of life on earth for the cheer of man, and he loves to see others enjoy themselves.

"Father John in some respects is the most remarkable man in Russia to-day, and certainly is the most talked of. He represents a type all by itself in the Russian Church, and no one has so vividly brought home to the people its power and potentialities with a complete leaving out of all the ostentation, pomp, and grandeur with which it formerly charmed and awed the people.

"Those who have been wont to consider Father John as a mystic or as a man of a monastic cast of mind have erred. He is the opposite. He took a wife, and he mingles freely in the common life of the people, and he enjoys a good joke. He has secularized religion and both by life and teaching has steadily striven to lift the common life to the level of religion. He is a strong advocate of the living help, and he turned his back on monastic orders just because he felt he was needed and could be a potent influence for good by remaining in the open life where those that needed him could constantly besiege the doors of his simple dwelling in Cronstadt when he is there and the crowds that gather at railroad stations during his many journeys through Russia which occupy the greater part of his time have shown that he was right.

"His influence reaches from the throne of the Czar to the meanest hovel in Russia. He takes from the abundance of the rich with both hands and scatters it as freely among those that need it. It is only through the remarkable gifts he receives that he has been able to maintain something like twenty-five asylums and institutions in different parts of Russia, of which he is the founder.

"One charm about Father John is his broadness. While orthodox in the essential meaning of that word, he makes no distinction between those that follow his and other beliefs. He bestows his blessing on all alike, for he recognizes as divine every channel through which a devout spirit and a realization of the highest life can flow into the human soul.

"In his study you will find a desk, a bed and some holy pictures. It is as simple as the cell of a monk. He spends little time there, however, for his time is mostly taken up with relieving suffering among the poor, comforting the dying, and on missionary journeys. Were a call to attend a deathbed at the other end of the empire to reach Father John in the middle of the night he would rise and take the first train.

"There are many in Russia who ascribe supernatural powers to Father John. He does not claim any, except the power of prayer. He is a firm believer in that, and the most remarkable thing is that his prayers are very brief. But one cannot look into his wondrous violet eyes without feeling that the look in them is not of this world. They seem to be looking, one minute far beyond the border line of life, and at other times they seem to penetrate into one's very soul. Strangely, also, those who have observed him during the last twenty-five years of his life—he is now over seventy—declare that age seems to have wrought no change in his appearance."

It's hard to imagine something like this appearing in a newspaper today, but in St. John of Kronstadt's lifetime, the American press was fascinated with him. Beginning in the early 1890s, news about St. John appeared quite regularly in US newspapers, complete with accounts of miracles (including even the raising of someone from the dead). But this *Wilkes-Barre Times* article stands out from all the rest. Here, you have one saint talking about another (a rare enough thing), and for a secular audience, no less.

Saint Alexander on the Death
of Saint Nikolai of Japan

SAINT NIKOLAI KASATKIN, the missionary bishop of Japan, died on February 16, 1912. He was remarkably well known in America, where both secular periodicals and Russian Church publications chronicled his ministry. Saint Alexander had a particular admiration for St. Nikolai, and when Nikolai died, Alexander wrote this eulogy in the March 14, 1912, issue of the *Russian Orthodox American Messenger*:

> An irreparable loss! The Orthodox Church is mourning. Her most worthy son, the apostle of her teaching, has departed from earthly life. Before the news of the decease of the Most Reverend Nikolai, the glorious light-bringer of Japan, all the small struggles and discords which are vexing the organism of the Russian Orthodox Church shrink into insignificance. "Nikolai of Japan": you have before you the most glorious page of the missionary work of the Orthodox Church, an Orthodox pastor's service of more than fifty years in a foreign land, and what service! He gave himself up wholly to his sacred task, and wedding his bride, the Japanese Church, he kept those sacred ties unbroken until his latest breath. A unique example! While he lived, there was no need to prove to enquirers and questioners of the vitality of the Orthodox Church, and its missionary tendencies: it was enough to say "Nikolai of Japan", and the whole world of other creeds and other faiths became silent in adoration: for all the powers of other creeds and other faiths could not show his equal among the ranks of their warriors!
>
> Let us prostrate ourselves before thy sacred tomb, O light-bringer of Japan, true servant of Christ! And let us pray:—Be thou the representative, in the heavenly habitations, of thy beloved Orthodox Church, and may God save her from all injuries and obstacles, and may He send forth other light-bringers, even in part like to thee to illumine the world with the light of the Gospel of Christ!

CHAPTER EIGHTEEN

Saint Sebastian on Society in 1899

THIS ISN'T A collection of primary sources, and I've resisted the temptation to reprint too much from old documents, but I have to make an exception here. Saint Sebastian Dabovich—the first saint to have been born on US soil—published a collection of his homilies in 1899 under the title *Preaching in the Russian Church* when he was a thirty-six-year-old priest in his birthplace, San Francisco. One of those sermons is "On the Condition of Society," where St. Sebastian talks about how degraded American society has become. He might as well have been writing it today. Here's the whole thing:

> How long will it thus go on! When will the baptized become active Christians, so that the pastors may give their attention to the conversion of the heathen? What a terrible battle we must fight. Already the fire of hell is in the world. Great cities are multiplying throughout the land. The farmer, as the word is defined in our dictionaries, is a thing of the past. It is now the land-owner with a mansion in the city, a yacht on the sea, and with a private train across the continent. There are comparatively but a few laborers in the fields—too poor to support families. The quiet country homes are becoming few, shall I say precious? I fear not so, because people are fast losing their ability to rightly estimate the value of things. Most of the cities in all the world

are overcrowded. The female portion of the population is most conspicuous. A stupid craze after unwholesome fashions is the one all-absorbing passion of the majority of women. There is no room for gardens and yards; most of the children in San Francisco are actually brought up in the streets. Oh, how few of them feel the blessed influence of a Christian home! Young men and young women are continually "on the go," as they say. And this "go" is a nervous, unsteady rush to "keep up with the times." And after all their hurry nothing is left but steam and vapor, for they are empty, as empty as the changing and vanishing world can be. Yet they fret and inquire: "Where shall we go to and what shall we see? What shall we do? Oh! what can we do?" If you promenade along the broad avenue or pass through the narrow lane, if you visit the meeting halls in the city or look into the factories, everywhere you see that same all-devouring gaze of the bold young woman, who stares with a kind of artificial movement of the eyes. And sometimes you hear even so-called Christians say that it is a weakness of character in one who has the downcast eyes of modesty, the blush of innocence. Such people do not know the live sense and fine impulse of a pure conscience. When a young man puffs tobacco smoke or shows his teeth with a disapproving smile in the presence of and at the conversation of older people, then society is wrong; something is the matter with his family.

In view of all this, beloved, the preacher of the Word of God is obliged by a terrible oath he has given before he received the gift in Apostolic succession at his ordination, to present to you the whole of the Truth, not a part of it.

The number of unmarried people is increasing. And there are some married people who say: "We do not want children, because we want to have as much pleasure as possible." This is a false position, for in a Christian marriage one kind of pleasure is not allowed continually. Christians marry for the sake of God and His law as much as they do for themselves. But Christians who remain single renounce marriage and live holy for the sake of God and Him alone. Thus we find that the family tie is

abused, as well as the single state. Courtship of young people just out of school is
not to be advised, because it often leads to
debauchery. A courtship running through
long years also gives occasion to sin and a
species of wrongdoing to God, for the heart
and its love are stolen from God and thrown
away on a man.

Throughout all the long centuries of
Christianity there have been in the Church
heroic members, young people of both sexes,
who by the grace of God have kept their

Saint Sebastian
Dabovich preaching

souls pure and intact, and have dedicated to the honor of God
the noblest attribute of their human life, namely, an untarnished
purity of soul and body. Such persons have had the courage and
such unbounded confidence in God's assistance that, although
living in the world and its dangers, though threatened by the
cravings of their own individual passions and by the temptations
of the devil, yet they have succeeded bravely in preserving this
treasure even in a frail earthen vessel, have carried it uninjured
through life's long journey here below, and have finally presented
it to their Lord.

Christian heroes and heroines, you who have imitated or who
still do imitate the sublime example of the Most Blessed Virgin,
the Church admires your spirit of sacrifice as she does that of
the holy martyrs, who in a few hours finished their contest and
proved their fidelity to God and their faith; because you have to
combat, to suffer, and to sacrifice your whole life through. With
joy and veneration do the angels look down upon you, for you
resemble themselves. With motherly affection and with mighty
power does the Holy Virgin Mary when you earnestly pray throw
her sheltering omophorion around you, for you are her pupils and
imitators. With the sweetness of divine love the heavenly Bride-
groom will fill your heart and more than compensate you for the
fleeting, transient, worldly love that you have laid down at His
feet. The eternal Judge will find you waiting like the wise and

prudent virgins who all through life carry in their hands the pure oblation of love and the burning light of good example. Therefore, faithful to the end, He will invite you to the eternal wedding feast in heaven. Amen.

CHAPTER NINETEEN

Bishop Nicholas
in Defense of the Alaskans

RUSSIA SOLD ALASKA to the United States in 1867. A decade later, a Presbyterian minister named Sheldon Jackson began missionary work in the territory—missionary work to convert indigenous Orthodox Christians to American Protestantism. In 1885, he was appointed to be the federal government's General Agent of Education in Alaska, and using that position, he divvied up Alaska among the various Protestant denominations. His aim was clear: These native people needed to be turned into good Americans. "It is the purpose of the government in establishing schools in Alaska to train up English speaking American citizens," he wrote to new teachers soon after his appointment. "You will therefore teach in English and give special prominence to instruction in the English language. . . . [Y]our teaching should be pervaded by the spirit of the Bible."[1] He explicitly aimed to eradicate the indigenous culture of the Alaskan tribes—a culture that included Orthodox Christianity, which by this point had become part and parcel of tribal identity.

In January 1899, Bishop Nicholas Ziorov had just been

---

1 Richard Dauenhauer, "Two missions to Alaska," *Pacific Historian* 26:1 (1982), 29–41.

Bishop Nicholas Ziorov

transferred out of America, soon to be replaced by St. Tikhon. One of Nicholas's last acts before leaving was to write a letter to President William McKinley, appealing on behalf of the indigenous Alaskans and singling out Sheldon Jackson as a particular villain. Here is the full text of the letter:[2]

Alaska stands in need of radical reform in all directions. A limit must be set to the abuses of various companies, more especially of the Alaska Commercial Company, which for over thirty years, has had the uncontrolled management of affairs and has reduced the country's hunting and fishing resources to absolute exhaustion, and the population to beggary and semi-starvation. A limit must be set to the abuses of officials who, as shown by the experience of many years, are sent there without any discrimination and exclusively on the recommendation of Alaska's irremovable guardian, Sheldon Jackson. And, lastly, Alaska must be delivered from that man. By his sectarian propaganda he has introduced dissension, enmity and iniquity where those evils did not before exist. It was the Orthodox Greek Church which brought the light of truth to that country; why, then, try to drive her out of it by every means lawful or unlawful?

In the name of humanity and justice, and freedom—of those very blessings for the sake of which you declared war against Spain—I make these requests. Will you be acting consistently if, while waging war for the liberty of Puerto Rico, Cuba and the Philippines for their human rights, you ignore all those things at home, in part of your own country which has been waiting thirty years for the blessings promised to it? And are not we Russians fully entitled to demand of you for Alaska that for which you have taken up arms against Spain?

---

2   The letter was published in newspapers across America. I took this text
     from the *Alaska Mining Record* (January 18, 1899).

The only thing that may possibly be brought up against us is that we practice the true faith, and have not yet divested ourselves of our sympathies for Russia, the land of our own faith. But is that really sufficient ground for blame and persecution? There is no danger whatever in that to American rule in Alaska, as some persons would probably have you believe, if only for the reason that our church never meddles with politics and our clergy never busied itself at home or abroad with intrigues.

Jackson's response was swift; within days, he fired back:

The greatest enemies to public schools in Alaska are the priests of the Greek Church. They have even imprisoned boys to keep them out of the schools. They do not want their children to learn English for fear that they may leave the Greek congregation. However, the cause of the Greek priests in Alaska is dying. They are not citizens, but are sustained by the Russian government, and have been required to renew their oaths of allegiance every time there has been a change in Russian authority. For the support of the Greek Church in the territory the Russian government pays annually the sum of $60,000. Their work is not progressing, and my opinion is that twenty-five years hence will see the end of the Greek Church in Alaska.[3]

Despite his best efforts, Jackson's prediction was proven false. Orthodoxy in Alaska survived the government-backed double onslaught of Protestantism and deindigenization and persists to this day.

---

3   *New York Evangelist* (January 19, 1899).

CHAPTER TWENTY

Saint Tikhon

SAINT TIKHON IS a massively important figure, not just for American Orthodoxy but for the whole history of the Church globally. The book *Glorified in America* has a long and fantastic chapter on his life. Professor Scott Kenworthy is working on a major book about him that will undoubtedly be the definitive work for generations. In the introduction to the current volume, I discussed Tikhon's famous proposal for the organization of Orthodoxy in America—an exarchate of the Russian Church that would have ethnic dioceses within it, led by their own ethnic bishops. It was an outside-the-box approach to a completely novel challenge. This alone reveals much about St. Tikhon and his pastoral vision.

What can I add, then, that tells you something about St. Tikhon you can't read elsewhere? Here are a few nuggets of lesser-known information.

Saint Tikhon's Brother

SAINT TIKHON'S YOUNGER brother, Michael, served as his secretary during his time in America. While in San Francisco, Michael became infatuated with an Italian opera singer named Tina de Spada. As she later told a reporter, "he used to send me flowers every day and he used to send me letters, all letters of admiration, written in very good Italian, although he spoke the language very little." They met only once, at the opera house. De Spada could speak neither English nor Russian, so in broken Italian, Michael professed his love for her. She was kind but didn't reciprocate.

In the fall of 1902, de Spada's father died in Italy, and she decided to leave San Francisco to be with her mother. Michael was devastated—not just figuratively heartbroken, but literally so. From the *San Francisco Call*, December 5, 1902:

> Wednesday night he retired early to his apartment at 1715 Powell street, where the cathedral is located. He was in such a condition of nervous prostration that Dr. Victor G. Vecki was summoned to attend him. He administered sedatives and left his patient apparently resting easily. But the knowledge that Tina de Spada would depart in the morning and that probably he would never see her again gripped his heart until it ceased its beating. When the family went to awake him in the morning he was dead.

When she reached Italy, de Spada learned of the tragedy. She later told the *San Francisco Examiner* (8/26/1908):

> I was very much astonished and very much shocked. It seemed so strange that a man whom I had met only once should have considered himself in love with me to that extent. But it is difficult to account for people's actions sometimes. I think that a few months afterwards I saw Mr. Bellavin's brother, Bishop Tikhon, in Naples, but I did not speak to him. I am very sorry for the whole affair about the death of Mr. Bellavin, but I do not think that I am in any way to blame.

After Michael's death, St. Tikhon returned to Russia for an extended visit, comforting his mother. His flock in North America was afraid that he wouldn't return, but he did, remaining in charge of the diocese until 1907.

Saint Tikhon and Americans

Saint Tikhon

IN HIS REPORT to the Holy Synod for 1902 (completed the following year), St. Tikhon wrote at some length about the relationship between his diocese and the heterodox Americans:[1] "By setting up in North America an independent see what was intended was, among other things, the acquaintance of the heterodox world with the Orthodox Church. How far has this objective been met? What is being done for this? Very little, as of yet." There were, he said, some liturgical books, some articles, pamphlets by St. Sebastian, but nothing more. "There are among our parishioners 20–30 Americans (sometimes in mixed marriages). That is all for the time being." But the possibilities were greater.

> There is, however, an interest among Americans in the Orthodox Faith, and it is growing all the time: in our churches here, and especially in New York, one often sees Americans, who very much like our rites and singing and who want to be acquainted with the doctrine of our Church, in attendance at services. . . . That this interest may not weaken and in fact bear noticeable

---

1   Translated into English in Kostadis, 205–215.

fruit, we must work further on it, so that Americans may come to know and understand us. The main thing here is the language, without which it is difficult for us to move ahead.

Saint Tikhon talked about Isabel Hapgood's forthcoming English translation of the Service Book and the need for more Orthodox books in English. And he emphasized the necessity *"for our missionaries here to acquire skill in the English language"* (emphasis his), as well as the need for an American Orthodox seminary, orphanages, hospitals, and other institutions, to better present Orthodoxy to Americans.

Saint Tikhon and Bishop Grafton

ON NOVEMBER 5, 1905, St. Tikhon ordained Ingram N. W. Irvine an Orthodox priest. It was a courageous action, and I cannot help but think that St. Tikhon's feelings on the matter were bittersweet. He knew—he must have known—that he was indeed ushering in a new "epoch in Church history," as Irvine put it. He knew Irvine's baggage and his potential value. (For more on Irvine, see chapter 25.)

More than that, St. Tikhon knew that by ordaining Irvine, he would irreparably damage the close relations he had built up with leading Anglicans, most especially his dear friend Bishop Charles Grafton.

Bishop Grafton was the Episcopal Bishop of Fond du Lac, Wisconsin, but he was much more than that. He was the head of Nashotah House, one of the preeminent seminaries in the Anglican world. (In the very year of Irvine's ordination, Nashotah House had awarded Tikhon an honorary doctorate.) Grafton was also one of the leading lights of Anglo-Catholicism, that High Church segment of Anglicanism that was closest to Orthodoxy. In his long life—he was seventy-five when Irvine was ordained— Grafton had done as much as anyone to foster close ties with the Orthodox churches, and virtually from the moment of St. Tikhon's arrival in America in 1898, Grafton became his close friend and confidant. Grafton represented the very best the Episcopal Church had to offer, and for Tikhon, his friendship was invaluable. Saint Tikhon must have known that, in accepting Irvine, he would lose his friend. On November 4, 1905—the day of Irvine's chrismation and ordination to the diaconate—Grafton wrote in a letter, "I have been very busy this last week in the endeavor to stop Bishop Tikhon from ordaining Dr. Irvine to the priesthood on Sunday the 5th November." He continued,

> [Tikhon] is a good, gentle, pious Christian Bishop who has been imposed upon. For the sake of the Russian Church I am sorry it should take up with a man who rightly or wrongly has been deposed from the priesthood. There was no necessity for it, for Dr. Irvine could have appealed to the Court of Review lately established, or to the House of Bishops sitting, as they do, in Council. The action of Archbishop Tikhon can only be based on the view that we are no part of the Catholic Church and so all relations between us must terminate, or on the ground that he has received authority from the Holy Synod to receive appeals from our courts. In the latter case I said that we had received no notice of such authority being delegated, and if we had, and had accepted it according to the Canon of the Universal Church which he was bound to respect, he could only hear appeals from bishops and not from priests who were confined to appeals within their own nationality or province.[2]

While well intentioned, Grafton was in error. Of course, his arguments display a fundamental ecclesiological misunderstanding: Grafton thought that the Orthodox and Anglican Churches were both parts of the "Catholic" (Universal) Church, and thus

---

2   B. Talbot Rogers, ed., *The Works of the Rt. Rev. Charles C. Grafton*, vol. 7 (Longmans, Green, 1914).

that the Orthodox had to respect the territorial rights and judicial decisions of the Anglicans. In Grafton's (and the Anglicans') view, St. Tikhon was roughly paralleled by the Russian ambassador. Ordaining Irvine was equivalent to the Russian ambassador declaring a convicted American criminal to be innocent and then bestowing a Russian consulship on him. The Russian ambassador had no such rights; he was in America for diplomatic purposes, but he had no jurisdiction here. The same basic restrictions— thought the Anglicans—applied to the Russian archbishop.

Incidentally, Grafton also misunderstood his own Church's appeals process. When Irvine was defrocked by his Episcopal bishop in 1900, the Episcopal Church had no mechanism by which he could appeal the punishment. They established a court of appeal in 1905, but that court was not able to make retroactive rulings. Irvine simply had no way of being reinstated in the Episcopal Church. Grafton concluded his letter with strong words:

> My telegrams will be published in next week's Living Church; our presiding Bishop has protested. The Archbishop has made a big, bad blunder. I asked the Russian Ambassador to interfere with his influence. But I fear Tikhon will steer his craft on the rocks. My hope is that God will in some way overrule this to good, for it is Satan's work.

Neither God nor the Russian ambassador prevented Irvine's ordination. Richard Hatfield—then an Episcopal priest, but now Fr. Chad Hatfield, best known as president of St. Vladimir's Seminary—wrote in 1992, "The friendship between Grafton and Tikhon ended with the ordination of [Irvine]. . . . The ordination of Father Irvine brought to an abrupt close the first phase of Orthodox-Anglican relations in the new world."[3]

---

3   V. Rev. Chad Hatfield, "Nashotah House, Bishop Grafton, and Saint Tikhon of Moscow," address at the Sequicentennial Convocation, Nashotah House, 11/7/1992, http://anglicanhistory.org/orthodoxy/hatfield.pdf

CHAPTER TWENTY-ONE

A Flying Machine and Suicide

Archimandrite Misael Karydis

ARCHIMANDRITE MISAEL KARYDIS spent twenty years as the priest in New Orleans, from 1881 until 1901. Two decades at a single parish is a long time, especially in the early years of American Orthodox history. Before Karydis, only one priest (that I know of) had ever served such a lengthy tenure—Hieromonk Nikolai Militov, who spent twenty-two years (1845–67) as pastor of the Russian church in Kenai, Alaska. Then came Karydis's long stretch in New Orleans, followed by those of Fr. Theoclitos Triantafilides (Galveston, 1896–1916) and Fr. George Maloof (Boston Syrian church, 1900–1920).

Karydis was an odd character. In 1888, he got into a fistfight with a Greek writer for a French newspaper. From the *New Orleans Daily Picayune* (8/24/1888): "A conversation was entered into and soon assumed the attitude of a heated debate. The language used by the reverend gentleman [Fr. Misael] was not very polite, and Mr. Nicolopulo reminded him of his insolence. Without more ado Misael struck Nicolopulo in the face." Despite the fact that Karydis, not Nicolopulo, had done the striking, the police arrested Nicolopulo for assault and battery. Eventually,

Nicolopulo was released, and the newspaper criticized the poor judgment of the officers.

All the contemporary sources tell us that Karydis came from Bulgaria, although I think he was ethnically Greek. Here is how the *New York Times* describes him in a June 6, 1901, article:

> The Rev. Michael Jevizoylon Karidis is pastor of Holy Trinity Church, on the corner of Dorgenois and Hospital Streets, here [in New Orleans]. His congregation is composed of Greeks. He came here from Bulgaria twenty years ago, and is supposed to have had some means. About eight years ago he showed signs of mental unbalance, and since then has been engaged in constructing a flying machine.

The *New York Sun* (6/7/1901) describes another invention that sounds a lot like a motorcycle: "a bicycle that would be a sort of automobile, the rider only guiding it. He made several applications for a patent, but could never perfect the invention."

Something snapped in Karydis at the beginning of June, 1901. It's difficult to reconstruct exactly what that was. According to the *New York Times*, "Last Sunday he donned a stovepipe hat for the first time in his life, and with a small grip left his house, announcing that he was going to collect some money that had been left to him." But his trip wasn't just about collecting an inheritance. The eldest member of his parish, Captain Nicholas Theodore, told the *New York Sun*:

> Ever since Sunday I had known that something was going to happen. I was sitting out in the yard when Father Misael came running to the gate. He said he wanted to see me quick. His shirt was open in the front and his face was very pale. A lot of little boys were following him and calling him Santa Claus. I told them they ought to be ashamed of themselves, and made them stop. Then the father came in and talked to me.
>
> He was pale and trembling all over. He did not look right. I

don't think he was quite right in his head. He had been working so hard and for so long on some kind of a thing to make a bicycle go that he was tired out. "I am tired of living," he told me. "My father is dead in Bulgaria and I want to go there. I think I will kill myself."

I told him that he ought not to talk of suicide, but that he should think of his congregation and the people for whom he had worked so long, and did my best to quiet him.

Father Misael traveled to New York City, where he visited the powerful Greek consul, Demetrius Botassi, who had ties to the New Orleans church. On the morning of June 5, 1901, Karydis checked into the Eastern Hotel. He spent most of the day in the hotel's café before retiring to his room a little after four in the afternoon. He ordered some dinner, and when the waiter brought it to him, he observed Karydis sitting at a table, writing something. Soon after this, a shot was heard. The hotel staff broke down the door to Karydis's room and saw that the priest was wounded. The newspapers differ on where the wound was— the *New York Times* and *Tribune* say that Karydis was wounded in his right side, but the *World* says that he was shot "over the heart," which sounds more plausible. Karydis reportedly told the hotel manager, "Let me finish my work. I want to die."

News of Karydis's suicide spread quickly. Before he had even died, one of the Orthodox in New Orleans, Marcos Papovich, received a telegram saying that Karydis was deathly ill in New York. "Papovich says he does not know the priest," the *New York Times* reported. "Karidis lived a rather secluded life." In a front-page story, the *Biloxi Daily Herald* (6/7/1901) said, "He had become demented from long work at a flying machine he was trying to invent. His workshop was a part of his home adjoining the church in which he had lived all alone for the past eighteen years." And then there's the *New York Sun*: "Not long before he died at the Hudson street hospital here the priest told Policeman

Durr that he had been accused of an assault on a boy in New Orleans."

Father Misael Karydis lingered for several hours, finally succumbing a few minutes before eleven o'clock at night.

CHAPTER TWENTY-TWO

A Saloon-Owning Priest in San Francisco

Father Constantine Tsapralis

FROM ITS FOUNDING in 1868, the Russian cathedral in San Francisco was a multiethnic community. In particular, Greeks and Serbs were an integral part of the church, and, at various times, an ethnic Greek (Fr. Kallinikos Kanellas) and an ethnic Serbian priest (St. Sebastian Dabovich) served the parish. By 1903, however, the Greeks of San Francisco wanted their own church. From the *San Francisco Call* (1/8/1903):

> While the Greek members of Bishop Tikhon's flock have nothing but the kindest feelings toward their spiritual director and the church which has sheltered and fostered the faith of their own land, they find the Russian language, in which the church services are now conducted, a decided impediment in the way of a proper and beneficial appreciation of the good Bishop's ministrations.

There were about two thousand Greeks in the city at this point, and they got together and formed an association with the aim of establishing their own Greek-speaking church. By the end of the year, all the arrangements were in place, and Holy Trinity Church was born. (Yes, they adopted the same name as the Russian parish they were leaving.) The community hired Fr. Constantine Tsapralis to be their priest. Upon arrival in San Francisco, Tsapralis attended the Divine Liturgy at the Russian cathedral. On November 16, Fr. Sebastian Dabovich sent this report to his bishop, St. Tikhon:

> It is my duty to report to your Grace that the Greek Community in San Francisco has begun building a new church in San Francisco on a plot of land purchased south of Market Street. They ordered a priest by mail for themselves who arrived and was present today at Divine Liturgy at the Cathedral church (he was standing in the altar). This priest (married) in the rank of sakellarios, Father Constantine . . . [Tsapralis, or Chaprales] has his credentials from his Bishop, Ambrose of the Diocese of Salaris [Fr. Sebastian is probably mistaken; it could be Salamis] (in the Kingdom of Greece), in the jurisdiction of the Holy Synod in Athens. He has a Holy Antimension that was given to him (he says) to celebrate Liturgy in the United States of North America. He was here with two Orthodox Greeks known to me.

On December 12, Tikhon sent a brief reply: "May God grant them all success."[1]

As St. Sebastian said, Fr. Constantine Tsapralis was a married priest. In 1904, he sent for his wife and son. Tsapralis was born in about 1869, so at this point, he was in his mid-thirties. Despite this, he and his wife went on to have four more children, the last of them when Fr. Constantine was in his mid-fifties.

In an article that used to appear on the Holy Trinity Greek Church website, Tsapralis was described as "durable," having

---

1   Both St. Sebastian's letter and St. Tikhon's reply were translated from Russian into English and published at https://www.holy-trinity.org/history/1903/11.16.Dabovich-Tikhon.html.

pastored the parish through many difficult times, including the devastating 1906 earthquake and various schisms in the decades that followed. He's also described as "kind and compassionate," "a good teacher," and "gentle with children." Here is one story about Tsapralis:

> In 1913, a Greek man named Prantikos was convicted of mur-
> der. Fr. Tsapralis was asked to go to San Quentin to administer
> the last rights [sic] before Prantikos was hung for his crime. The
> event, described in the *San Francisco Call Bulletin*, said that Fr.
> Tsapralis was reading prayers on the way to the gallows. He was
> described as a strong, tall man. On the gallows, his knees buck-
> led and he wavered at the sight before him. The prison chaplain
> put his arm around him to support him because he was worried
> that he might fall through the gallows. Fr. Tsapralis continued
> reading prayers and he witnessed the hanging. The prison chap-
> lain later described him as a kind, gentle soul.[2]

For several years in the early 1900s, Tsapralis owned and operated a candy store, which has also been described as a "saloon."
If it really was a saloon (in the sense that we understand it), this
would be uncanonical—an Orthodox priest is expressly forbidden
from operating a drinking establishment.[3] Eventually, Tsapralis
sold the place—to his wife. The *Morning Oregonian* (11/18/1911)
reported, "But before selling he neglected to liquidate a bill of
$300 for a soda fountain and other fixtures in the shop. A

---

2   This story was included on a page about Tsapralis on the website of Holy
    Trinity Greek Orthodox Church of San Francisco, but it is no longer
    available.

3   See canon 9 of the Sixth Ecumenical Council, which forbids any clergy-
    man from operating a tavern—although St. Nikodemos of the Holy
    Mountain notes in the *Pedalion*, "If, on the other hand, he owns a tavern,
    but employs others to serve in it, this does not amount to causing him
    any harm or impediment; according to Zonaras. It is better, however, for
    him to sell it, and buy some other more decent property that is more in
    keeping with the profession of clergyman."

collection agency sued, and, securing judgment, had an execution issued against the candy store." The sheriff came and seized store property, but Mrs. Tsapralis protested, arguing that the store was her property, not her husband's. The case went to court, and Fr. Constantine admitted having owned the store. I don't know how the case turned out.

After Fr. Constantine's wife died, he was raised to the rank of archimandrite. He served the Holy Trinity community for more than three decades, finally stepping down in 1936. He died in 1942, at the age of seventy-three.

CHAPTER TWENTY-THREE

Saint Raphael: Antioch or Russia?

SAINT RAPHAEL WAS born in Beirut in November 1860. His family was from Damascus, but they were in Beirut as refugees due to anti-Christian riots by the Druze in Damascus. The following year, they returned to their home.

In his late teens, Raphael worked as a schoolteacher; he was then tonsured a monk and briefly served as assistant to the patriarch of Antioch before entering the Ecumenical Patriarchate's theological school at Halki. This was a big deal: the Patriarchate of Antioch had no seminaries, and Raphael was the lone Antiochian student admitted to Halki. He spent seven years there, and in his next-to-last year he was ordained a deacon.

Returning to Syria, Raphael traveled throughout the patriarchate, accompanying Patriarch Gerasimos of Antioch. The patriarch gave Raphael the job of preaching to the faithful, since he was one of the few educated clergymen in the patriarchate, and ordinary village priests were not allowed to give homilies. But this didn't last long; Raphael was restless and curious, and soon he entered the Kiev Theological Academy in the Russian Empire.

But Raphael wasn't able to finish his studies: Fr. Christopher Jabara, the head of the Antiochian metochion in Moscow, had made himself unwelcome in Russia because of his heresies, and the patriarch of Antioch asked the Russian Church to ordain St. Raphael to the priesthood so he could take over the metochion. Despite holding this important position with the patriarchate, Raphael wrote pseudonymous articles attacking the Brotherhood of the Holy Sepulchre, the ethnically Greek monastic brotherhood that controlled the Patriarchates of Antioch and Jerusalem and, in St. Raphael's view,

Saint Raphael Hawaweeny

mistreated the indigenous faithful. When Patriarch Spyridon of Antioch discovered that Raphael was behind the articles, he suspended him, and in 1893, Raphael was granted a canonical release to the Russian Orthodox Church.

For a couple years, he taught Arabic and anti-Muslim polemics at the Kazan Theological Academy, but then word reached him that the nascent Syrian community in New York City needed an Orthodox priest.

Saint Raphael was the perfect person for the massive job he undertook: to minister to the scattered Antiochians across the sprawling continent of North America, under the general oversight of the Russian Mission. In his early years, in the mid- to late-1890s, he undertook three significant pastoral tours, visiting communities and outposts all over the country. In 1898, he began intentionally recruiting priests from Syria to come to America. The same year, he published his translation of *Divine Prayers and Services* into Arabic. The publication of this book, affectionately known as the "five-pounder," was a major accomplishment, coming at a time when the indigenous Antiochians in Syria were still under a Greek-controlled patriarchate and didn't have many educational or literary opportunities.

In 1899, the Antiochians wrested back control over their patriarchate, electing the Syrian-born Meletius Doumani as patriarch—the first Arab Orthodox patriarch of Antioch in over 170 years. Immediately, the Holy Synod tried to bring back their most gifted and accomplished son to serve the patriarchate: St. Raphael was nominated for the see of Lattakia in 1899 and then elected for Zahle in 1901. That same year, he was offered the position of auxiliary to the metropolitan of Beirut. Each time, he refused, insisting that his work in North America was unfinished.

Finally, in 1903, the Holy Synod of Russia elected Raphael as vicar bishop of Brooklyn, to be responsible for the Syro-Arab Vicariate of the Russian Archdiocese under the oversight of St. Tikhon, the Russian archbishop of North America. This time, Raphael accepted, and he was ordained to the episcopacy in 1904.

The Consecration of Saint Raphael

THE FIRST THING to know about St. Raphael's episcopal ordination is the crowd—the enormous, crushing crowd. Two thousand people—some worshippers, some sightseers—were crammed like sardines into the cathedral on Brooklyn's Pacific Street. Throw in a generous portion of incense and hundreds of burning candles, and the place was one hot, dense mass of humanity. "There were half-smothered cries of women and children," the *Boston Globe* reported (3/14/1904). At least three women fainted and had to be carried out of the building.

Adding to the chaos were the newspaper photographers, one of whom chose to take a picture at the moment of consecration. From the *New York Sun* (3/14/1904): "[T]he photograph fiend, who apparently respects religion no more than any other material for a subject, startled the congregation and the clergy by exploding a flashlight cartridge. The building was soon filled with smoke, making the rest of the ceremony very indistinct for some time."

It was quite a ceremony. No fewer than four now-canonized saints participated—Raphael, Tikhon, Alexis Toth, and Alexander Hotovitzky. Afterward was a big dinner, attended by a lot of people (between 150 and 500; the newspapers don't agree, though I'm inclined to believe the smaller figure). It was a fast day, but that didn't stop the feasters from having an impressive menu. From the *New York Tribune* (3/14/1904): "The menu was vegetables, oysters and lobsters, Damascus artichokes, fried fish, lettuce salad, peas a la Syriene, cabbages a la Turque; desserts, mishabbak, cornstarch; fruits, apples and oranges; Turkish coffee." Presumably no one left hungry.

As far as the general public was concerned, the consecration was a decidedly Russian affair. The newspapers referred to it as taking place on the tsar's orders, and at the celebratory dinner, the tsar was toasted and the Russian national anthem was sung. One of the first public acts of the new Bishop Raphael was to visit the Russian ambassador in Washington.

These facts did not please the local Greeks one bit. They saw the ordination as an act of Russian imperial expansion, and it contributed to the growing Greek fear that the Russian Church aimed to spread its influence across Orthodoxy worldwide. The Greek consul in New York chose not to attend the consecration, and his absence made headlines.[1] A few weeks later, on Holy Friday, Bishop Tikhon tried to visit Holy Trinity, one of the Greek churches in New York. Father John Erickson writes, "He was barred from entering by its angry trustees, who feared a Russian takeover of their parish properties."[2]

The Greeks may not have been happy with the consecration,

---

1   "Greeks Angry at the Czar," *New York Sun* (March 15, 1904), 12, and
    "Fear Russian Rule of Church," *New York Tribune* (March 15, 1904), 6.

2   Erickson, *Orthodox Christians in America*, 73.

but the Episcopalians certainly were. Bishop Tikhon invited his good friend, the Episcopal Bishop Charles Grafton of Fond-du-Lac, Wisconsin, to attend. That fact alone means little; non-Orthodox religious leaders are often invited to witness such events. But Grafton's invitation was different, at least in the eyes of the Episcopalians themselves. Supposedly, Bishop Tikhon's invitation included a request that Grafton actually participate in the ceremony as the third consecrator, along with Tikhon and Innocent![3] In reality, it is inconceivable that Tikhon actually intended for Grafton to be one of the consecrators. Such an act would require full communion between the Orthodox and the Episcopalians, and, as later events would prove, Tikhon was unwilling to unilaterally declare such a union. He had great respect for the Episcopalians and for Grafton in particular, and he may even have privately believed in the legitimacy of their holy orders, but he by no means would have permitted Grafton to actually participate in the service.

In any case, Grafton proved unable to attend due to illness, but a delegation of other Episcopalians came in his stead. Some of Grafton's representatives were allowed to stand in the altar during the ceremony.

Of course, St. Raphael's ordination meant the most to his own Syrian flock, which now had their own bishop. Right away, though, some ambiguity arose: was the new Bishop Raphael a hierarch of the Russian Church, leading a vicariate of the Russian Archdiocese of North America? Or was he, perhaps, a bishop of Antioch, leading a diocese of the Antiochian Patriarchate?

---

3   C. Lewis Leicester, "What Might Have Been," *The Christian East* 13:2 (Summer 1932), 79–80. Quoted in Andre G. Issa, *The Life of Raphael Hawaweeny, Bishop of Brooklyn: 1860–1915* (unpublished M.Div. thesis, St. Vladimir's Orthodox Theological Seminary, May 1991), 46.

Antioch or Russia?

WITH THE RETURN of indigenous leadership of the patriarchate, St. Raphael's ties with Antioch immediately became close. According to Paul Garrett's essay "The Life and Legacy of Bishop Raphael Hawaweeny," St. Raphael was "consulted before virtually every important decision in the patriarchate and informed of the outcome directly thereafter."[4]

Following St. Raphael's election as bishop by the Russian Holy Synod, St. Tikhon issued a decree on the establishment of a Syro-Arab Vicariate under the Russian diocese. In the decree, St. Tikhon instructed that the names of both Raphael and the Russian bishop be commemorated at the liturgical services in each Syro-Arab parish in America.

When Raphael was ordained to the episcopacy in March 1904, Patriarch Meletius of Antioch wrote to St. Tikhon, "Since His Grace, Bishop Raphael, having received the grace of the episcopate through the laying-on of your blessed hands, became a bishop of our Syrian children within the boundaries of North America, and since we together with our brothers, the metropolitans of the holy See of Antioch, do still consider him as a member of our body, since he comes from our midst, and we number him as one of us in faith and in virtue of his responsibilities over our Syrian children, dispersed in North America, we consider it our most important duty to send the present Patriarchal Letter to you, in order to bestow our blessing, from the depth of our heart, upon that election, which occurred through the inspiration of the Most Holy Spirit."[5]

For his part, St. Tikhon, while affirming Raphael's

---

4   Paul D. Garrett, "The Life and Legacy of Bishop Raphael Hawaweeny," in George S. Corey, et al., eds., *The First One Hundred Years: A Centennial Anthology Celebrating Antiochian Orthodoxy in North America* (Englewood, NJ: Antakya Press, 1995), 19.

5   Issa, 46–48.

membership in the Russian Church, stated his "certitude" that Raphael "would never break the most intimate spiritual ties with his mother Church of Antioch," and he asked the patriarch to guide and advise the new bishop. Soon after Patriarch Meletius's letter, the Holy Synod of Russia issued a certificate of ordination to Raphael.[6]

In 1905, St. Tikhon drafted a famous proposal to form an Orthodox exarchate in North America. This exarchate would include overlapping ethnic dioceses, and the ethnic bishops in charge of each diocese would come together in a national synod, headed by the Russian archbishop. It was a fairly ingenious idea, but the plan was never implemented. In that proposal, St. Tikhon wrote that St. Raphael "is the second auxiliary to the diocesan bishop of the Aleutian Islands, but is almost independent in his own sphere."

In his magazine, *Al Kalimat*, St. Raphael himself wrote that his consecration was "by the order and permission of Meletios, the Patriarch of Antioch," and that "Patriarch Meletios counted the new parish of Brooklyn, New York, as one of the parishes of Antioch." Saint Raphael went on to say that Patriarch Meletios declared that he "had instituted the new diocese as one of the dioceses pertaining to the See of Antioch and thus it is in actuality, notwithstanding its nominal allegiance to the Russian Holy Synod." He also said, "The territorial jurisdiction of the See of Antioch became much more extensive during the time of his beatitude [Patriarch Meletios], for Syrians who emigrated to many other countries still retained their spiritual relations with and continued to acknowledge and yield allegiance to their mother church, the Holy Church of Antioch."[7]

---

6   Issa, 49–51.
7   Translated and published in the Michigan Supreme Court decision *Hanna v. Malick, Northwestern Reporter* vol. 193, 802 (193 N.W. 798 [Mich. 1923]).

A 1912 report by an official commission of the Episcopal Diocese of New England stated, "These Orthodox . . . are all apparently under Bishop Raphael. This Syrian Bishop derives his authority from the Orthodox Patriarch of Antioch, but is closely connected with the Russian Archbishop in New York."

While the relationship between the Syro-Arab mission and the Russian Archdiocese may indeed have been "nominal," the relationship did exist, and it existed chiefly in the person of St. Raphael himself. His relationship with Russia and Antioch was ambiguous, and this ambiguity was strengthened by his own words and actions. In *Hanna v. Malick*, a legal dispute between factions of a Syro-Arab parish in 1923, the judge observed with some frustration, "[A]t first the writings of Bishop Raphael gave to the Patriarch of Antioch jurisdiction over the Syrian branch of the Orthodox Church in the United States, and later gave expression to language indicating that all the branches, including the Syrian branch, of the Greek Orthodox Church in America, were under the jurisdiction of the Holy Synod of Russia."

In practice, as the writings of both Ss. Tikhon and Raphael suggest, St. Raphael was pretty much independent. Neither he nor his clergy were present at the famous All-American Sobor in Mayfield, Pennsylvania, in 1907. There's no evidence that any Syro-Arab students attended the Russian seminary.

None of this was a problem during St. Raphael's lifetime, because no one questioned his authority, and he had good relations with both Russia and Antioch. The trouble came after his untimely death in 1915. Quoting again from the judge in *Hanna v. Malick*:

[A] meeting was held of the Syrian priests who were present at the funeral, and a division of minds existed and was then expressed as to whether or not Raphael, as Bishop of Brooklyn, was subordinate to the Holy Synod of Russia or to the Patriarch of Antioch, and whether the successor of Raphael as Bishop of Brooklyn should be a Syrian, or whether he might be a Russian.

That division, born pretty much the moment Raphael died, wasn't fully healed for six decades. His flock divided into warring camps—the Russy, who pledged allegiance to Russia, and the Antacky, who preferred subordination to Antioch.

To make matters worse, Raphael had no obvious successor, and the Russian leadership dragged their feet on choosing a bishop to replace him. It took two years for them to pick Bishop Aftimios Ofiesh as the new bishop for the Syro-Arabs, and Ofiesh proved to be the wrong man for the job. Meanwhile, a visiting Antiochian bishop, Metropolitan Germanos Shehadi of Baalbek, was in America already on a fundraising tour when Raphael died. Metropolitan Germanos decided to stick around and try to start his own diocese, even though the Antiochian Holy Synod ordered him to return to Syria. Eventually, the Patriarchate of Antioch established its own fully authorized archdiocese in 1923–24.

Saint Raphael came to America under the Russian Church; he was consecrated by Russian bishops and received a consecration certificate from the Russian Holy Synod. At the same time, he was in close, regular contact with the Patriarchate of Antioch and told his people that his diocese was "a diocese of Antioch . . . notwithstanding its nominal allegiance to the Russian Holy Synod." Given that ambiguity, it's no surprise that St. Raphael's flock divided into Russy and Antacky camps the moment he was gone.

Saint Raphael's Memorial Liturgy, 1915

CHAPTER TWENTY-FOUR

Saint Raphael and the Battle of Pacific Street

IN 1905, NEW York's Syrians were divided into two main camps—Orthodox and Maronite. Each group had a corresponding newspaper—*Miraat Ul Gharb* (*The Mirror of the West*) for the Orthodox and *Al Hoda* for the Maronites. *Miraat Ul Gharb* was clearly the weaker of the two publications, appearing only once a week and having a smaller circulation than the daily *Al Hoda*. The papers were engaged in a war of words, and slanderous articles appeared in both.

Finally, St. Raphael could stand no more of it, and he called for the editors to stop publishing such trash. The *Al Hoda* crowd, which called itself the Champagne Glass Club, told him to shut up—that "his place was in the church" (*New York Sun*, 8/27/1905). In speaking up, St. Raphael made himself a target, and *Al Hoda*'s editor, Naoum Mokarzel, took direct aim at the bishop. He accused St. Raphael of numerous offenses, including trying to incite the Orthodox to violence against the Maronites. *Miraat Ul Gharb* responded, and the back-and-forth attacks continued. Rather than stopping the battle, St. Raphael's intervention unwittingly made things worse.

In late August 1905, the leaders of the Champagne Glass Club went to the police with a remarkable story. According to the Champagne Glass Club, on August 15, St. Raphael assembled his congregation and told them that they needed to defend his name with their lives—that if one or two of them might have to die in defense of his honor, then so be it. On August 20—again, according to the Champagne Glass Club—Raphael claimed that he was "as great as Grand Duke Sergius of Russia" and needed to be defended accordingly (the Grand Duke had been assassinated earlier that year). I am convinced that both of these claims are utter fabrications, but if you're in doubt, read the next allegation of the Champagne Glass Club. From the *Brooklyn Daily Eagle* (8/28/1905):

> Another speech was made on Wednesday, August 23, in which the bishop made a statement to the effect that he was wounded by the attack of certain Syrian papers which attempted to stain his morality, and that if such a fact be established and he were proved to be immoral, every marriage that he had performed during the last twelve years among the Syrians in New York and elsewhere would be annulled. Thereupon he called the younger element of his congregation to rise in his defense and several of them who were present provided with arms took such arms and deposited them on a table in the church, in accordance with an established Oriental custom, saying they would defend him with the last drop of their blood.

This is just plain absurd; the Champagne Glass Club overreached. It is unimaginable that St. Raphael, an extremely well-educated Orthodox theologian, would claim that sacraments administered by an immoral clergyman were invalid. We covered that ground back in the early fourth century, when the Church recognized Donatism to be heretical. No doubt the Champagne Glass Club would respond by saying that, even if Raphael didn't believe it, he would have made such a claim to incite his flock to violence. But that's even more absurd—the two Syrian camps already hated each other, and the Orthodox didn't need any encouragement to fight their Maronite counterparts. Even a hypothetically wicked bishop would have gained nothing for his cause with public pronouncements and actions like the ones Raphael was accused of.

Of course, St. Raphael did nothing of the sort. Here is his version of what happened, as he told it to the *Brooklyn Daily Eagle*:

> We held a meeting in the basement of the church so that I could calm and restrain my people. I wanted the members of my church to ignore the men who are abusing me. I wanted to advise them to keep their tempers and do nothing to any enemy of mine. I told them that I had forgiven Maluf and Markozel and that they must forgive them. I begged them to keep peace and to have nothing but brotherly love in their hearts.

Forgiving Mokarzel—even feigning forgiveness—would have been extremely difficult for most of St. Raphael's flock. Consider this quote from the *Al Hoda* editor in the *New York Times* (8/28/1905):

> He [Raphael] asserts that his morality has been attacked. I say nothing about his private life—his wine, his card playing. I have not put it in my paper. I respect his church and wish my church to be respected. I am a Roman Catholic. I have heard that the Bishop has said he would crush me, do me bodily and moral injury. He has called together his congregation and appointed a committee of six desperate men to take vengeance upon me and others. Well, I am willing to die for the truth.

I think that is what they call "talking out of both sides of your mouth." If Mokarzel is telling the truth, he's doing a pretty lousy job of it. And apparently, in *Al Hoda*, he was much more slanderous than in the above quote, and his opposite number in *Miraat Ul Gharb* wasn't holding back, either. According to the *New York*

Tribune (8/28/1905), it had gotten so bad that the Syrian men forbade their wives to read the papers.

The police seem to have been more amused than anything else by all this intra-Arab bickering. From the *Sun*: "The big sergeant behind the desk of the Church street police station last night smiled at the idea of bloodshed, and said that no extra police had been placed in the Syrian quarter, though the men on post had been told to exercise vigilance."

ooooo

THROUGHOUT THE FIRST half of September, the Syrian community was balanced on the edge of a knife. The tense situation was complicated by several factors:

One of the richest Syrian merchants in New York was a man named John Abdulnour (in fact, the *Brooklyn Daily Eagle* of September 19 describes him as "the wealthiest Syrian in America" and "the leader of the Syrians"). Abdulnour was apparently a Maronite, but his wife was Orthodox, and she would occasionally travel from their "palatial" home in Staten Island to attend St. Nicholas Orthodox Cathedral in Brooklyn. Late in the summer of 1905, Mrs. Abdulnour filed for a divorce—with the reported encouragement of St. Raphael (*Tribune*, 9/20).

Another issue, which I've briefly touched on already, is the fact that St. Raphael did not simply remain silent in the face of slander. He didn't call for vengeance as the Champagne Glass Club claimed, but he also didn't take the attacks lying down. According to the *Eagle*, Raphael sued a Maronite editor named Maloof for libel. The amount? Twenty-three thousand dollars—that is, over three quarters of a million dollars today. I wouldn't be too harsh on St. Raphael, as libel suits were exceedingly popular at the turn of the last century. In any event, he agreed to accept an apology and drop the case, but that did nothing to quell the ever-increasing resentment that each side felt for the other.

Finally, there is the issue of Lebanese nationalism. In 1905, there was no state called Lebanon—today's Lebanon and Syria were, at that time, still a part of the Ottoman Empire. But Naoum Mokarzel aimed to change all that. He was as passionate a Lebanese nationalist as there has ever been, and he was directly instrumental in the eventual establishment of the Lebanese state.[1] But Lebanese nationalism was far more of a Maronite sentiment than an Orthodox one, and Mokarzel no doubt felt that St. Raphael's relative tolerance of the Ottomans and out-and-out loyalty to the Russians was a betrayal of his heritage. To Mokarzel and his ilk, all things were subordinate to the ideal of Lebanon; to St. Raphael, fidelity to one's faith always trumped the idea of national identity.

ooooo

ON THE AFTERNOON of Friday, September 15, about twenty Syrian men, representing both the Orthodox and Maronite parties, came to blows in the business center of the Syrian enclave. They were armed with guns and knives, but thankfully only one shot was fired, and it missed its target. A policeman bravely rushed into the fracas, breaking up the fight and arresting three men. One of the arrested Syrians, Haiss Nahas, had a slight head wound—the day's only injury, caused when he was knocked to the ground by Navis Harris. Harris, for his part, claimed that Nahas had fired a shot at him.

Nahas, Harris, and another man were hauled into police court. Harris appears to have been Orthodox, and he was represented by the prominent attorney Charles Le Barbier. Just as the case came up before the magistrate, the other party—Nahas, he of the head wound—was brought in. Le Barbier's jaw dropped when he

---

1   Michael W. Suleiman, "The Mokarzels' contributions to the Arabic-speaking community in the United States," *Arab Studies Quarterly* (March 1999).

realized that he had represented Nahas in a previous case and thus had an unavoidable conflict of interest. Both prisoners were locked up, with bail set at five hundred dollars apiece. When another Syrian tried to bail out Harris, the police recognized him as one of the men involved in the fight. He was arrested but was soon set free by the merciful magistrate.

The street fight took place in broad daylight on Friday afternoon, September 15, in the heart of the Syrian colony. But this incident was more of a minor skirmish than an actual battle. The combatants apparently took the weekend off, although St. Raphael reportedly accused Mokarzel of attacking him in print (*New York Times*, 9/19/1905). This would hardly have been the first time *Al Hoda* had gone after Raphael, and the *Times* reference isn't terribly clear, but it's possible (probable, even) that St. Raphael addressed the controversy in his Sunday homily. Come Monday, the Syrian colony was a powder keg.

By Monday, tensions had reached a breaking point. That afternoon, three Syrians had a dust-up and were arrested. Then, at seven o'clock that night, an Orthodox merchant named Nicolo Abousamra boarded a ferry boat. Two men attacked him with a stick, leaving a nasty lump on his head. Abousamra thought they had a dagger, but he was able to escape to a more crowded part of the boat.

Abousamra made it home, where he told his business partner, Sakir Nassar, about the attack. According to the *Brooklyn Daily Eagle* (9/19/1905), "they decided that it might be as well to have the bishop call on them last night and talk the thing over. For they felt sure that there were assassins lurking about to kill the bishop and they wanted to warn him and plan some form of protection." Though it was by now the dead of night, Nassar hurried off to find St. Raphael. As it turned out, the bishop already had a bodyguard with him: "for the bishop has been worrying about the shadows that lurk about him when he goes abroad, and it is his habit to take some of his parishioners along with him when he goes out at night" (*Eagle*). Saint Raphael went at once to visit Abousamra, and at least some of his accompanying parishioners were armed.

Saint Raphael and his entourage never made it to Abousamra's. Saint Raphael lived at 320 Pacific Street; Abousamra was at 114 Pacific. On the way, the St. Raphael's party had to pass by 137 Pacific—the home of none other than Naoum Mokarzel. For his part, Mokarzel had conveniently invited a dozen friends over, and at least some of these friends were packing heat. (None of the sources say so, but I strongly suspect that Mokarzel's friends were the other members of the Champagne Glass Club.)

Why did St. Raphael go to the home of his archenemy in the middle of the night? The *New York Sun* (9/19) reported that Raphael got the rather wild idea that, if only he could sit down with Mokarzel and talk face to face, they could make peace and end all the violence. Alternatively, the Orthodox parishioners may have taken the initiative to go to Mokarzel's house, and St. Raphael may have joined them in an effort to prevent a fight. Another explanation, offered by St. Raphael himself, appeared in the *New York World* (9/19):

> I have enemies who are seeking to kill me. I have been warned time and again that I will be assassinated and for many weeks I have not dared to leave my home unaccompanied at night. Whenever I go out I get several of my parishioners to go with me and this was the case last night when I went out to visit a sick friend.
>
> Neither I nor those with me had any part in the riot, nor did we make an attack upon the home of Mr. Makarzoe [sic]. We were passing peaceably through Pacific street when the shooting began. I am convinced that it was a feigned pistol duel, with the purpose of murdering me by hitting me with what would appear to be a stray bullet.

One reason it's hard to get a handle on what happened is the fact that the newspapers don't agree with each other. The *Sun* reports that St. Raphael and several parishioners went into Mokarzel's house and spent about an hour there in a relatively peaceful meeting. Things eventually turned violent, the meeting broke up, and a shootout began. At least, that's the *Sun's* story.

The *New York Times'* version of events basically follows St. Raphael's story. According to the *Times*, "The minute the Hawaweeny party entered [Mokarzel's house] the fight began. It was rough and tumble in the parlor for a few minutes, and then the combatants went to the street and fought there." No hour-long meeting in this version. Honestly, I think the *Times*, rather than the *Sun*, has it right. Consider the facts:

» It was nearly midnight.
» The Orthodox were on their way to visit an assault victim, Abousamra.
» Saint Raphael and his followers believed that assassins were after him.
» There were a dozen Orthodox men, some of whom were armed.
» There were a dozen Maronite men, some of whom were armed.
» The two groups hated each other's guts.

I say there's no way in the world, under those circumstances, that a dozen Orthodox men could have approached Mokarzel's house—full of armed Maronites—and not had an immediate fight. Saint Raphael's story sounds reasonable, and I'm inclined to believe him.

In any event, a moment or an hour after the Orthodox group passed by Mokarzel's house, a gunfight broke out. Here is how the *Brooklyn Daily Eagle* (9/19) describes the scene:

> It was clearly a pitched battle, for the combatants were dancing about, here and there, taking refuge when they could and again

take pot shots at each other. There were others on the street in addition to the combatants, some of the men from the nearby house of the fire patrol, and Captain Cashman, the head of the fire patrol company. The men of the patrol were gingerly trying to stop the shooting, and when the uniformed policeman appeared ran in with him and put the shooters to flight.

The police officer—a fellow named Patrick Mallon, or Nallin (his name has as many spellings as New York had newspapers)—had heard the shots and bravely rushed into the battle. Police reinforcements soon arrived, and the Battle of Pacific Street finally ended. About twenty shots had been fired, but fortunately, no one died and only two men were injured.

Officer Mallon saw one of the Syrians "running for all he was worth" (*Times*) away from the fight, and he chased after the man. As it turns out, this was none other than St. Raphael himself.

Soon enough, Officer Mallon caught up to the bishop and arrested him. According to the officer, St. Raphael brandished a revolver and even tried to pull the trigger. The *Brooklyn Times Union* (9/19) says that St. Raphael snapped the revolver three times and then hid under a truck and had to be pulled out by his coattails. Saint Raphael vehemently denied pointing a revolver at the officer and said that he had never even handled a gun in his life, and would never do such a thing. More on all that in a moment.

Most of the Syrian fighters escaped, but several were arrested and locked in jail. Some women tried to bail out St. Raphael, but the magistrate said that, for the time being, the bishop was safer behind bars than out in public. The physical battle was over, but St. Raphael's fight for his reputation, and his freedom, had just begun.

ooooo

DID ST. RAPHAEL pull a gun on a cop or not? The next day's newspapers told competing stories. On one end of the spectrum was the *Times*, which didn't even mention a gun. At the other extreme was the *World*, which reported not only that St. Raphael had a revolver but that he "snapped" it at Officer Mallon. Accounts began to crystallize on August 20. In that day's issue of the *Sun*, we find this: "[Officer] Nallin says he saw two men break away. He gave chase. One of them was the Bishop, who was hot-footing it toward home. Nallin grabbed the episcopal coat tails. It was then, Nallin avers, that the Bishop turned around and shoved a pearl handled pistol in his face. He snapped it twice, but it didn't go off."

The *Tribune* (9/20), also citing Officer Mallon's sworn testimony, reported that St. Raphael had snapped the revolver three times rather than twice. The *Sun* also reported Officer Mallon's accusation that St. Raphael had actually fired the revolver in the battle before turning it on the policeman. And here's the *Brooklyn Daily Eagle* (9/19):

> [Officer] Nallin declares, and swore to his declaration in a complaint made against the bishop, that the prelate held the pistol at him and snapped it more than once. It did not go off, for maybe there were rim firing cartridges in a center firing gun; but this the police cannot know, for they have not found the bishop's revolver, if he had one. Hawaweeny, the policeman says, then took to his heels in a most undignified way and ran away. Nallin was after him like a shot, for there were other policemen by this time attending to the other men in the shooting party, and he caught the bishop, as has been explained, hiding behind a wagon in the express company's stable.

What about St. Raphael's own version of the incident? Here is what he told the *Brooklyn Times Union* (9/19):

We had gone only a short distance when men began to shoot at me. I ran up the street, and fearing that I might be shot, I went into a carriage factory and secluded myself under a truck. I had no pistol, and never had. It would be unpriestly for me to go armed. If I had a pistol I would not know how to use it. Indeed, it would be more dangerous to me than anybody else. I am a man of peace. I try to quell strife, not to provoke it.

He told the same story to the *World* (9/19):

As soon as the firing began I fled and took refuge in a carriage shop. I did not have a revolver at any time during the excitement and this policeman who says I did knows that he is telling a deliberate falsehood. He admits that he did not find any weapon in my possession when he made me a prisoner.

According to St. Raphael's followers, his arrest was part of a pre-arranged plot, which allegedly included the police. The *Tribune* (9/20) offered this report:

The friends of Bishop Raphael assert that his arrest was the result of a plot. Men were especially brought from Asbury Park and Fishkill, it was said, by his enemies to assault his followers. N. Maloof, one of the faction opposed to the bishop, was arrested Monday for assaulting one of the latter's friends. He threatened, it is alleged, that Bishop Raphael would be arrested before midnight, and he was. The bishop's friends say that he carried no revolver, but that one was supplied for the occasion by his enemies. He ran away when the detectives arrived because he believed he was being pursued by the men who threatened his life.

We are left with three possibilities:
1. Officer Mallon was mistaken,
2. Officer Mallon was lying, or
3. St. Raphael was lying.

Let me say something up front as we begin our analysis of the available evidence: I am a huge admirer of St. Raphael. He is, without question, my favorite American Orthodox historical figure. My own son's middle name is Raphael, in his honor. It is impossible for me to be completely objective about this case, because I am admittedly biased in favor of St. Raphael. At the same time, I cannot simply ignore inconvenient evidence or refuse to pursue possibilities that might leave St. Raphael looking less than clean. To be an honest historian, I have to look at everything. And so I will.

Is it possible that Officer Mallon was mistaken? Of course. The incident happened after eleven o'clock at night, and this was 1905, so we can be certain that it was very dark. Accounts indicate that Officer Mallon chased after two men—St. Raphael and someone else. It is entirely plausible that the other man pointed a gun at the officer. Also, the newspapers indicate that many people came out into the streets to see what had happened. According to the *Tribune*, by the time Officer Mallon arrived at the scene, the mob "numbered nearly two hundred persons." The two dozen or so combatants were scattering in all directions, trying to avoid being either shot or arrested. So there were plenty of people in the street at the time.

Even Police Inspector Cross, who took charge of the case, was skeptical of St. Raphael's guilt. Inspector Cross received a letter from a Russian official, attesting to the bishop's good character, and Cross responded, "I am investigating the matter, and I am satisfied that the Bishop is innocent of all the charges and accusations that have been made against him, and I shall be pleased to have you communicate this information to the Consul-General of Russia" (*Sun*, 9/22). The inspector questioned Officer Mallon, who, the *Brooklyn Daily Eagle* (9/22) reported, said "that he could not be mistaken about it and that the bishop had pulled a revolver on him and snapped the trigger, just as he had sworn in court."

But in the subsequent weeks, the officer's testimony changed. On November 16, 1905, the *Brooklyn Daily Eagle* (11/16) reported, "The officer who said that the Bishop had drawn a revolver on him was not so very sure of the matter and that case against the Bishop was dismissed."

It's worth noting that most low-level policemen, like Mallon, weren't trained in police academies like our officers today. Mallon may have been a police officer, but his value as a witness isn't necessarily any better than that of the average man on the street.

This leads us to our second possibility—that Officer Mallon was lying. Besides being uneducated, many of New York's policemen in 1905 were, to one degree or another, corrupt. Just a few months before all this chaos, another Officer Mallon had been convicted of murder. I haven't been able to track down our Officer Mallon's first name, much less his biography, and it doesn't help that literally every newspaper uses a different spelling of his name. But regardless of the spelling you use, there is a distinct possibility that Officer Mallon was Irish. And if he was Irish, he was probably a Roman Catholic. Given that the Syrian war was between two religious factions, and one of those factions was itself under the pope of Rome, it's certainly possible that Officer Mallon lied to benefit his coreligionists. I don't have any evidence for this, but it's something that must be considered as we try to determine the truth.

Finally, there is the remote possibility that St. Raphael himself was lying. Let us, for a moment, try to set aside the fact that we're dealing with a canonized saint and try to approach this with as open a mind as we can. Saint Raphael Hawaweeny was an Orthodox bishop. He had good reason to believe that his life was in imminent danger. He left his house late at night to visit a parishioner who had been beaten earlier that day. Bishop Raphael brought with him a bodyguard of parishioners, at least some of whom were armed. Stop for a moment—might he have been armed himself? He might have been, but I think not. His best option would have been to run for the hills if anyone attacked, and that is precisely what he did. He probably was not armed. But what if one of those parishioner-bodyguards had thrust a revolver into his hand at the last moment? Is it possible that he took it—not intending to use it, mind you, but simply took it into his hand? I think we must admit that this is possible, albeit remotely so. Bishop Raphael may have had a revolver on his person when he ran from the gunfight.

He ran and was chased by someone. We now know that someone to be Officer Mallon, but did the bishop know this? Almost certainly not. As we've seen, it was very dark, and Bishop Raphael was running from a veritable riot. Surely he thought—I would have thought—that his pursuer was one of those Maronite enemies coming to get him. In that situation, would it have been reasonable for him to pull out that revolver and point it at the pursuer? I think so. I probably would have done the same thing. I don't think he would have intended to actually fire the gun, but he probably thought that his life was in imminent danger. Pointing a gun at your apparent attacker is a pretty normal reaction. Once he learned that his pursuer was not an attacker but a policeman, would he have thrown the gun away? Almost certainly.

But—continuing just a little longer with the unlikely theory that Bishop Raphael was guilty—why would he compound the problem by lying about it afterward? Why not just admit the mistake? It's very possible that the bishop considered his position, and his flock, and the likely consequences (not just to himself, but to his ministry) of admitting to assaulting a police officer. He may well have felt that a sin—lying—would be better than the destruction of his ministry. And it's hard to blame him if he did think along those lines.

Is the theory I just laid out possible? I think it is. Is it plausible? Is it likely? No, it is not. Given what we know of St. Raphael, given the realities of New York policemen in 1905, given that the alleged revolver was never found, given the specific circumstances of the case (nighttime, a crowded street, the probable assumption by the officer that all those at the gunfight were participants)—given all that we know, I feel pretty confident that St. Raphael never wavered in telling the truth. I do not believe that he tried to shoot a police officer.

We'll leave this with the assessment of St. Tikhon, from his annual report to the Holy Synod: "It is comforting to note that although they implicate Bishop Raphael's name in all this, he himself is clean in the matter."[2]

---

2   Kostadis, 229.

CHAPTER TWENTY-FIVE

The Most Famous Convert in American Orthodox History

Father Ingram Nathaniel Irvine

INGRAM IRVINE WAS the most famous convert in American Orthodox history.

On its face, this seems like an absurd statement, since most of you reading this will never have heard of him. The most famous person who is a convert to Orthodoxy in America is probably someone like Tom Hanks, but that's not what I'm talking about—he's famous and happens to be an Orthodox convert, but he's not famous *because* he's an Orthodox convert. In his own day, Ingram Irvine was nationally famous because of his conversion to Orthodoxy. It made front-page headlines. It was major news. No other conversion to Orthodoxy in America has generated anything close to that kind of attention.

Irvine was born into an Anglican family in Ireland in 1849. He claimed to be a descendant of Oliver Cromwell, the seventeenth-century Lord Protector of England. Irvine moved to America as a teenager, attended General Theological Seminary in New York, and was ordained an Episcopal priest in 1874. At his first parish assignment on Long Island, he earned the nickname "the Spurgeon of Brookhaven" for his excellent preaching. ("Spurgeon" is a reference to a then-famous Protestant preacher named Charles Spurgeon. It's the nineteenth-century American Protestant equivalent of calling someone "the Chrysostom" of his milieu.)

Fr. Ingram Irvine obituary photo, Brooklyn Daily Eagle, *Jan. 24, 1921.*

Irvine moved from parish to parish in the years to come. He and his wife had four children, but only one survived to adulthood. By 1883, he was in Quincy, Illinois, dean of the Episcopal cathedral there. It was in Quincy that Irvine experienced his first major church controversy, going to battle with his own bishop. Irvine's version of the story is that the bishop facilitated a secret, illicit marriage involving a man who had illegally divorced his previous wife, and Irvine objected. The bishop's faction accused Irvine of various things, the worst of them being that he'd allegedly taken improper liberties with a young woman who'd been taken into the Irvines' home. There were issues with the young woman's testimony (she said the incident had occurred on New Year's Eve, but Irvine wasn't in town on New Year's Eve; and she'd accused several other men before—a doctor, a dentist, and a Long Island minister). At an ecclesiastical court, Irvine was acquitted of all the worst charges but was found guilty of (this is the term they used) "certain specifications," and he was suspended for a year. He appealed; in the end, the bishop apologized, and Irvine left town.

Irvine ended up in Philadelphia, where he proved to be just as much of a lightning rod as he had been in Illinois. Some of his vestrymen (equivalent to parish council members) were coming to church drunk, and Irvine wouldn't give them communion. Another ecclesiastical trial was held, and Irvine was vindicated, but he was also out of a job. He landed in central Pennsylvania, at St. John's Church in Huntingdon, under his former seminary classmate, Bishop Ethelbert Talbot. (Incidentally, Talbot himself had previously been in North Dakota, where he'd run across the Bulgarian Monk, and he would go on to become the presiding bishop of the entire Episcopal Church in America.) Talbot made Irvine promise that he would not stir up any trouble in his new assignment and that, if Talbot asked Irvine to resign, he would.

Predictably, Irvine soon found himself embroiled in yet another conflict, this time with the richest woman in the church—a divorcée who'd married a man who was himself divorced. Irvine learned of this and refused to give the couple communion. They appealed to the bishop, who sided with the couple. After an ecclesiastical trial, Irvine found himself defrocked. At this point it was 1900, and Irvine was past fifty.

He refused to take this lying down; he tried every avenue to restore his name, from ecclesiastical courts to the Supreme Court of Pennsylvania. The case made headlines nationwide. Finally, after five years, Irvine surrendered in 1905.

It seems that he went to Philadelphia at this point, where he befriended St. Sebastian Dabovich, who was serving in a parish there. Irvine got the idea that he should become Orthodox. He would claim that this was a result of divine revelation, on the Feast of Pentecost, no less. More cynical observers would see this as an opportunistic last-ditch gambit. In any case, Irvine argued that his conversion to Orthodoxy was sincere. He wrote, "God the Holy Ghost, on the morning of Whitsunday [Pentecost], 1905, in St. Mary's Church, Philadelphia, in response to the inquiry of my soul, 'Lord, what wilt thou have me to do?' commanded me in an irresistible way, 'Go and work for the Holy Eastern Church.' And I was obedient unto the voice."[1]

Saint Sebastian put Irvine in touch with St. Tikhon, the

---

1   Ingram N. W. Irvine, *A Letter on the Anglican Church's Claims* (1906).

Russian bishop in New York. This put Tikhon in an awkward position: he was close to the Episcopalians, especially the respected Episcopal bishop Charles Grafton. Accepting a defrocked Episcopal priest would irreparably damage St. Tikhon's relationships. But he could find no reason to refuse Irvine, and in early November 1905, Irvine was received into the Orthodox Church via chrismation. He was then tonsured a reader, ordained a deacon, and, on November 6, ordained to the priesthood by St. Tikhon, who was assisted by St. Raphael.

Practically every newspaper in America put this news on the front page. The *Washington Post* did a cover spread on the story on November 26. The Episcopalians were aghast. Saint Tikhon's friend Bishop Charles Grafton, whose Nashotah House seminary had just given Tikhon an honorary degree, was deeply hurt. Tikhon offered to return the degree. Grafton accepted. Their friendship was never the same.

The Episcopalians were upset for two reasons. First of all, some viewed St. Tikhon as essentially a religious ambassador of Russia to America. It was all fine and good for him to administer his Russian flock, they said, but he had overstepped his bounds by interfering in the life of an autocephalous church. At least, that's how the Episcopalians saw things. Of course, the Orthodox response was that the Episcopal Church was not another autocephalous Orthodox Church, and thus the Orthodox were under no obligation to acknowledge some kind of Episcopal jurisdiction over all of America.

The deeper issue was the Episcopalians' concern about their holy orders: by ordaining a man who'd been an Episcopal priest, St. Tikhon was implicitly rejecting the validity of Episcopal holy orders. Saint Alexander Hotovitzky, Irvine's sponsor at his ordination, responded to this by saying, "The matter of Anglican Orders is quite an open question. Until something definite is learned concerning it, we cannot here presume to set a precedent.

Were we to go ahead and accept Dr. Irvine [without first ordaining him], we would put ourselves in the place of schismatics, and
surely would be regarded so by the Eastern Church." He went on
to say, "If the fact that we stick to the rules our Church has set is
to hurt us with our friends, we will be very sorry, but I cannot see
that we can act differently."[2]

Irvine was fifty-six when he was ordained. He was given the
name Father Nathaniel, since Nathaniel was one of his middle
names. Saint Tikhon put him in charge of "English work"—
mostly doing services in English and writing articles. Saint
Tikhon was transferred out of America in 1907. As soon as
his successor, Platon, arrived, St. Alexander Hotovitzky wrote
a long letter to the new archbishop, briefing him on Irvine's
situation.[3]

> It became obvious to all that we are dealing with a man of
> exceedingly loose moral attitude, of shameless arrogance. In his
> manners and actions Fr. Irvine characterized himself as end-
> lessly deceitful, evasive, smooth talking, crafty, litigious. At all
> times he did not manage to endear for even a brief period a single
> person—on the contrary, everywhere [. . .] he displayed discord,
> irritation, insecurity, and so forth. In justification of his actions
> he provided nothing of substance to the matter; rather he slung
> mud in abundance at his enemies, though he might have only just
> before praised them. Thus, in order to put favorably in his light
> that his wife barely lives with him, he was not hesitant to say that
> she is half mad, as if she is his cross, whereas everything is con-
> firmed to the contrary. It goes without saying, after all, that these
> features repel every decent man from such an individual.

---

2   *Russian Orthodox American Messenger*, November Supplement (1905),
    375–387.
3   I found this letter in Irvine's file in the archives of the Orthodox Church
    in America. Aram Sarkisian provided a translation.

The letter goes on. And on. Saint Alexander tells of how Irvine got himself into debts, didn't repay them, and left the New York cathedral footing the bill. Irvine hung around with shady characters, took advantage of a man down on his luck—basically, he was a scumbag. Saint Tikhon tried to salvage things as best he could. He moved Irvine to a different church and tried to get him to focus on productive work, to no avail. Saint Alexander was at his wits' end. He saw no future for Irvine in the Orthodox Church.

That was enough for Archbishop Platon, who transferred Irvine to St. Raphael's Syro-Arab mission. Somehow, St. Raphael seems to have managed Irvine well enough to avoid major issues. He gave Irvine the job of serving as his English secretary, along with teaching Sunday school at the Syrian cathedral in Brooklyn and writing articles for St. Raphael's periodical, *Al-Kalimat*. It was Irvine who drafted St. Raphael's letter against the Episcopalians (covered in chapter 31).

The Syrian parents drove Irvine crazy. In a private letter, he complained to the Russian Archbishop Platon:

> My work amongst the Syrians has nearly broken me down. I am a nervous wreck; and, am told that, I must take a rest. You know, Your Grace, they are a people different from all others. They have a lovely Bishop, but the people here run wild after material gain. Rome and Protestantism spoiled them in Syria; and, here they have gone madly after money and dress. But besides, the children are encouraged to go to any Church or Sunday School where they can have a good time. I have done my best to teach the doctrines of the Orthodox Faith but there never has been one Liturgy said in English; yet the children all know English better than Arabic.[4]

His articles for *Al-Kalimat* were mostly directed at the Syrian youth, but in one article, he wrote to their parents, harshly rebuking them.

---

4   OCA archives.

You say that you like to take them visiting or to the Park or some where else on Sunday afternoon. You cannot, you say, take them during the week, for it would be taking you away from your business. Strange excuse! You do not want to rob yourself out of a Dollar but you do not care whether you rob God out of the souls of your children for whom He shed His Precious Blood upon the Cross.

Oh, foolish parent, who hath bewitched you! What demon is it which has blinded your eyes, dulled your understanding and filled you with unnatural love for your children? Do you think that love only means the satisfying of the eye, the ear, the palate and the body? Alas, these are the last to be thought of. I do not say that you must not make your children happy and take good care of them. Far from this. They ought to be treasured as jewels. But we will take it for granted that you send your children to Sunday School. Which Sunday School is it? You belong to the Holy Orthodox Church? "Yes," you say. Well then do you think that if your children go to a Roman Catholic, Protestant Epis-copal, Methodist, Baptist, Presbyterian, Maronite, Lutheran, Congregational or what other Religious Body you thus may select that they are instructed in the Doctrine, Discipline and Worship of the Church to which you belong? Why you are wild to think so. If you want your children to grow up in your Faith, the Faith of the Holy Martyrs of the first eight Centuries you will never have them do so unless they are sent to their own Sunday School.

If nothing else, Irvine was a skilled writer. And he wrote a lot—a small book against Anglicanism, an open letter to the Ortho-dox bishops on the problems facing Orthodoxy in America (in which Irvine suggested that the church should adopt the motto, "Aggressive Orthodox Catholicity, for Truth's Sake"), a slew of articles for *Al-Kalimat*, editorials for the *Vestnik*. His views were all over the map. In his open letter to the bishops, he proposed shortening the services and adding musical instruments; a few years later, he said that Orthodoxy should retain the Julian calendar and not switch to the Gregorian, since the Old Calendar "is a standing protest against the encroachments of Rome on the rights of Christendom and suggests investigation on the part of seekers after Ancient ways and truths amongst Protestants."

When St. Raphael died in 1915, Irvine eulogized him. "We see him now in his true light, great and good, learned, and, yet humble as a little child, a brave champion for the Orthodox Faith, yet filled with love for all mankind."[5] He lobbied hard against the election of Aftimios Ofiesh as Raphael's successor on the grounds that Aftimios was a Freemason. "I will never recognize him as a Bishop," Irvine wrote. "I can not serve God and Mammon in the Episcopate."[6]

Once Aftimios took over the Syro-Arab mission in 1917, Irvine got out, transferring back to the Russian archbishop. In 1920, when Irvine was seventy-one, an American-born Irish nationalist and Episcopal priest named James Mythen converted to Orthodoxy. The Russian archbishop, Alexander Nemolovsky, immediately ordained Mythen a priest and elevated him to archimandrite. For a stretch in the early 1920s, Mythen wielded enormous power in the Russian Archdiocese. He began to gather a cadre of American converts around him—a group that became known as the English-speaking Department. In July 1920, Mythen started a short-lived church in New York, the American Orthodox Catholic Church of the Transfiguration, the first all-English, all-convert parish in history. Late in his life, Irvine's dream was coming true.

Soon after the parish was established, there was a break-in, but nothing was stolen. Irvine served the liturgy as planned, and afterward, he consumed the gifts. Here's how the *New York Times* (8/16/1920) describes what happened:

---

5   *Russian Orthodox American Messenger* 19:5 (March 2/15, 1915), 70–72.
6   February 5, 1917, letter kept in the OCA archives.

[W]hen he drank the sacramental wine from the chalice at the end of the service, Canon Ingram N.W. Irvine became conscious of an agonizing pain in his mouth, throat and stomach. Believing that in some manner the chalice had been filled with acid instead of wine, he acted immediately to save his own life. By his promptness he escaped without serious injury, though he was very sick for a day or more.

The bottle of unconsecrated wine was not tainted, so the convert priests of the parish concluded that someone had poisoned the chalice itself. I'm skeptical about this explanation, since no one else got sick from the Eucharist—if such a thing is even possible, apart from divine chastisement. That makes me wonder if this was, in fact, an instance of divine chastisement. That, or perhaps another example of Irvine's melodramatic character.

Six months after this incident, on January 23, 1921, Irvine died at his home in Brooklyn. Although he seems to have still been Orthodox at the time of his death, his funeral was served by an Episcopal priest—and not in a church but in Irvine's home.

In the years that followed, Mythen and his convert friends (several of whom were also ordained priests) quickly washed out of the Orthodox Church. The English-speaking Department lived on. Some additional convert priests joined the group, and their new leader, Fr. Michael Gelsinger, became a hugely influential figure in the Antiochian Archdiocese under Metropolitan Antony Bashir. But Irvine's memory was forgotten; at best, he's a sort of odd footnote in American Orthodox history.

In his writings, Irvine comes across as bold, principled, and devoted to the Orthodox Faith. But then there's St. Alexander Hotovitzky's damning and detailed letter to Archbishop Platon, accusing Irvine of being a man of extraordinarily poor character. There seems little question that Irvine was a difficult and combative man who made enemies much more easily than he made friends. That such a great priest as St. Alexander would view Irvine as a toxic deadbeat is enough for me to conclude that Irvine was no saint; at the same time, St. Raphael seems to have been able to rein in the worst aspects of Irvine's character and get some use out of his obvious skill as a writer.

CHAPTER TWENTY-SIX

The Translator

Isabel Hapgood

IF YOU'VE HEARD about Isabel Hapgood, it's undoubtedly because of her 1906 translation of the Orthodox service book into English—a volume that's sometimes called simply "the Hapgood."

Some may be surprised to learn that Hapgood herself was never Orthodox; she was an Episcopalian all her life. She was born in Boston in 1851 and raised in Worcester, Massachusetts. Her father was from an old New England family, and Isabel was a very respectable young woman. She was given a first-class education, and she was particularly drawn to linguistics. She spent most of her twenties mastering not only the Romance and Germanic languages but also Slavic languages such as Russian, Polish, and Church Slavonic. And she didn't just want to read these languages; she hired a Russian woman to train her in spoken Russian, and pretty soon, Hapgood was fluent in Russian.

She never married, which gave her the flexibility to pursue her interests without the constraints of a husband or children. She translated works from French, Spanish, Portuguese, Dutch, Polish—and especially from Russian. She was quite taken with Russia.

In the late 1880s—in her late thirties—she spent two years in Russia with her mother, traveling and visiting the sights of the country. By this point she was a well-respected translator, and she was warmly received by all kinds of dignitaries, including Konstantin Pobedonostsev, the powerful ober-procurator of the Holy Synod. She attended imperial balls, and she even became friends with the novelist Leo Tolstoy, staying at his estate for an entire summer.

Hapgood wrote a book about her experience in Russia, *Russian Rambles,* published in 1895. Throughout the 1890s and early 1900s, she wrote countless articles about all things Russian for trendy American magazines such as *Harper's Bazaar* and *The Independent.* In 1895, she published an account of her meeting with St. John of Kronstadt—she had heard all about St. John, who was already in his lifetime famous as a wonderworker (even in America, where he routinely made headlines). She tried to get introduced to him to no avail, until by chance she met him in a railway carriage:

> His clear, brilliant blue eyes were very searching, but gentle, and in nowise alarming seen thus at short range. He looked through me for a moment, then grasped one of my hands firmly in his, and softly patted me on the shoulder with the other, in an unconventional manner which must have aroused the envy of all the Russians who beheld the scene. After standing thus for what seemed to me a long time under the scrutiny of those eyes, he tightened his clasp on my hand and said: "You will have strength; yes, you will have strength!" Then he blessed me—a voluntary blessing from him is regarded as an honor and prophetic of good fortune—gently refused the handkiss due him, and clasped both my hands instead. That is a fair and characteristic specimen of a favorable interview with Father Joann, and of his prophecies. Like the prophecies of the Delphic oracle, one has to live through the fate before it is possible to interpret it.[1]

---

1   *The Independent* (August 8, 1895), 5.

Hapgood was attracted to Orthodoxy, particularly Russian Orthodox worship. She wasn't necessarily interested in converting to Orthodoxy herself; her attraction was less a matter of conviction than of aesthetics. Hapgood wrote about attending a vespers service in Kiev and hearing the beautiful singing of the choir, and she said that she "shifted her stance from that of a foreign observer [. . .] to that of a devout worshiper experiencing the sublime."[2]

Returning to the United States, she became acquainted with Bishop Nicholas Ziorov and told him of her desire to translate the Orthodox church services into English, so that English-speaking people could fully experience the beauty of Orthodox worship. Bishop Nicholas was very excited about this and gave her a complete set of service books in Slavonic. This was the beginning of her great translation project.

It took her eleven years, from 1895 to 1906. After Bishop Nicholas was transferred, his successor, St. Tikhon, was an equally enthusiastic supporter of Hapgood's work. This original service book was published in 1906, and it's been in continuous use ever since. It's still widely used today in parishes all over the United States.

The other prominent non-Russian in the Russian Mission was Fr. Ingram Nathaniel Irvine, who loathed Hapgood. But he could not find a word to say against her translation of the Service Book—even Irvine had to admit that it was an astounding achievement—and so he publicly claimed that St. Alexander Hotovitzky, rather than Hapgood, was the real brains behind the translation. Saint Alexander was aghast at this, writing to Irvine to demand a retraction. Of Hapgood, Hotovitzky wrote:

---

2   Quoted in Marina Ledkovsky, "A Linguistic Bridge to Orthodoxy: In Memoriam Isabel Florence Hapgood," lecture delivered at the twelfth annual Russian Orthodox Musicians Conference, October 7–11, 1998, Washington, DC.

The Service Book was compiled by Miss Isabel F. Hapgood, on her own initiative. To her belongs the original idea of this work; hers are the plan and the execution of it, which have required arduous labor and expenditure of strength for the space of several years, as she was compelled to study our Liturgical books, and the Church Slavonic and Greek languages, and so forth. Anyone who has the slightest conception of the complicated structure of the Orthodox religious services, in their entire extent, will make no mistake if he applies to this labor the epithet "gigantic," both as to its design and its importance; and the merits of Miss Hapgood's liturgical English in this work are confirmed by learned ecclesiastical authorities of the Episcopal Church.

In comparison with this enormous mass of labor—in truth a most precious and unselfish gift from Miss Hapgood to our Church—my share in it, (as an Orthodox priest, who has rendered, so far as occasion required, only what aid was indispensable,) is merely of secondary importance; and, especially when her name is omitted, does not deserve to be mentioned.[3]

Hapgood was close friends with Fr. Alexander and his wife throughout their time in New York, from his 1895 arrival until his return to Russia in 1914.

It would be a mistake to view Hapgood merely as a translator of services. She was very involved in the inner workings of the Russian Mission in the early 1900s. She was one of the key organizers of the St. Nicholas Cathedral choir in New York City in 1903. She got financial backing for the choir and arranged for it to give glamorous concerts for the American public. In 1914, the choir gave a private performance for President Woodrow Wilson at the White House.

The next year, in 1915, Hapgood wrote a letter to the Russian

---

3   Quoted in Stuart H. Hoke, "A Generally Obscure Calling: A Character Sketch of Isabel Florence Hapgood," *St. Vladimir's Theological Quarterly* 45:1 (2001), 84.

archbishop, Evdokim, on the subject of the cathedral choir. This letter was published in the *Vestnik*, the official magazine of the Russian Mission. Hapgood opens the letter boldly: "I am going to be very frank. There is no one else who can tell you about the American public and the conditions connected with Concerts as well as I can." She then proceeds to argue that the cathedral choir should aspire to be a musical organization on par with the great Boston Symphony. She goes on, "I now wish to repeat to you, with great emphasis: The Cathedral Choir, properly constituted large enough, is immensely more important to your Church and Mission in this country than twenty little new parishes."[4]

Hapgood's rationale is basically that a great professional choir would show off all the aesthetic beauty of Orthodox worship, which would attract well-to-do, paying audiences. It would, in Hapgood's words, "win more friends for your Church." It's clear that she's not talking about making converts, but rather about making more people like her—non-Orthodox "friends." She says, "A prejudiced person who hears the Cathedral Choir will (if it is really fine), wish to know about the services of your Church which have inspired such music, such singing, such interpretation of spiritual emotion. They will become helpful friends of Russia and of your Church." She concludes her letter, "Please let us have a splendid choir!"

It was a bad look for Hapgood; for all the good she did the Orthodox Church—and she did it a lot of good—the truth is that she loved Orthodoxy for her own reasons, but not as the Ark of Salvation. Hapgood's enemy, Irvine, seized the opportunity and fired back with a vicious letter in the next issue of the *Vestnik*. "Our Archbishop was not called by the Holy Ghost to conse-crate Choir Leaders for roving Singing-Bands to help and please new Orthodox churchgoers—'Episcopalians' and Protestants in

---

4   *Russian Orthodox American Messenger* 19:20 (Aug. 20/Sept. 2, 1915), 311–314.

general to whom Miss Hapgood refers. . . . Christ and His Holy Apostles went forth, and sent forth their representatives, without Singing Bands to tickle 'itching ears,' or please the sensual." He accused Hapgood of espousing a "musical heresy" and said that she, as a Protestant, had no business telling an Orthodox bishop how to run his diocese.[5] Privately, Irvine was even harsher, calling her "that vixen Miss Hapgood" who has "damned the church for years."[6]

That unfortunate incident aside, Hapgood remained a friend of the Orthodox Church. She was in Russia when the Revolution broke out in 1917. She had to escape, and upon returning to the United States, she worked to help the cause of the suffering Russians. She continued to write for all kinds of publications, always advocating on behalf of the Russian people, up to her death in 1928. She died in New York at the age of seventy-six. Although she never converted to Orthodoxy, she is one of the most significant figures in early American Orthodox history.

5   *Russian Orthodox American Messenger* 19:23 (September 10/23, 1915), 368–370.
6   April 30, 1917, letter from Irvine to Archbishop Evdokim, Irvine file, OCA archives.

CHAPTER TWENTY-SEVEN

Helen Keller's Teacher

Michael Anagnos

HELEN KELLER WAS one of the most famous women in America in the early twentieth century. Both deaf and blind, she overcame her disabilities to become a bestselling author and popular lecturer. Keller's tutor, Anne Sullivan, became rather famous in her own right for her role in training the young Keller. In 1962, Anne Bancroft won the Academy Award for Best Actress for her portrayal of Sullivan in The Miracle Worker. Less well-known, but just as significant, is the man who brought Keller and Sullivan together—Michael Anagnos, an Orthodox immigrant from Greece and the longtime head of Boston's Perkins Institute for the Blind.

Anagnos (shortened from Anagnostopoulos) was born in a mountain village in Epirus in 1837. The son of a peasant, he grew up tending his father's flocks and studying in the village school. He eventually earned a scholarship to a better school and ultimately was admitted to the University of Athens. There, he was so poor that he couldn't afford textbooks and had to copy the required readings by hand. He worked his way through college, graduated, and then studied law.

After law school, Anagnos began a career, not in law, but

in journalism. In his mid-twenties, he became editor of an Athens newspaper, *Ethnophylax* (*The National Guard*). From that post, Anagnos opposed the government of King Otho, which led to his arrest and imprisonment. In 1866, he supported the cause of revolutionaries in Crete. As it turned out, a certain American, Dr. Samuel Howe, was also a supporter of the Cretan revolutionaries and had come

Helen Keller with Michael Anagnos, 1891.

to the region to engage in relief efforts. Howe hired Anagnos to be his assistant, and when Howe returned to the US, Anagnos joined him.

Dr. Howe happened to be the founder of the Perkins Institute for the Blind in Boston, and he gave Anagnos a position as teacher of Greek and Latin, as well as the job of private tutor to the Howe family. Before long, Anagnos and Howe's daughter Julia had fallen in love, and they were married in 1870. As Dr. Howe's health declined, he gave Anagnos more and more authority at the Perkins Institute, and after Howe's death, Anagnos became the institute's head.

Anagnos was perfect for the job. Right away, he raised one hundred thousand dollars (roughly two million today) to publish books for the blind, and he made sure that every public library in Massachusetts had copies. He set up vocational training programs for blind people and started a kindergarten for blind children (raising another hundred thousand to keep it going). Helen Keller was the institute's most famous product: she was sent to Anagnos by Alexander Graham Bell, and Anagnos paired her with twenty-year-old former student Anne Sullivan, who herself was visually impaired. Anagnos led the Perkins Institute for thirty years, affecting the lives of countless blind individuals. After his death, one student offered this remembrance (reprinted in Annie S. Beard's *Our Foreign Born Citizens*, 1922, which has been a major source for this chapter):

> His strength comforted our weakness, his firmness overcame our wavering ideas, his power smoothed away our obstacles, his noble unselfishness put to shame our petty differences of opinion, and his untiring devotion led us all to do our little as well as we could. . . . Better than all, he taught us to the best of our ability to be men and women in our own homes.

Besides his role at the Perkins Institute, Anagnos was a towering figure in Boston's Greek community. He also served as president of the National Union of Greeks in the United States, and he may well have been the most famous Greek person in America in his day. He made many trips back to Europe, where he donated tens of thousands of dollars to fund schools in Greece, Turkey, Serbia, and Romania. After Anagnos's death in 1906 on a visit to Romania, the *Boston Evening Herald* (7/16/1906) published a tribute from T. T. Timayenis of the Boston Greek community:

> He was the man who taught the Greeks of America to learn and adopt everything that is good in the American character, the only man whom all Greeks revered and implicitly obeyed; the man who did good for the sake of the good; the man who conceived the idea of establishing a Greek school in Boston; the man who expected every Greek to do his duty toward his adopted country—America.

At his funeral, Fr. Nestor Souslides—the parish priest and Anagnos's close friend—broke down while delivering the eulogy; according to the *Boston Globe* (7/16/1906), "Tears streamed down from the eyes of the preacher before the conclusion of his address and he was so overcome by his emotions that he was obliged to step for a moment into his study before he could give the benediction." The parish community vowed to hold annual memorial services for Anagnos in perpetuity.

Michael Anagnos ca. 1900.

CHAPTER TWENTY-EIGHT

The First Black Priest in America

Father Raphael Morgan

The Morgan story is so utterly improbable that one tends to dismiss it as a hoax.[1]

FATHER RAPHAEL MORGAN was the first black Orthodox priest in America. His story is both utterly remarkable and rather mysterious: we have bits and pieces of information that have survived the past century, but there's a certain arbitrariness in stringing those moments into a narrative. We'll try, though.

Morgan was born in Chapelton, Clarendon, Jamaica, either on April 23, 1863, or October 7, 1866. Those are two very specific dates. Here's why: Fr. Raphael's given name was Robert Josias Morgan, and I found two listings of babies named Robert Josias Morgan in the baptismal records of the Anglican parish in Clarendon, Jamaica. It's possible that the two boys were cousins, but my best guess is that they were brothers and that the first died in infancy. It was common back then for parents to reuse the name

---

1   Gavin White, "Patriarch McGuire and the Episcopal Church" in Randall K. Burkett and Richard Newman, eds., *Black Apostles: Afro-American Clergy Confront the Twentieth Century* (Boston: G.K. Hall & Co., 1978), 164.

of a dead child when they had another. So the most likely birth date for our Morgan is October 7, 1866.

His father died before he was born, and at a young age, Morgan embarked on an amazing life of travel, financed by unknown means. He went first to Panama and Honduras, then to the United States. The purpose of these initial journeys is unclear, though it is possible that Morgan was pursuing an education. He next traveled to Germany, where he worked as a Christian missionary, then to England, and finally to Sierra Leone in Africa. At some point amid his travels (the precise date of which is indeterminate), Morgan became a minister in the African Methodist Episcopal Church and then joined the Church of England. In Freetown, Sierra Leone, he studied Greek and Latin at an Anglican school and met his future wife, Charlotte. Next he worked as an Anglican lay reader and missionary in Liberia for "a number of years," and it was in Liberia that he got married, in December 1888. After a visit to the United States, Morgan returned to England to study for holy orders in the Anglican Church. Upon completion of his studies, he returned to America and was ordained a deacon in June 1895. He served in Wilmington, Delaware (where he also taught in local public schools), Charleston, Richmond, Nashville, and Philadelphia.

The family moved around a lot. They had five children, only two of whom survived infancy: a daughter named Roberta and a son named Cyril Ignatius.

At some point around the turn of the twentieth century, Morgan began to question his faith. He embarked on a sweeping three-year study of Anglicanism, Roman Catholicism, and Orthodox Christianity, concluding that the Orthodox Church "is the pillar and ground of the truth."[2] Rather than simply

---

2   Frank Lincoln Mather, ed., *Who's Who of the Colored Race: A General Biographical Dictionary of Men and Women of African Descent* (Chicago, 1915), 226. The biographical entry on Morgan appears to use Morgan

convert to Orthodoxy, however, Morgan began another phase of travel. He journeyed to Russia in 1904 and was present at the anniversary service of the coronation of Tsar Nicholas II and at the memorial service for the late Tsar Alexander III. He was treated as an honored guest, and his photo reportedly appeared in numerous Russian periodicals. He also visited many monasteries and holy sites of the Russian land.

In an open letter written at the end of his month-long stay, Morgan spoke in glowing terms of his experience in the country and his regard for the Orthodox Church. After expressing a desire for the union of Christendom, he concluded, "I must say, that my stay in Russia did me personally much good: I feel now firmer and stronger spiritually than I did before I came."[3] He also visited Turkey, Cyprus, and the Holy Land.

Another three years of study followed, this time under the tutelage of Greek priests in America. Morgan's reasons for affiliating himself with the Greeks rather than the Russians are unclear. The Russians had bishops resident in the United States; they had seminaries and administration. The Greeks were far less formally organized and were nearly two decades away from having their own bishops in America. Moreover, Morgan indicates that he had just spent an edifying month in Russia and held the Russian Church in high regard. Still, he chose to place himself under the Greeks. While no explanation for this choice is apparent, it is possible that Morgan, who was living in Philadelphia, simply developed a relationship with the local Greek congregation and thus chose to ally himself with them.

On January 7, 1906, Morgan was present at the Christmas services of the Greek church in Philadelphia. The *Philadelphia Inquirer* reported the next day that "Rev. R.J. Morgan of the

---

himself as its primary source.

3   *Russian Orthodox American Messenger,* October & November Supplement (1904), 380–382.

American Catholic Church, an off-shoot of the Protestant Episcopal Church, assisted."

The next year, in June 1907, Morgan traveled to Istanbul
armed with two letters. One, from Fr. Demetrios Petrides, the
Greek priest in Philadelphia, introduced Morgan to the Patriarchate of Constantinople and recommended him for reception
into the Orthodox Church and ordination to its priesthood. The
other, from the Greek congregation of Philadelphia, seconded
Petrides's recommendation and also stated that if Morgan were
unsuccessful in establishing an Orthodox parish for black Americans, he would be welcome to serve as an assistant priest for the
Philadelphia community. Metropolitan Joachim of Pelagoneia,
one of the few hierarchs of the patriarchate with a knowledge
of English, was assigned to Morgan's case, and he recommended
that Morgan be baptized, chrismated, ordained, and then sent
back to America to "carry the light of the Orthodox faith among
his racial brothers."[4]

In August, Metropolitan Joachim baptized and chrismated
Morgan in the presence of three thousand people, and on August
28 (Dormition on the church calendar), Morgan was ordained
to the Orthodox priesthood. He was given the name Father
Raphael, which he adopted in place of Robert. The Holy Synod
of Constantinople sent Morgan back to Philadelphia with vestments, liturgical books, a cross, and twenty pounds sterling for
traveling expenses. He was granted the right to hear confessions,
but the Synod denied his request for an antimension and Holy
Chrism, possibly wanting to wait until Morgan had received further training in liturgics from Fr. Demetrios Petrides in Philadelphia. As soon as he arrived back in the United States, Morgan
baptized his wife and children into the Orthodox Faith.

---

4   Paul G. Manolis, "Raphael (Robert) Morgan: The First Black Orthodox
     Priest in America" (Athens, 1981).

ooooo

ONE OF THE mysteries surrounding Morgan's life relates to his missionary activity. There are hints of conversions among his fellow blacks, but the details are hazy at best. On January 8, 1910, the *Philadelphia Record* published an article on the "Orthodox Community of All Saints," an initiative led by Morgan that included two former Protestant clergymen (one Episcopal and one Methodist) as well as "a considerable number of laymen." This community seems not to have been a parish but perhaps more of a planning committee, with the ambitious aim of starting multiple churches and schools, using English as the primary language for worship. This would make it one of the earliest English-language Orthodox efforts, particularly notable because it took place under the Ecumenical Patriarchate (which, at the time, was focused on ministering to ethnic Greeks in the diaspora, using the Greek language). But other than that one 1910 newspaper article, we don't know anything about Morgan's All Saints project.

A year earlier, in 1909, Morgan's wife, Charlotte, filed for divorce. This was in an era before no-fault divorces were the legal norm (no-fault divorces allow either party to end the marriage for basically any reason, usually citing "irreconcilable differences"). Back then, to get a divorce, a person had to prove some specific grounds to a court: infidelity, abuse, abandonment, and so forth. Charlotte Morgan's allegations against her husband were extremely serious: she testified in detail about alleged physical and verbal abuse as well as infidelity. Remarkably, the court documents and the transcript of her testimony have survived, and they paint a rather chilling picture of the marriage. Charlotte brought with her the Morgans' former landlady, who corroborated the abuse allegations. Father Raphael didn't show up in court, but in a written filing he denied the accusations and instead claimed that Charlotte had abused him (which would also have been grounds for divorce). The judge granted Charlotte the divorce.[5]

Even before this, the Morgans had split up their children: thirteen-year-old Roberta lived with Fr. Raphael, while nine-year-old Cyril Ignatius lived with his mother. After the divorce, Fr. Raphael traveled with his teenage daughter to Europe, and when he returned to the United States at the end of 1911, she wasn't with him. He had left her in Greece, where she spent the rest of her adolescence and early adulthood, finally returning to America in 1924. Think about that: a black teenager from America dropped off in Greece by her father to live for the next dozen years. What's the story here? Why did he leave her there, and what was her life like? Unfortunately, we have no answers.

Father Raphael continued his life of travel, visiting his home country of Jamaica in the summer of 1913 for a speaking tour of the island. Among his stops was Chapelton, the place of his birth. In late December, the Russian warship *Rossija* stopped in Jamaica, and Morgan concelebrated the Divine Liturgy with the Russian priest aboard the ship. In addition to Russian, English was used in the service for the benefit of the many Syrian-Jamaicans in attendance. According to the local newspaper, the *Gleaner* (12/27/1913), Morgan was in contact with St. Raphael Hawaweeny: "Father Raphael states that he is now in communication with the Syrian Orthodox Bishop of Brooklyn with regard to the Syrians here, and hopes that ere long something will be done in regard to their spiritual welfare."

Morgan's next appearance in the historical record is September 19, 1916, when he published a letter to the editors of the leading Jamaican newspapers, critiquing the famous Jamaican preacher Marcus Garvey, who was on lecture tour in America. A group of

---

5   Matthew Namee, "The Fr. Raphael Morgan Divorce Documents," *Ortho-dox History* (September 3, 2019), https://orthodoxhistory.org/2019/09/03/the-fr-raphael-morgan-divorce-documents/

concerned Jamaican-Americans residing in Philadelphia, led by Morgan, took issue with Garvey's reactionary tone. "We, having attended his lectures," wrote the Philadelphia Jamaicans, "found them to be pernicious, misleading, and derogatory to the prestige of the Government and the people [of Jamaica]." At the heart of the issue was Garvey's dismal portrayal of race relations in Jamaica, which at the time was a part of the United Kingdom. The letter was signed first by Morgan and then by twelve others. In response, Garvey wrote a letter of his own claiming that Morgan's letter was "a concoction and a gross fabrication" written as part of a conspiracy against him.

After this, we lose track of Morgan. Father John Perich of St. Tikhon's Seminary tracked down Morgan's death certificate, which shows that he died on July 29, 1922, in Philadelphia. The cause of death is listed as "acute dilation of the heart." He was fifty-six years old. It seems that Morgan remained Orthodox until the end, as his death certificate is signed by Fr. Thomas Daniels, the priest of Annunciation Greek Orthodox Church in Philadelphia.

ooooo

MORGAN'S LEGACY IS a bit muddled. A black man from Jamaica discovered Orthodoxy and became a priest in 1907: this alone is absolutely amazing and obviously significant. The fact that he did so, not under the missionary-minded St. Tikhon, but under the more ethnically focused Ecumenical Patriarchate, is all the more notable. We don't know much about his missionary efforts, and it doesn't seem as if his work had a direct lasting impact on Orthodoxy in America (which is not to say that it might not be an inspiration for present-day evangelism).

We do know that Morgan was, at one point, associated with another black Jamaican clergyman in the Episcopal Church, George Alexander McGuire, who, years later, created the non-canonical African Orthodox Church and became its "patriarch." Eventually, some Ugandan men in Africa joined the African Orthodox Church, but when they realized that it was not actually Orthodox, they approached the Patriarchate of Alexandria and converted. This was the beginning of modern Orthodox missions in sub-Saharan Africa—one of the great stories of Orthodoxy in modern times. Father Raphael Morgan was not directly connected with any of that, but it's possible that he was some kind of inspiration for McGuire in creating his church.

Morgan's personal life is riddled with question marks: What are we to make of the extremely serious abuse allegations made by Charlotte Morgan and the landlady? Why did Fr. Raphael leave his teenage daughter in Greece? What did he do in the final years of his life, between his 1913 Jamaica visit and his death in 1922? All we have for that nine-year period is the 1916 exchange of letters with Marcus Garvey.

Perhaps, in the years to come, more evidence will emerge, giving us a more complete understanding of this remarkable story.

CHAPTER TWENTY-NINE

The Stormy Petrel of the Cloth

Father Demetrios Petrides

FATHER DEMETRIOS PETRIDES was born on the Greek island of Samos in 1863. He was married and had children, but his wife died before he came to America. Back in Greece, his daughter fell in love with a young man, and they wanted to get married. The man's father opposed the marriage and disowned his son when they went through with it, but Fr. Demetrios supported the young couple and took his son-in-law under his wing. Soon, the son-in-law left for America to earn money, as so many Greek men did in that era. In 1907, Fr. Demetrios was asked by the Church of Greece to become the new priest at Annunciation Church in Philadelphia, and he brought along his daughter, reuniting her with her husband.

The Philadelphia Greek church had a notable catechumen, a black man from Jamaica named Robert Morgan, whom we met in the previous chapter. A couple months after arriving in the United States, Fr. Demetrios wrote a letter to the Ecumenical Patriarchate, recommending Morgan for reception into the Orthodox Church and ordination to the priesthood. The patriarchate agreed, and in July 1907, Morgan traveled to Constantinople, where he was baptized and then moved through the ranks of the clergy, becoming a priest. He returned to Philadelphia, becoming the assistant priest to Fr. Demetrios at Annunciation parish, and for a while, Morgan lived in the Petrides family home.

Like so many of his fellow priests, Fr. Demetrios traveled throughout his region of the country, ministering to the Orthodox people he found who didn't have a priest. One time, he went to Ithaca, New York, to do a baptism. After the service, unbeknownst to Fr. Demetrios, a sixteen-year-old Greek girl had advertised that she would go into a "spirit trance." Greeks had traveled from all over to witness the spectacle. Father Demetrios caught wind of what was going on, and he burst into the room, stopped the girl's trance, and told the people that spiritualism is against the teachings of the Orthodox Church. This was the sort of man he was—completely unafraid to stand up for what was right, no matter what.

It was this gumption that got him run out of Philadelphia. The Philadelphia church was dominated by a rich layman, Constantine Stephano, who was a millionaire cigarette magnate. Stephano and Fr. Demetrios did not get along. Things came to a head in 1912, when Stephano sent the following message to Fr. Demetrios—this is almost unbelievable:

> Constantine Stephano commands you to appear at his office every evening at sunset and salaam low upon entering his presence. Then you are to stand erect, with folded arms, with your eyes cast downward, awaiting a word from Stephano before sitting down or otherwise changing your position. If you are not asked to be seated you are to remain in this position until Stephano leaves his office, and when he passes through the door you are to salaam low again and depart with bowed head.

Stephano was obviously trying to humiliate the priest, and Fr. Demetrios would have none of it. He responded, "I will not thus humiliate myself before this maker of cigarettes."

In the early twentieth century, Greek parishes in America had only a loose connection to the church authorities in Athens or Constantinople. As a practical matter, the parishes were run by lay boards of trustees, which would hire and fire priests at will. Constantine Stephano arranged for Fr. Demetrios to be ousted from the Philadelphia church by the slim margin of seven votes.[1]

But, characteristically, Fr. Demetrios left with his head held high. In September of 1912, newspapers in Georgia began reporting that a daring Greek priest was coming to Atlanta. One newspaper called him "the stormy petrel of the cloth."[2] Another paper said that he was famous for his "lambasting of the rich Greeks who loved money for the sake of power." He was warmly welcomed by the Greeks in Atlanta, who seemed to have a good idea of the sort of priest they were getting.

But Fr. Demetrios was not simply focused on his fellow Greeks. At the turn of the twentieth century, an active dialogue was taking place between the Orthodox and the Episcopalians. This led to the creation of a group called the Anglican and Eastern Orthodox Churches Union. The Orthodox members of the group included clergy from various ethnic backgrounds, including Antiochians, Russians, and Greeks. Previously, St. Raphael Hawaweeny had been involved with the group, and for several years in the teens, Fr. Demetrios was the organization's Greek representative.

As the teens wore on, he developed diabetes, and in the days before insulin, that was a death sentence. As his health declined, tragedy struck: Fr. Demetrios's son George died while still a young man. On March 7, 1917, Fr. Demetrios wrote this letter to a friend:

---

1   "Priest Won't Salaam to Rich Tobacconist," *Syracuse Journal* (July 20, 1912), 12.
2   *Columbus Enquirer-Sun* (September 15, 1912), 10.

My warmest thanks to you for your participation in our mourning and for your condolences, and for the wonderful selection of expressions for the death of my beloved boy, my George, my brave one. Ah! It is impossible to describe on this lifeless piece of paper the pain in my heart. I was not able to save him! I made every effort, much surpassing my strength. My God! What a torture it is. My eyes were changed into oceans and my tears had no end. But even going through this, blessed be the name of the Lord.[3]

Six months later, Fr. Demetrios himself succumbed to diabetes, dying on September 4, 1917, a month shy of his fifty-fourth birthday.

---

3   Letter provided to me by the Jannoulis family, descendants of Fr. Demetrios.

CHAPTER THIRTY

The Odd Adventures
of Father Philip Sredanovich

FATHER PHILIP SREDANOVICH is one of the odder characters in American Orthodox history. Perhaps not as odd as the
embellishing Agapius Honcharenko or the wandering Bulgarian
Monk, but in all my studies, I've run across few parish priests
stranger than Sredanovich.

Sredanovich was born in Montenegro in 1881. I read somewhere that he was educated in Russia, although I can't seem to
track down the precise source. (This is supported by the 1920
US Census, which says that Sredanovich's wife was born in Russia.) He came to the US just after the turn of the twentieth century; by 1906, he was pastor of St. Nicholas Serbian Church in
Wilmerding, Pennsylvania. A couple of years later, while serving
in Butler, Pennsylvania, he made his first newspaper headlines.
From the *Washington Post* (12/11/1908):

> The Rev. Philip Sredanovitch, pastor of the Greek Orthodox
> Church and editor of Justness, today announced a discovery,
> which, if it works out, will put Newton, Franklin, and Edison in
> the amateur class. The pastor-editor declares that he has invented
> a means by which the rotation of the earth on its axis may be

taken advantage of in travel, and that by standing still one may go around the world in 24 hours.

He says he has found a way by which men may lift themselves above the earth to a point where they will stand still while the earth, rotating from west to east, will do their traveling for them. The secret is jealously guarded by the pastor and his wife, whom he credits with suggesting the idea. He asks $100,000 for the invention.

Sredanovich says: "We will hoist ourselves above the earth and await the coming of the desired place, then we will lower ourselves where we desire to be. In this way we may go from America to Europe in less than eighteen hours. My secret is how to stand above the earth and not be affected by the earth's attraction."

He says his invention makes it possible to get away from gravitation and still not be lose [sic] in space.

He does not say how one may get away from the swirling earth and take his stand in the ethereal world, but any one with $100,000 may find out. So far as is known, the pastor has invented no airships nor announced any scheme for climbing a sunbeam.

This has to be a joke, right? An educated clergyman couldn't seriously think that you could circle the globe simply by "hoisting" yourself above the earth—could he?

Sredanovich bounced around a lot. Here is an incomplete list of the places he served:

» Wilmerding, Pennsylvania
» Butler, Pennsylvania
» Kansas City, Missouri
» South Bend, Indiana
» Gary, Indiana
» Kansas City, Missouri (again)
» Butte, Montana
» Milwaukee, Wisconsin
» Steelton, Pennsylvania

» Johnstown, Pennsylvania
» Butte, Montana (again)

In Fr. Philip's day, it was quite common for priests to spend only a couple of years (or less) at one parish before moving on to the next. But Sredanovich's travels seem to have been caused as much by his own personality as by the era in which he lived. In November 1920, he was "fired" from his post in Kansas City and responded with four successive lawsuits in the span of three months. In one suit, he asked for twenty-five thousand dollars, charging that "church officials were instrumental in causing slanderous remarks to be printed against him" in a Serbian newspaper. A few days later, he filed another lawsuit, this time merely seeking $120 in back pay. (I don't know the outcomes of these cases; my only source is the *Kansas City Times*, 1/25/1921.)

After leaving Kansas City, Sredanovich went to Butte, Montana, where he took over Holy Trinity Serbian Church. One day, in November 1922, he was walking down the street when a group of teenage boys started to bother him. One picked up a rock, at which point Sredanovich took off for his house. He went inside, got his pistol, and returned to the street. The youths continued to taunt Sredanovich, who responded by shooting one of the boys in the foot. The injured eighteen-year-old was taken to the hospital, and Sredanovich was arrested and charged with second-degree assault (*Idaho Daily Statesman*, 11/30/1922).

Sredanovich soon left Butte, but he returned to the parish in 1949, spending the last three years of his life there. He died in 1952 and is buried at St. Sava Serbian Orthodox Monastery in Libertyville, Illinois.

CHAPTER THIRTY-ONE

Saint Raphael and the Episcopalians

A T THE TURN of the last century, relations between the Orthodox Church and the Anglicans were quite warm. They cooled a bit in 1905, when St. Tikhon ordained the former Episcopalian priest Ingram Nathaniel Irvine to the Orthodox priesthood, but even so, many on both sides of the dialogue felt that full union would eventually happen.

In England in 1896, a body was formed called the Anglican and Eastern Orthodox Churches Union. A dozen years later, in 1908, a group of high church Episcopalians decided to establish an American branch of the organization. Several Orthodox leaders attended the first meeting in New York City, including the Syrian bishop Raphael Hawaweeny, Fr. Benedict Turkevich (representing the Russian Archdiocese), and Fr. Methodius Kourkoulis (representing the Greeks). During the meeting, St. Raphael was elected to be the Orthodox vice president.

The Episcopalians had an ambitious agenda: they wanted the Orthodox to recognize their holy orders as valid. Indeed, they wanted to be recognized as a fully fledged sister church, just as "Orthodox" as the churches of Constantinople or Russia or Antioch. The Orthodox in the group, and St. Raphael in particular, had much more modest goals. They wanted to promote friendly dialogue, with initiatives such as seminarian exchanges.

All the while, St. Raphael faced a monumentally difficult pastoral situation. His flock was scattered across North America, and many lived far away from any Orthodox church, Syrian or otherwise. In 1909, the Episcopalians suggested that he have the Anglican Book of Common Prayer translated into Arabic, so that the Syrians could worship with the Episcopalians. Raphael responded that it would be better for the Episcopalians to buy some Orthodox service books for their churches, so that the Syrians could use them if they visited.

In June 1910, Raphael went even further, granting formal permission for his people to seek the ministrations of Episcopal clergymen in the event that no Orthodox priest was available. He was careful to specify, "in this matter I am only speaking for myself *personally*, as an Orthodox Bishop, and in no way binding my brother Orthodox Bishops in North America. I *speak alone for the Syrian people*" (emphasis his). And he tried to set forth some rules (I'm summarizing here, not quoting directly unless noted):

» For weddings, where no Orthodox priest is available, the Syrians should get a blessing from Bishop Raphael first, and if an Orthodox priest of any ethnicity is nearby, he should perform the ceremony.

» For baptisms, if no Orthodox priest is available, the Orthodox practice of threefold immersion should be used, and the Episcopalian clergy should push for the child to be chrismated by an Orthodox priest as soon as possible.

» "When an Orthodox Layman is dying, if he confesses his sins, and professes that he is dying in the full communion of the Orthodox Faith, as expressed in the Orthodox version of the Nicene Creed, and the other requirements of the said Church, and desires the Blessed Sacrament of the Body and Blood of Christ, at the hands of an Episcopal Clergyman, permission is hereby given to administer to him this

Blessed Sacrament, and to be buried according to the Rites and Ceremonies of the Episcopal Church. But, it is recommended that, if an Orthodox Service Book can be procured, that the Sacraments and Rites be performed as set forth in that Book."

This is a pretty shocking policy, especially coming from a saint. And it was a huge mistake. It led to confusion among the faithful and facilitated the poaching of Orthodox Christians by Episcopal priests. Within fifteen months, St. Raphael knew that he had made a grave error.

And he repented.

On September 25, 1911—fifteen months after issuing his letter of permission to the Episcopalians—St. Raphael formally withdrew from the Anglican and Eastern Orthodox Churches Union. He sent a letter to the Union tendering his resignation and then sent a pastoral epistle to his flock, admitting his error and rescinding his June 1910 letter.

In his letter to the union group, he wrote,

There is a great and growing misunderstanding on the part of the Laity to wit, that, there is actually a union, or that, there will be, in the very near future, a corporate Union, between the Protestant Episcopal Church and the Holy Orthodox in America at least. The result is that the Laity in some sections are being confused in their doctrinal belief as well as growing careless about other requirements of the Holy Orthodox Church. In fact they neither know what to believe nor to reject,—much less which Church it is their duty to sustain.

All of this was made worse by the Episcopalian priests:

Some of the Protestant Episcopal Clergy have taken upon themselves, through misunderstanding, to offer their services to

Orthodox people, when even Orthodox Priests were within calling distance to minister to them; thus conveying the idea that, they, the Protestant Episcopal Clergy, were accepted as Holy Orthodox and that, there was no need of the ministrations or pastoral care of their own Orthodox Bishops and Clergy.

Thus, St. Raphael respectfully withdrew from the Union. He followed this with a 2200-word pastoral epistle, in which he stated, "I am convinced that the doctrinal teaching and practices, as well as the discipline, of the whole Anglican Church are unacceptable to the Holy Orthodox Church." Therefore, "I direct all Orthodox people residing in any community not to seek or to accept the ministrations of the Sacraments and rites from any clergy excepting those of the Holy Orthodox Catholic and Apostolic Church." But St. Raphael didn't stop there. It was not enough for the Orthodox to avoid the ministrations and sacraments of non-Orthodox bodies. He went on, "I further direct that Orthodox Christians should not make it a practice to attend the services of other religious bodies, so that there be no confusion concerning the teaching or doctrines."

This example of repentance and public acknowledgement of error by an Orthodox bishop is a model for all.

CHAPTER THIRTY-TWO

Father Basil Kerbawy's Beard and the Mayor of New York

FOR THREE TUMULTUOUS decades—1907 to 1938—Fr. Basil Kerbawy was the dean of St. Nicholas Syrian Orthodox Cathedral in Brooklyn. Apparently, in 1911, he was having some issues related to his beard, and things got so bad that he wrote to William Gaynor, the mayor of New York. I can't resist reprinting their correspondence. Here is Kerbawy's original letter, which got picked up by numerous newspapers:[1]

> Most Honored Sir—I want to know if it is a crime to wear a beard? I suppose that this may appear to be a foolish question to you, but to me it means a great deal. I am the pastor of St. Nicholas Greek Orthodox church on Pacific street, Brooklyn, and my profession calls for the wearing of a beard. When I go out on the street the boys and young men mistake me for a Jewish rabbi and insult and assault me.

---

1 For Kerbawy's letter and Gaynor's response, see, for example, the *New York Herald* (April 27, 1911), the *Washington Post* (April 28, 1911), the *Wilkes-Barre Times-Leader* (April 28, 1911), the *Columbus Enquirer-Sun* (April 29, 1911), and the *Boston Globe* (May 1, 1911). Gaynor's response is also published in *Some of Mayor Gaynor's Letters and Speeches* (New York: Greaves Publishing Company, 1913), 40–41.

Fr. Basil Kerbawy

They often throw decayed vegetables at me. If I were a rabbi, would that be an excuse for loafers to assault and insult me? I am a citizen and as such should be protected from assault.

I have borne the insults and assaults patiently up to last Saturday night, when an incident occured that made me lose all patience. I was alighting from a car at Seventy-third street and Thirteenth avenue, Brooklyn, when a little loafer hit me with a decayed vegetable, which I believe was a more than ripe tomato. This exhausted my patience. I went for the lad, who, luckily for him, escaped.

Hoping that you will do what you can for me and gain for me the protection I deserve, I am sir,

Very respectfully,

BASIL M. KERBAWY.

The mayor didn't take long to reply. On April 12, 1911, he wrote to Kerbawy:

Reverend and Dear Sir: Your letter informing me that as you walk about the city visiting the homes of your parishioners people apply opprobrious names to you, and throw empty cans and rubbish at you, and otherwise assault you, on account of your beard, is at hand. You ask me, "Is it a crime in the City of New York to wear a beard"? No, it is not. I wear one myself and nobody ever takes any notice of it. How is it they take notice of your beard? Have you trimmed it in some particular way, contrary to the Scriptures? For you know the Scriptures say, "Ye shall not round the corners of your heads, neither shalt thou mar the corners of thy beard."

Yes, if they assault you, and throw cans at you, you have a right to defend yourself to the last extremity; but if you find it necessary I will have a detective go around with you for a few days until we arrest some of those who are wronging you. Are you certain that it is your beard which is the cause of the trouble?

Kerbawy actually took the mayor up on his offer of a detective. From the *New York World*:[2]

> The clergyman will be a striking figure with his tall, shiny hat and ruddy face almost hidden by the luxuriance of his black beard. It is not of such a length, being very neat in its trimming, but it is so abundant that only mere patches of the priest's red cheeks show above it. Softly behind Father Kerbawy will tread a sleuth ready to promptly pounce upon the first person along the way who shies sticks, stones, objurgation, tomato, or even a spit-ball at the worthy priest.

Kerbawy's reply to the mayor? "It was very kind of the mayor to give such prompt attention to my case. I shall probably write to let him know that my whiskers are trimmed in full accordance with the Scriptures."

---

2   Reprinted in the *Washington Post* (April 28, 1911).

CHAPTER THIRTY-THREE

What Happened to Saint Sebastian's Miter?

I F YOU READ one of the many articles on the life of St. Sebastian Dabovich, you might run across a story about his miter (that is, his archimandrite's crown). Saint Sebastian had been elevated to archimandrite by St. Tikhon in 1905, and Tikhon gave Sebastian a miter on the occasion. According to St. Nicholai Velimirovich, who became friends with St. Sebastian years after this happened, the crown was worth one thousand rubles in gold. In an April 22, 1900, article, the *San Francisco Call* claimed that one of Tikhon's miters (which may or may not be the one he gave to Dabovich) was worth two thousand dollars—that is, over sixty thousand in today's money.

Saint Nicholai reported, "But Fr. Dabovich quickly sold that precious gift and gave it to the church towards paying its debts."[1]

That's one version of the story. Here's another, from Fr. George Gray's *Portraits of American Saints*: "[Father Sebastian] sold St. Tikhon's mitre (which he had been awarded when he was made an archimandrite) and used the money in an attempt to alleviate

---

1   Hieromonk Damascene, "Archimandrite Sebastian Dabovich: Serbian Orthodox Apostle to America," *The Orthodox Word*, 252–253 (2007).

St. Tikhon's sufferings at the hands of the communists."[2]

So St. Nicholai has St. Sebastian selling the miter right after he got it—presumably 1905 or '06. But the other story puts the sale sometime after the 1917 Bolshevik Revolution.

As it turns out, neither story seems accurate—and they're both off by about half a dozen years. What really happened is this: In 1912, Serbia was in the midst of the Balkan Wars. And although he was born in America, St. Sebastian was a patriotic Serb. In October, he decided to auction off many of his most valued personal possessions to raise money for the Serbian war effort. Here's an article about the auction, from the *Los Angeles Times* (10/25/1912):

St. Tikhon's miter, from the San Francisco Call, *1900*

> The Balkan war between the Serbs and Turks, has developed many cases of self-sacrifice among the Serbs in and around Los Angeles, but probably none greater than that of Father Sebastian Dabovitch, bishop of the Orthodox Eastern Catholic Church, who has for two years been working among the Slavs and Greeks of this city, to induce them to higher ideals in living. He has built a small chapel on Boyle Heights and has just begun to get his work on a better footing, when he feels called upon to sacrifice his personal belongings for the benefit of the hospital work in the Serb army.
>
> At the meeting of the Friday Morning Club this morning, in the Woman's Clubhouse, the following historic relics will be offered at auction to the highest bidder above the minimum price named:

---

2   George A. Gray and Jan V. Bear, eds., *Portraits of American Saints* (Diocesan Council and Department of Missions, Diocese of the West, Orthodox Church in America, 1994), 66–67.

A bishop's gorgeous miter, handmade and painted in Russia, by nuns, to be sold to the highest bidder above $100; a jeweled pectoral cross and chain, made by a Serb jeweler in Bosnia, minimum bid, $100; twelve sacred hand-paintings on panels of steel minimum $50 for the set; beautiful icon of the Savior, which belonged to a Russian nobleman, who had it with him in the campaign against Napoleon at Moscow, minimum, $50. Four decorations—Order of St. Sabbas, from the King of Servia; Order of Danilo, from the King of Montenegro; Order of St. Anne, from the Emperor of Russia; a medal from the Emperor of Russia, in memory of Alexander III; minimum bid for all, $25. A handsome medium-size hand-made rug, made by the Christian peasant girls of Macedonia; minimum bid, $50.

These were St. Sebastian's most prized possessions, and it must have pained him to auction them off. The whole lot was being offered for a minimum of $375, which works out to just shy of $12,000 in today's money. The minimum of $100 for the miter is roughly $3,000 today. Actually, that suggests that St. Sebastian's miter might not be the same one featured in the 1900 *San Francisco Call* article. The miter in the *Call* was valued at two thousand dollars in 1900; it's almost inconceivable that the minimum bid a dozen years later would be a measly hundred bucks. Most likely, then, St. Tikhon gave St. Sebastian a different miter.

Saint Sebastian wasn't alone in trying to raise money for the war effort. A few days before the auction, the Greeks and Serbs of Los Angeles had combined to raise an impressive ten thousand dollars—equivalent to over three hundred thousand today.

When I first wrote about St. Sebastian's miter on my website years ago, I poked around a bit to see if anyone knew what had become of it. My searches turned up nothing: the miter appears to have simply vanished. I can't imagine that something so obviously precious was ever destroyed, so presumably it's either in a museum somewhere, or it's sitting in someone's private collection.

CHAPTER THIRTY-FOUR

Orthodoxy and Theosophy

Vera Johnston

I N THE EARLY 1900s, a woman named Vera Johnston was involved with the Russian cathedral in New York and the seminary in Tenafly, New Jersey. With a name like Johnston, you might think she was a convert, which is what I thought when I first ran across her name. But Vera Johnston was actually a cradle-born Orthodox Christian. She was born in the Russian Empire, in what is now Ukraine, and her maiden name was Zhelihovsky. She was born in 1864, and her mother was also named Vera.

Before her marriage, the elder Vera, the mother, was named Vera Blavatsky. That last name, Blavatsky, might sound familiar to some of you. The elder Vera's sister—our Vera's aunt—was a lady by the name of Helen Blavatsky, also known as Madame Blavatsky, the founder of the theosophy movement.

Theosophy has been described by some as a modern version of Gnosticism. It has a lot of occult and pagan elements, drawing in particular on Hinduism. Helen Blavatsky herself spent time in India. Beliefs included reincarnation, ancient pagan deities, secret teachings. Essentially, we're talking about neo-paganism. They certainly had a kind of syncretistic place for Christianity, as one of the many pieces of the "truth" that could lead you into true

Vera Johnston

knowledge, but basically, this was a neo-pagan movement.

Helen Blavatsky had founded the theosophy movement in the 1870s. In 1886, her niece Vera—the future Vera Johnston—spent some time with her aunt and read drafts of her book *The Secret Doctrine*. Vera was in her early twenties at this point, and her mother was a follower of Aunt Helen, so it was only a matter of time before young Vera herself became a theosophist.

In 1889, Vera published an article called "Modern Magic" in the *Theosophist* journal, and by this time she had apparently joined the movement. The year before this, in 1888, she had married Charles Johnston, an English follower of Blavatsky. Johnston himself was one of the leaders in the theosophy movement and was especially noted for his translations of Hindu scriptures from Sanskrit into English. Vera and Charles spent some time in India themselves, and both wrote and translated numerous theosophical articles in the coming years. For example, in 1895, they coauthored an article called "The Priestess of Isis and Her Accusers." This was par for the course with Vera and Charles.

Helen Blavatsky died in 1891, and in 1896, Charles and Vera Johnston moved to New York City. Vera was still a very visible figure on the theosophical scene, speaking at conventions and translating articles.

Sometime after the turn of the century, the Johnstons became associated with the Russian Orthodox cathedral in New York. The details of this are very sketchy. What I'm giving you is incomplete research. I haven't been able to find many materials on Vera Johnston's life after 1900 or so, and of course this is the period in which we're most interested, because this is when she was associated with the Russian Mission.

So please understand, much of this is a mystery. But I'm going to give you what I have.

In 1912, the Russian Archdiocese moved its seminary to Tenafly, New Jersey. Both Vera and Charles Johnston were professors. I don't know what subject Vera taught, but Charles is listed in 1918 as Teacher of English Language. During this period, Vera ran the seminary's booth at a Russian bazaar in New York City. Both Johnstons were deeply involved in the work of the Russian Mission.

Also in 1915, Vera wrote an article in the *Constructive Quarterly* called "The Coming of Archbishop Evdokim," talking about the arrival of the new Russian bishop. One passage in particular seems to reveal something of Vera's own religous outlook:

> In the principle thus simply and eloquently enunciated by Archbishop Evdokim, what vistas there are of reconciliation, of genuine peace and good-will among men and nations: the differences between nations, in their religious as well as their secular life, are not stumbling-blocks but *revelations of the wisdom of God.* The mind of Christ is so wide, so deep, so rich, that no one race, nothing less than all humanity, suffices to embody and reveal it. [Emphasis in original.]

The same year, also in the *Constructive Quarterly*, she translated an article called "Byzantium the Preserver of Orthodoxy."

So it seemed, when I learned these things, that Vera Johnston had converted—or returned—to Orthodoxy. She was involved almost on a day-to-day basis with the life of the Russian Mission. The thing is, she doesn't seem to have given up theosophy. Her husband, Charles, who was also involved in the Russian Mission, remained a major figure in the theosophical movement.

In early twentieth-century New York, a splinter theosophist

group was formed, calling itself the Order of the Living Christ. While small, this group included some of the city's elite—Wall Street executives, professors, Episcopal priests, and so forth—as well as Charles and Vera Johnston, whose ties to Helen Blavatsky helped bring legitimacy to the Order. The Order was essentially an attempt to merge Christianity and theosophy. The group believed in reincarnation but adopted the externals of Anglo-Catholicism (traditional Anglicanism). They revered the works of Helen Blavatsky and her associates but also had a deep fascination with early Christian mysticism. Members saw it as perfectly acceptable to be a part of the order and still participate in the life of, for instance, the Episcopal Church. It is likely that Vera Johnston shared this philosophy, and she may well have considered herself an Orthodox Christian while simultaneously adhering to beliefs that Orthodoxy recognizes as patently heretical. All this, while teaching future priests at the official seminary of the Russian Archdiocese in America.

Vera Johnston died in 1923, just shy of sixty. Charles passed away eight years later. It is likely that documents survive—perhaps in the OCA archives—which can help us to better understand the Johnstons' role in the Russian Mission and the extent to which their theosophical ideas were known by the Russian clergy who employed them.

CHAPTER THIRTY-FIVE

Henry Ford and the Julian Calendar

O NE OF THE most obvious practical issues facing early Orthodox Christians in America was the difference between the church calendar—the Julian calendar—and the civil (Gregorian) calendar. In the nineteenth century, twelve days separated the two calendars; after the turn of the century, the difference was thirteen days. And since the new calendar wasn't adopted by any of the world's Orthodox Churches until the 1920s, the calendar discrepancy was something every American Orthodox Christian dealt with.

Newspaper reporters were amused by the difference, and every year there would be a spate of articles on the "Russian Christmas" or the "Greek New Year." For instance, here's something from the *Philadelphia Inquirer* (12/24/1905):

When the thousands of children of this city upon whom the favor of good old St. Nicholas will fall this year have lost the keen delight first occasioned by the sight of their toys there will be about three hundred little ones who will still be wondering what Christmas morn will bring forth. There will also be about one thousand adults who have not yet satisfied their inclination for gift-giving.

It will not be until the seventh day of January that Christmas Day will dawn for these people.

It is due to the fact that they are communicants of the Greek Orthodox Church that their Christmas is so belated in comparison with that of the Western churches, the difference in time—thirteen days—being caused by the Greek Church's adherence to the Julian calendar. All the Western churches use the Gregorian calendar, it having been adopted early in the eighteenth century.

Even before a portion of global Orthodoxy adopted the new calendar in the 1920s, some American Orthodox people thought a change should be made. On Pascha in 1906, Greek laborers in Gurley, Arkansas, got into a fight over "whether the modern or the Greek Church calendar should be observed in celebrating the Christian festival." The fight turned into a drunken riot, and it got so bad that the National Guard had to be called in. At least seven men died, and many more were injured (*New York Times*, 4/17/1906).

In 1914, Henry Ford fired between eight and nine hundred Orthodox employees for missing work to celebrate Christmas on the Julian calendar. This was about six percent of the entire Ford workforce. A Ford official issued a statement saying, "if these men are to make their home in America they should observe American holidays. It causes too much confusion in the plant . . . when nearly a thousand men fail to appear for work."[1]

The following year, the Greeks in Columbia, South Carolina, took matters into their own hands. From *The State* (1/8/1915):

> Yesterday was Christmas day, under the Julian calendar, which is that retained by the Greek Orthodox church, but the Greek colony in Columbia, comprising upwards of 100 persons, lacking a church, did not observe the day. Louis Malloy, proprietor of a

---

1   Sharmila Rudrappa, *Ethnic Routes to Becoming American* (Rutgers University Press, 2004), 151.

restaurant, said that he and his fellow countrymen in Columbia had adopted the Gregorian calendar and therefore their Christmas is December 24.

In light of the Ford Motor Company incident, it's easy to imagine why individual Orthodox Christians in America might observe Christmas on the Gregorian calendar even if all the Orthodox churches remained on the Julian. But I haven't seen any examples of Orthodox parishes adopting the Gregorian calendar prior to the wider switches to the new calendar that began in the 1920s.

CHAPTER THIRTY-SIX

Saint Raphael the Innovator

I N 1906 AND every decade thereafter until 1936, the US Census Bureau conducted a Census of Religious Bodies, collecting data from individual congregations across the country. These censuses are treasure troves of information about Orthodoxy in the early twentieth century. In 1906 and 1916, the Census Bureau asked questions about the language of worship. As you might expect, in 1906, virtually all Orthodox church services were conducted in non-English languages—mainly Greek, Slavonic, or Arabic.

In 1916, for most everyone, nothing had changed:

- » Both of the Albanian parishes used exclusively Albanian.
- » The four Bulgarian parishes used Bulgarian and Slavonic.
- » The 87 Greek parishes used exclusively Greek.
- » Both of the Romanian parishes used exclusively Romanian and Slavonic.
- » Of the 169 Russian parishes, 166 used exclusively Slavonic. Two used a combination of Slavonic and English, and one used exclusively English.
- » Eleven of the twelve Serbian parishes used exclusively Slavonic and/or Serbian. One Serbian parish used exclusively English.

In total, there were 276 parishes in the United States in 1916, not counting the Syrians. Of those, 272 (98.55%) worshipped entirely in foreign languages, and just two used English only. None of this should come as a surprise. The vast majority of American Orthodox Christians in 1916 were either immigrants or the children of immigrants. And the vast majority of American Orthodox clergy were also immigrants, most of whom had been educated and ordained in the Old World.

But what about St. Raphael's Syrians? Here's what the 1916 *Census of Religious Bodies* reported:

> Of the 25 organizations, 13, with 4,361 members, reported services conducted in English only; and 12, with 7,230 members, reported services conducted in foreign languages alone or with English. Of these, 4 organizations, with 1,230 members, reported the use of Arabic alone or with English; 5, with 2,900 members, Arabic, Greek, and English; and 3, with 3,100 members, Arabic, Greek, Russian, and English. In 1906 all the organizations then represented reported the Syro-Arabic language only.

This is stunning. Ten years earlier, the Syrians were like everybody else, worshipping exclusively in their native tongue. In 1916, everybody else was pretty much the same—98.55% foreign. But in just a decade, the Syrians had changed dramatically. By 1916, at least 21 of the 25 Syrian parishes (84%) used at least some English in their church services, and over half (13 of 25) served entirely in English.

Saint Raphael became a bishop in 1904 and died in 1915; thus, the period for which we have data, 1906–16, almost matches his years as a bishop. What was behind the rapid adoption of English in his parishes?

Firstly, and probably most importantly, in 1906, Isabel Hapgood's landmark English translation of the Orthodox service book was published. Another significant moment came in 1907, when Fr. Ingram Nathaniel Irvine, a recent (1905) convert priest, transferred from the Russian archbishop's jurisdiction to St. Raphael's. Irvine was generally in charge of "English work" and began publishing (with St. Raphael's blessing) English-language articles in St. Raphael's magazine, *Al-Kalimat*. These articles were primarily directed at Syrian children and their parents.

More generally—and at this point I'm just speculating—another factor may have been the weaker national identification with Orthodoxy among the Syrians. What I mean is this: to be a Russian, a Greek, or a Serb was to be Orthodox. National identity and religious affiliation were intimately intertwined, to the point that they were one and the same. But it was not so among the Syrians. They came, not from their own nation-state, but from the Ottoman Empire. And they also came from a region of great religious pluralism—back in Syria, they lived alongside Melkites, Maronites, Muslims, and Druze. In other words, while the Slavonic, Greek, and Serbian cultures (and languages) were closely identified with Orthodoxy, the same could not be said of Syro-Arab culture and language. And it's possible (though I can't prove it) that this distinction was a major factor in the spread of English among the Syrians, while the rest of American Orthodoxy was still firmly attached to foreign languages.

But the key to this open approach to English was undoubtedly St. Raphael himself, who was constantly adapting and adjusting to meet the needs of his people. We see it in other areas, too—for example, St. Raphael was an early adopter of electricity, having electric lights installed in his Brooklyn cathedral and encouraging his parishes to do the same. The same flexibility led him into his 1910 error with the Episcopalians, but it also motivated his 1911 correction.

Unfortunately, in the area of language, his encouragement of English didn't outlive his episcopate. By the 1930s, when Metropolitan Antony Bashir was the primary leader of the Antiochians in America, English had fallen out of use, to the point that in 1939, Bashir spoke of his own push for English as if it were a completely novel thing.[1]

∞∞∞

SAINT RAPHAEL'S PARISHES were distinctive in other ways, too. I did a brief study on priestly stability and found that, out of 135 parishes across all ethnic groups in 1911, only 29% had the same priest four years later. The Syrians under St. Raphael were the outliers: 71% of their parishes had the same priest in 1915 as they did in 1911, by far the highest percentage of any group.

Why did the Syrian Mission perform so well compared to the Russians, Greeks, and Serbs? The Greek and Serbian parishes were basically independent entities, with parish councils recruiting, hiring, and firing priests without any real involvement from bishops. The Russians had a bishop and a diocesan structure, but their priests were often moved around frequently, doing tours of duty in various American parishes before (often) returning to Russia. The Syrians had their own bishop, so the power of parish councils was much more limited than it was with the Greeks and Serbs; also, the whole idea of tours of duty wasn't really present among the Syrians. Saint Raphael made an effort to identify the right priest for a given parish, and it made no sense to him to move a priest unnecessarily. In some cases (one being Fr. Nicola Yanney, profiled later in this book), St. Raphael would ask the local parish community to nominate one of their own to be their priest.

∞∞∞

SAINT RAPHAEL SEEMS to have been particularly interested in the new technology of electric lighting. He had it put into his

---

1   Esther Coster, "Archbishop Is Americanizing Syrian Orthodox Church," *Brooklyn Daily Eagle*, Feb. 4, 1939, 5.

Brooklyn cathedral, and early in 1914, on a pastoral visit to consecrate a new church in Beaumont, Texas, he decided that the
fledgling parish needed electric lighting, so he personally raised
five hundred dollars ($15,000 today) to have it installed.[2] He was,
among other things, a brilliant fundraiser.

In a biography of St. Raphael composed shortly after his
repose, his archdeacon, the future bishop Emmanuel Abo-Hatab,
wrote this of him:

> All his works are famous and well-known and it was not long
> before the community flourished under his care and brought
> forth sweet fruits, so many were the churches he founded, the
> schools established, the associations he formed, and the good
> works he did. In the center of his diocese, that is in Brooklyn, his
> chief concern was to improve the cathedral that he had erected,
> adorning it with holy icons, precious vessels, and honorable vest-
> ments. Then he installed electrical lighting and renovated it as it
> is today. He strove to establish an orphanage for the community
> and for this purpose acquired the house adjacent to the church.
> He expended great effort to pay off its mortgage so that the house
> (known as the Community House) could become property of the
> church and be turned into an orphanage, even if it took a long
> time for this idea to be actualized. He made it possible to find the
> necessary funds to undertake his righteous charitable projects for
> the church and the community. He undertook the work spending
> what was necessary and the community did not feel burdened or
> taxed. This is on account of his good management and his well-
> known ways of dealing with money. In all parts of the diocese his
> voice was heard and influential among his children as a means of
> collecting donations for building churches, establishing schools,
> and undertaking charitable projects. When it was necessary,
> he did not hesitate to personally collect funds for the churches
> under his direction, leaving no other way to achieve charitable

---

2   Issa, 96.

work except his methods. In addition to all of this were his counsels and wise guidance that caused peace to prevail among rivals, brought agreement to those who differed and united those who were divided. In sum, he was a shepherd and a father whose flock knew his voice and whose children knew his kindness compassion and love. He is a father even more than a leader and a servant even more than a master. He did not set aside his concern for his diocese until the moment of his death. Remember that two days before his death he was reading the letters arriving to him and signing the responses to them with his own hand. Indeed, he was concerning himself with the diocese and giving us direction in how to manage it two hours before his death, when we said farewell to him, not knowing that it was the final farewell, since we could not believe that a man in such a state as his, tending to the major duties of his center, could die without giving any prior signs of death.[3]

---

3   Unpublished translation by Samuel Noble.

CHAPTER THIRTY-SEVEN

A Well-Traveled Saint

Father Jacob Korchinsky

FATHER JACOB KORCHINSKY had a globetrotting ministry that calls to mind the much better-known travels of St. John Maximovitch. Father Jacob's ministry ended in martyrdom.

He was born in 1861 to a wealthy family in Ukraine, then part of the Russian Empire. Initially he became a schoolteacher, but soon after his marriage at twenty-five, he was ordained a deacon. This wasn't just a stepping stone to the priesthood; Fr. Jacob remained a deacon for over eight years. During this time, he studied at the Odessa Theological Academy. After his graduation in 1895, he was one of the great crop of remarkable young clergymen recruited by Bishop Nicholas Ziorov to come to America. This group included, among others, St. Raphael Hawaweeny, St. Alexander Hotovitzky, and St. John Kochurov, along with the elderly Fr. Theoklitos Triantafilides.

All of those men were brought over to serve in the contiguous United States, but Fr. Jacob was ordained a priest and sent to Alaska, to be a missionary to the native people. Within two years, he received a commendation for "converting to Orthodoxy more than 250 savages." In 1900, he moved to Edmonton, Alberta, becoming the first resident Orthodox priest in Canada.

He built a church there and traveled widely in the region. That year, in a single day, he baptized thirty-three children in Shandro, Alberta. You get the sense, reading about Fr. Jacob's life, that this kind of thing was not really out of the ordinary for him. Several years later, in 1906, St. Tikhon wrote to the Holy Synod concerning Fr. Jacob, "He did much to convert the heathens to the Christian Faith and returned many Uniates to the Orthodox Church. He set the foundation for parish life in many places, built churches and assisted the unfortunate with his acquired medical knowledge."

Soon, though, Fr. Jacob—by now in his forties—had to return to his homeland, the Diocese of Kherson and Odessa, because his wife had become ill. He took over a parish on the Black Sea and later became the rector of the Kherson prison. After two years of prison ministry, he applied to return to America, and he was sent to the booming heartland of the Russian Mission: Pennsylvania, where thousands of Uniates were converting to Orthodoxy. He served in Erie, Carnegie, and Mount Carmel, Pennsylvania; Newark, New Jersey; and Youngstown, Ohio. In time, he became dean of all the clergy in Pennsylvania.

At some point, probably in 1913 or '14, Fr. Jacob was sent to minister in Mexico City. While there, he adopted an orphaned infant named Dominica.[1]

In 1915, the Russian Orthodox community in Hawaii (joined by the Episcopal bishop of Hawaii) sent a formal request to the Holy Synod of Russia, asking that a priest be sent to them. Father Jacob, now fifty-four and newly elevated to the rank of protopresbyter, was chosen for this job and sailed across the Pacific Ocean. He celebrated a landmark liturgy in Honolulu on Christmas Day, December 25, 1915/January 7, 1916.

While in Hawaii, Fr. Jacob happened to meet a group of

---

1   A letter from Dominica's granddaughter, in Russian, is published at http://www.rusvera.mrezha.ru/515/14.htm.

ethnically Russian Latvians who were sailing from Australia to Egypt, via Honolulu and the brand-new Panama Canal. These Latvians told him that there were Russian Orthodox people in Australia. Soon after this, Fr. Jacob read this in the *Vestnik*, the official publication of the Russian Mission in America:

> [I]n Australia, there live thousands of Russian people, who are spiritually ministered to by a Greek priest who visits once a year. His services are conducted unwillingly and without a sense of piety, even though he receives a large amount of money for his services. It has also been reported that a self-styled "priest" has arrived in Australia from North America who has exploited the unsuspecting Russians with excessive fees for baptisms and weddings, so much so, that they complained to the police and the "priest" was arrested.[2]

Father Jacob had heard enough. He wrote to the Russian Consul-General in Melbourne, who asked Fr. Jacob to come to Australia immediately. He arrived in March. In the months that followed, he visited seven hundred fifty families and five hundred isolated individuals, baptizing sixteen children along the way. But he contracted malaria due to the excessive heat, and in July, he returned to Russia. He wrote this to Archbishop Evdokim Meschersky:

> We have elected a committee to oversee church life, but my illness brought on by the excessive heat, has caused me to take to my bed and has deprived me of being of any further use. . . . I most respectfully plead that Your Grace does not forsake the Russian Orthodox in Australia and especially their next generation of youngsters. I beg that Your Grace may raise the question of the Church in Australia at the forthcoming All Russian General Council and if it be appropriate to appoint me as the permanent priest for Australia.

---

2   *Russian Orthodox American Messenger* (January 1916).

The Holy Synod ended up placing Australia under the jurisdiction of the bishop of Tokyo. Father Jacob, meanwhile, needed money. He had spent all his own funds on his missionary work. All the while, his wife and three-year-old daughter had remained in America, and Fr. Jacob wanted to go to them. He was given both permission and money, but then World War I intervened. Father Jacob was assigned to be a chaplain at the military hospital in Odessa, serving there from December 1916 to August 1917. In time, his wife and adopted daughter made it to Odessa as well. Father Michael Protopopov, whose excellent history of Russian Orthodoxy in Australia is an important source for information on Fr. Jacob, writes:

> Upon being demobilised from military service, Korchinsky was again faced with the problem of having nothing to live on. On 29 August 1917, he again wrote to the Holy Synod asking that he be assigned a pension, as he was so poor that he needed to live in a rural village where the folk fed him out of compassion. A second resolution was made by the Holy Synod for a pension to be granted to Korchinsky, but no documentary evidence is available to confirm a pension ever having been paid. Nor is it known if he returned to his family in Pennsylvania.

I think we can be pretty sure that Fr. Jacob did not receive a pension, considering that he made his request only a couple months before the October Revolution turned everything upside down. And he never returned to Pennsylvania, either. Like so many faithful Orthodox clergy, he suffered arrests and persecution by the Bolsheviks. To protect his adopted daughter, he gave her to a close friend, who raised her, although she continued to consider Fr. Jacob to be her father.

For years, the ultimate outcome of Fr. Jacob's life was unknown. Then, in 2006, Soviet files from Odessa were uncovered, revealing that Fr. Jacob had been arrested on July 23, 1941, and was executed by gunshot on July 19. He was eighty years old.

Bishop Job of Kashira, who served as administrator of the Moscow Patriarchate parishes in Canada from 2005 to 2018, said this of Fr. Jacob's end:

> From the materials handed over to me by Mother Superior Seraphim (Shevchik) of the Archangel-Mikhailovsky Monastery in Odessa, it is clear that Father Jacob was not in any schism, did not renounce the priesthood, did not betray any of the parishioners. During the interrogations of the investigation, the priest answered truthfully. Although, due to circumstances, he did not perform divine services, he kept a priestly pectoral cross, utensils and some liturgical books. And why did he need to hide something or be afraid of death at the hands of atheists? After all, he, an eighty-year-old elder, had already lived his life and approached its natural sunset.[3]

Father Jacob has yet to be formally added to the calendar of saints by the Ukrainian Orthodox Church, but this seems to be only a matter of time.

---

3   Bishop Job of Kashira, then administrator of Moscow Patriarchate parishes in Canada, discusses Fr. Jacob in a July 20, 2015, interview in Russian, available at http://www.orthedu.ru/news/obzor-smi/13292-udi-vitelnaya-zhizn-svyaschennika-iakova-korchinskogo.html.

CHAPTER THIRTY-EIGHT

The Tragic Life
of Father Vladimir Alexandrov

THE LIFE OF Fr. Vladimir Alexandrov reads like the plot of a Russian novel. Alexandrov was a priest in the Russian Mission in the late nineteenth and early twentieth centuries. He began his career in 1896 as the choir director of the multiethnic St. Spiridon Church in Seattle, Washington. The following year, he chanted at the first-ever Orthodox liturgy celebrated in Canada. After his ordination in 1898 (or '99), he remained in Seattle as the pastor of the church, and he made repeated trips into Canada, receiving Uniate converts into Orthodoxy.

In 1904, tragedy struck. From the *San Jose Evening News* (January 28, 1904):

> Rev. Vladimir V. Alexandrof, pastor of the Greco-Russian Orthodox church gave his five year old son Nicholas a teaspoonful of strychnine last evening. Three physicians were immediately summoned, but before they could do anything the child died in convulsions. Both Rev. and Mrs. Alexandrof are prostrated over the terrible mistake.
>
> Alexandrof thought he was administering penopeptine in accordance with the physician's instructions, but picked up the bottle containing strychnine instead. The medicines were in

bottles of [the] same size. The Alexandrofs had only two children, and it is a little girl which is left to them. Rev. Sebastian Dabovich of San Francisco has been telegraphed for and will arrive in time to conduct the funeral services next Saturday.

The Alexandrovs no doubt had strychnine in the house to kill rodents, but it was in the same generic type of bottle as the actual medicine and apparently kept in the same place. (Incidentally, I looked up penopeptine but found no results.)

Normally, if a priest takes a life—even by accident—he cannot continue serving at the altar. Saint Tikhon, who was the Russian bishop at the time of the tragedy, must have decided against a strict application of the canons in this case.

After losing his son, Alexandrov was transferred out of Seattle, serving in a succession of parishes: Allegheny, Pennsylvania; Ansonia, Connecticut; Chicago (as successor to St. John Kochurov); and San Francisco.

ooooo

IN 1915, WHILE serving as dean of the San Francisco cathedral, Alexandrov participated in the Fourteenth International Lord's Day Congress, held across the bay in Oakland. He gave a paper, "The Church and the Sabbath: Position of the Greek Church."[1] Speaking of the Sabbath in Russia, Alexandrov acknowledges the significant Jewish minority in the country and its desire for an official rest day on Saturday as well as Sunday. He doesn't think such a thing should or would happen, but he does say, "Besides, we are probably on the eve of possible Jewish political independence in historic Palestine, where, if God helps them again to establish their political entity, they will have their own Kings, or

---

1   The Rev. Vladimir V. Alexandrof, "The Church and the Sabbath: Position of the Greek Catholic Church," in *Sunday the World's Rest Day* (The New York Sabbath Company, 1916), 133–139.

Presidents, and of course, their own up-to-date laws and privi-leges, and in all these, I for one, wish them God-speed."

Alexandrov also notes that a small percentage of American Christians attend church on Sundays, relative to Christians in Europe. "On Sundays, the churches are quite often only half filled or wholly empty while the moving picture houses as well as some of the theatres of the poorer class, often with very bad shows, are overcrowded," he said. His solution? That churches offer Christian-themed movies on Sunday afternoons and eve-nings. According to Alexandrov, in Russia, "besides the usual services on Sundays, semi-religious meetings were offered to the people in buildings of various schools and public institutions, in which moving pictures from the Bible were produced illustrating the life of Christ, His Mother and the Saints, and at the same time short lectures were delivered, accompanied by choir and general singing; and the success was grand."

In Alexandrov's view, the same sort of thing should be adopted in America. But he doesn't stop there. "I believe," he writes, "that the so-called Kinematograph or moving picture industry should be under the control of the State for educational and religious uses in such a way that it shall not harm but help people mentally and spiritually." He then echoes the ideology of the future Soviet regime: "If we have a 'pure food law,' why may we not also have a 'pure thought law'?"

Finally, from the article, we get a little bit of additional biographical data: "During my twenty years' work in the United States and Canada," writes Alexandrov, "I have built about four-teen churches," and ministered to Orthodox of all nationalities.

ooooo

IN 1917, IN between the February and October Revolutions, Alexandrov visited Russia. Upon his return to San Francisco, he discovered that his wife had disappeared and nineteen thousand dollars were missing from his bank account. The culprit in both cases was Fr. Vasily Dvornikoff, Fr. Alexandrov's assistant priest. Dvornikoff and Mrs. Alexandrov were lovers and had run off to Buenos Aires, Argentina, with all the Alexandrovs' money. Father Alexandrov sent a public letter to the newspapers:[2]

October 7, 1917.

Mrs. Rose V. Alexandrof, wherever she may be.

Dearest Wife: October first I returned from Russia finding you missing. I know from your letters your desire to join me in Russia. No matter what may have happened to you, please know my absolute faith in your goodness, truthfulness and love for me and children and pay no attention whatsoever to the slandering false stories.

Nobody believed them, as your noble and exemplary record of wifehood and motherhood for twenty years with me, known by many, stands well in your favor, and if you fell victim of pre-arranged criminal plot of robbery of those whom you and I were helping in their needs and who having robbed you, still, are trying to defame you, please do not for a moment hesitate to communicate with proper authorities and me, as I care so much more for you when you are suffering.

Trust in God's mercy and help and in my everlasting devotion to you and that soon our hearts' wounds will heal and we will become still happier. My trip to Russia was especially successful. I received special honors for my services to my fatherland in connection with this God-blessed country and have full hope that we shall enjoy life with our dear children better than ever before. My address is 834 Cabrillo street, telephone Pacific 8381, San Francisco, Cal.

REV. ARCHPRIEST VLADIMIR ALEXANDROF.

---

2   *San Francisco Examiner* (October 8, 1917), 3–4.

Dvornikoff was indicted by a grand jury on the charge of grand larceny, and he was arrested upon his arrival in Buenos Aires. Mrs. Alexandrov was with him.[3]

So Fr. Alexandrov had lost both his son and his wife in some of the worst ways possible. I'm not sure exactly what happened to him in the years immediately after 1917, though I suspect he returned to Russia. In 1923, he was made a bishop of the Bolshevik-backed Living Church. He returned to America and to his old parish, St. Spiridon in Seattle. He was obviously a damaged man, and he became a thorn in the side of the Orthodox community.

In 1932, "Bishop" Alexandrov filed a lawsuit in King County Superior Court, trying to take control of the St. Spiridon Church property. Alexandrov won, but the St. Spiridon parishioners stripped the church of everything—icons, holy vessels, and so forth. Alexandrov was left with an empty church and essentially no congregation.[4] On June 28, 1932, Alexandrov visited James Wickersham, a US Congressman from Alaska. Wickersham wrote in his diary, "Archbishop Vladimir Alexandrof who claims to own the Russian Church property in Alaska called—I do not care for him—He is a troublesome Soviet agent if I am not mistaken."[5]

The Living Church itself wasn't to last much longer, and in July of 1933, Alexandrov was received into the Roman Catholic Church, which recognized him as a bishop. He lived in obscurity

---

3   Documents and articles related to this episode are available on the webite of Holy Trinity Orthodox Cathedral, San Francisco, https://www. holy-trinity.org/history/1917/.

4   "Historical Perspective: Orthodoxy in Seattle," *The Orthodox Vision: The Official Publication of the Diocese of the West of the Orthodox Church in America* (Winter 2004), 5–6.

5   Wickersham's diary entry may be found on the website of the Alaska State Library—Historical Collections, https://library.alaska.gov/hist/ hist_docs/wickersham/ASL-MS0107-diary041-1932.pdf.

and retirement until his death in Baltimore in 1945. The *Baltimore Sun* printed a three-sentence death notice, referring to Alexandrov as "Arch-bishop elect."

CHAPTER THIRTY-NINE

The Equal of Martyrdom

Father Nicola Yanney

FATHER NICOLA YANNEY'S early biography is interesting but not necessarily uncommon. He grew up near the Balamand Monastery. He got married in his late teens, and he left his village to come to America, to try to make a life for his family that was better than what was available in Syria. In this, he was like so many others, including my own family and many of yours. America was the land of opportunity, and seeking that opportunity meant leaving behind home and family and community.

Nicola and his wife Martha went first to Omaha, and Nicola worked as a peddler—again, like a lot of young Syrian immigrants at the time. They had kids, they moved to a little homestead not too far from Kearney, Nebraska, and they planted modest roots. I don't know what their expectations were or whether they had expectations. I do know that they were pious Orthodox Christians who had gone years without even seeing a priest, much less confessing or taking communion or having their kids baptized.

And then one day, something unexpected happened. The year was 1899. Nicola and Martha had been in Nebraska for almost six years. A few years earlier, a dynamic young Syrian priest named Fr. Raphael Hawaweeny had come to New York to minister to the scattered Syrian Orthodox immigrants in America. And now, in the late summer of 1899, St. Raphael made it all the way to the remote town of Kearney, Nebraska. Here is how St. Raphael himself described the visit in his missionary journal:

> On Tuesday, September 7th, I departed Omaha and went further west to the city of Kearney, where I arrived after midnight instead of arriving at 3:30 PM as planned. [. . .] When I arrived in Kearney almost all of our Syro-Arabs came to greet me at the station. From the train they took me to the house of their elder in an open carriage. It was so cold that I was shivering all the way and warmed up only at the fireplace in the house of my hosts, and paid for it with sniffles. We all stayed up until four in the morning, after which time everyone went home to get some rest. The next morning, I felt so bad that I wasn't able to serve the Divine Liturgy, but only a Typica service.

So, pausing there for just a moment—this account starts to tell you something about St. Raphael and how devoted he was to his people. His train was delayed eight hours; he arrived, exhausted, after midnight; it was cold and he felt sick—and then he stayed up until four in the morning visiting with his people. And then, after barely a nap, he woke up in the morning for a church service, even though he felt so bad he couldn't serve the Liturgy. Saint Raphael continues:

> In the evening, I felt better, and offered to the members of the local community to go on horses to the farm of one of the Orthodox Syro-Arabs who lives there with his family and brother, located about 18 miles to the northeast of Kearney. At 9 PM with 15 people with me on four horse-drawn carriages, we departed for our journey. The weather was beautiful, the road was even, and it was a full moon. My companions enjoyed it so much that the entire trip they were singing church and national songs.

So St. Raphael, who was sleep-deprived and fighting a bad cold, heard about this farmer—Nicola Yanney—and his family, who were living way out in the country. And he volunteered to travel to them in the middle of the night. This was his own idea. This is the good shepherd who leaves the ninety-nine sheep and seeks after the one who is lost. In this case, not lost spiritually—the Yanneys were spiritually quite strong—but isolated in the wilderness. He could have sent some of the Kearney Syrians to bring the Yanneys back to the city, but no—he went to them himself. That's the kind of pastor St. Raphael was.

We arrived at the house of our farmers at about one in the morning. From all the noises and firing from handguns of my companions, the farmers ran out from their house and learned that their priest has arrived, and they were so overjoyed that, with tears and thanksgiving, they embraced us and kissed the ground, my hands, and my feet, thanking the Lord God, who granted them to see an Orthodox priest after seven years without one. Truthfully, we all cried as well, seeing such joyous greetings from them. The wife of the farmer cried more than anyone from her joy. She was mourning so much that living in such a distant place, she was deprived of an ability to ever see an Orthodox priest who could confess and commune them, and most importantly, would baptize her four children, the oldest of which was six years old. Now her sorrow has turned to joy, and not believing her eyes, she continually crossed herself, raising her hands to heaven, thanking the Lord for this unexpected mercy.

The home was very small. We all stayed in one room. From exhaustion, some started falling asleep on their chairs, others on the floor, and I was offered a small couch. In the morning everyone, with piety, attended the Matins service. After that, I served the Blessing of Waters and blessed the house and their entire farm. Having spent the entire day there, we returned to Kearney in the evening. The next day, this farmer, with his whole family and the brother, came to Divine Liturgy and for the baptism of their children.

This was Nicola's first encounter with St. Raphael, and more than that, it was his first encounter with a proper Orthodox missionary. He'd known priests and monks in Syria, but Raphael was something different—he was a pastor with a flock that wasn't concentrated in a village but scattered across a continent. And Raphael's devotion and self-sacrifice to care for the most isolated of his people left a deep impression on Nicola that became apparent during his own years as a missionary priest.

Eventually St. Raphael left, and life continued for the Yanneys. They had four little kids, and Martha was expecting their fifth. Nicola was twenty-nine years old—five kids before the age of thirty. And then something went wrong. Martha wasn't well. She went into labor too early. There was no one to help, and even the best doctors at the time probably couldn't have done anything. Martha died in childbirth. Nicola was a widower at twenty-nine, with five children.

And then he watched helplessly as his newborn baby wasted away and died, too, just days later.

Infant death was much more common back then than it is now, and it was also a lot more common for women to die in childbirth. But that doesn't take away from the agony Nicola and his surviving children experienced.

But it's what happened next—what Nicola did after being widowed—that really begins to set him apart. Before him were at least two paths—one narrow and one broad. The broad path would have been remarriage, and one could hardly have faulted him if he had chosen that path. He had little kids who needed a mother. He was a young man, only twenty-nine years old. He easily could have justified mourning for a time and then finding a new wife among the many Syrian immigrants who were flooding into the United States, even making their way as far as Nebraska.

The narrow path was kind of an unheard-of path. It wasn't as if the priesthood was a viable career option—America didn't have seminaries at that point, and there wasn't even an Antiochian bishop here yet. Orthodoxy had barely begun to take root, and there was only a smattering of parishes in the whole country of any ethnic background. But a little over a year after Martha's death, the Orthodox Syrians in Kearney wanted a parish of their own, and they decided as a group that Nicola should be their priest. And he agreed to bear this cross. It meant that he would never remarry, and it also meant that he'd have to sacrifice time with his children for the sake of his priestly ministry. He could hardly have foreseen just how big that sacrifice would be.

While all this was going on, St. Tikhon, the Russian archbishop, had arranged for St. Raphael to become a bishop himself, giving the Syrians their own hierarch. In early 1904, Nicola traveled from Kearney to New York City to be present at Raphael's consecration, and then to be ordained a priest. This was his first big trip away from his children, who stayed with family. After his ordination, Fr. Nicola spent time with St. Raphael in Brooklyn and then returned home to Nebraska. But he wasn't just coming back to pastor the fledgling parish in Kearney— St. Raphael gave him responsibility for an enormous geographic area, covering a territory roughly equivalent to the modern-day Diocese of Wichita and Mid-America. Saint Raphael may have been the shepherd to the lost Antiochian sheep

Fr. Nicola Yanney

of North America, but as a practical matter, that was too much territory for one man to cover in an effective way. So Fr. Nicola would be his deputy, himself a shepherd to the lost Antiochian sheep of the American Plains.

Father Nicola's missionary travels are exhausting to read. If I actually tried to convey an accurate sense of these travels, your eyes would glaze over, and I would never finish this chapter. So it will have to suffice to say that he routinely spent six-plus months at a time away from home, leaving behind his four children in the care of his brothers. We're talking about trips across vast areas of land, mostly by train and sometimes by horse and buggy, nights spent in all manner of uncomfortable and makeshift beds, cold, heat, loneliness, discomforts of every sort. Again, this would go on for many months at a time.

Father Nicola didn't choose to travel so much because he wanted to be away from his family. It's important to understand this and to understand the difference between Fr. Nicola and St. Raphael. I've spent a lot of time studying the life of St. Raphael and praying to him. He's a great saint who sacrificed a lot, but he also was restless by nature. He didn't like to sit still. So his work in America suited him perfectly—he was always on the move, and when he wasn't on the road away from New York, he always had projects to occupy him there, such as building a cathedral and establishing a cemetery. And he was a monk, with no children and nothing to miss when he was traveling.

Father Nicola was very different: from all the evidence we have, he seemed to be more of a homebody, happy to spend months on end working diligently on his little farm (which he had to give up when he became a priest). He was a single parent, with four small children whose mother had died. His correspondence with his children reveals how deeply he loved them. He was not some kind of escapist who wanted to be away from home to avoid family life. He wanted to be with his children, farming the land, and he sacrificed that for the sake of his ministry, to bring the sacraments to Syrian immigrants who otherwise would starve spiritually.

Three years into his priesthood, in April 1907, Fr. Nicola set off on one of his long missionary trips. He expected to be away from his children for many months. But in June, he was in Colorado when he received word that his eleven-year-old daughter Anna was very sick, near death. He rushed home, but by the time he arrived in Kearney, she was unconscious. She died on June 7, and Fr. Nicola had to serve her funeral. He wasn't able to say goodbye, or hear her confession, or give her communion. It is hard to imagine what he must have felt. Surely, an event like this would have broken some men—his service to Christ meant that he wasn't there for his daughter as she lay dying. But Fr. Nicola did not curse God or abandon his post.

It would have been completely understandable if Fr. Nicola had cancelled his long missionary journey at this point. His daughter was dead, his sons needed him, and his parish in Kearney needed him, as they too mourned the loss of Anna. How could you blame him for staying home for a long while? But no— Fr. Nicola remained in Kearney for only two or three weeks, and then he was back on the road, back to seeking out those scattered Antiochians and serving liturgies and baptisms and weddings and funerals. Again, he was not an escapist, running away from his grief—he no doubt wanted to be home, but his duty to God came before all else.

In all this, Fr. Nicola's model was St. Raphael. Over the coming years, Fr. Nicola continued his dual ministry as priest of St. George parish in Kearney and as a traveling missionary throughout the Plains. Saint Raphael's Syrian diocese was growing, and with more priests, there was a hope that Fr. Nicola might have fewer travel obligations. Raphael himself made a return visit to Kearney in September of 1914, and he pushed for the parish to build a new church. Things were looking up.

But on the very day of St. Raphael's arrival in Kearney that September, storm clouds began to appear over the Syrian diocese: Metropolitan Germanos Shehadi, an Antiochian bishop from Syria, arrived in America. Germanos was ostensibly here for a fundraising trip, to raise money for an agricultural school in his diocese back in Syria. But he also conveniently came to the safety of the United States just as World War I erupted in the Old World. Saint Raphael was wary of Germanos's true motives, but he gave him a blessing to visit the Syrian parishes.

For a few months, everything seemed relatively stable. Saint Raphael was only fifty-four years old, but all his missionary work had put a great strain on his body. He started showing signs of weakness not long after he returned to New York from Kearney, and by the end of 1914, he was bedridden. The end came the following February—on February 27, 1915, Fr. Nicola received a telegram in Kearney, informing him that the great bishop was dead. He served a trisagion for Raphael's soul on Sunday, and on Tuesday he boarded a train for Brooklyn to attend the funeral.

The Syrian diocese pretty much collapsed right then, at the funeral. Syrian priests streamed into Brooklyn in the days following St. Raphael's death, and as they gathered together, they found themselves in disagreement. Some said that Raphael was under the Russian Church, and so the Russian hierarchy would consecrate a new Syrian bishop. Others disagreed, pointing out that St. Raphael himself had said that his diocese was "a diocese of Antioch, notwithstanding its nominal allegiance to the Russian Holy Synod." So which would it be—Russia or Antioch? The Russy-Antacky schism had begun.

Part of the problem was that St. Raphael had no obvious successor. The main pro-Russian candidate was the highly ambitious, highly political Archimandrite Aftimios Ofiesh. His rival/ally was the very young—early-to-mid-twenties—Archdeacon

Emmanuel Abo-Hatab, who had been St. Raphael's assistant in his final years. Neither of these men was a worthy successor to the great Raphael.

On the other side was that troublesome but charismatic Antiochian metropolitan, Germanos Shehadi. Germanos had taken a shine to America, and America had taken a shine to him. Many Syrians thought that of course Germanos should be Raphael's successor. But there were two problems: one, the Russians weren't on board with this, and two, the Patriarchate of Antioch didn't actually want Germanos to stay in America. Over the years, they would keep ordering him to return to Syria.

It's interesting—nobody has ever suggested it, but it seems to me that the best candidate to succeed St. Raphael may actually have been Fr. Nicola himself. He never would have been nominated—he was far too apolitical, too humble, too unambitious. He wasn't part of the circle of influencers in the Syrian diocese—people like Ofiesh and Abo-Hatab and the married archpriest Basil Kerbawy of the Brooklyn cathedral. But he was canonically eligible, morally upright, and completely self-sacrificing as a pastor. Who knows what would have happened had the Syrians at the time been more open-minded and considered him? He would have been much more worthy than any of the men who were actually in the running, and much more in the mold of St. Raphael himself.

But that's all speculative—no one considered Fr. Nicola as a candidate. Everyone was forced to pick a side—did you want Aftimios or Germanos? Which was also framed as, should we be under Russia or under Antioch? In hindsight, there was no right answer. Saint Raphael had been highly ambiguous when he talked about Russia and Antioch, and he'd left behind no protégé, no successor. To be blunt, both Aftimios and Germanos were unworthy—anaxios. World War I was raging. The Russian Church waited two years before consecrating Aftimios, and by then Russia itself was in the throes of revolution. In the meantime, Germanos kept picking off parishes and refusing to go back home to Syria.

In the end, Fr. Nicola chose Germanos, which to him would have been less about Germanos personally (he didn't know him that well) and more about choosing Antioch (and not choosing the unacceptable Aftimios). I can't fault Fr. Nicola for that choice. He was totally removed from church politics, trying to make the best decision in an impossible situation, with two very poor options. He suffered for that choice—Emmanuel Abo-Hatab, on behalf of Aftimios and the Russy faction, went around suing all the priests that sided with Germanos, trying to seize their parish property. He filed a lawsuit against Fr. Nicola and won. In 1918, Emmanuel's lawyers were in the process of trying to seize Fr. Nicola's house when the Spanish flu pandemic hit.

In 1918, as troops returned home from the First World War, they brought with them a deadly strain of the flu. It's estimated that the Spanish flu killed up to one hundred million people globally. In America, about 28 percent of the population caught it, and over half a million people died. There was widespread panic, and at various times, governments would order quarantines. The flu spread in three waves. The first and least deadly wave came in the spring of 1918. The second began in late summer, peaking in October, when it killed 195,000 Americans in one month.

As all this was happening, Fr. Nicola was busy. He was dealing with the Russy-Antacky lawsuit and the prospect of losing his house. His son and daughter-in-law were expecting their first baby—his first grandchild. And in September, his new bishop, Metropolitan Germanos, visited Kearney. After Germanos left, Fr. Nicola went on his usual missionary journeys. He probably first heard about this new wave of the flu during his travels, in early October. He visited Wichita, where a citywide quarantine was already in place, so he couldn't serve the Divine Liturgy in the new church of St. George—the first Orthodox church in Wichita. While he was in Wichita, he anointed the sick, and he served a funeral for a sixteen-year-old Syrian girl who died while he was in town. There's a decent chance that Fr. Nicola caught the flu there, in Wichita.

Then he went back up to Nebraska, visiting scattered groups of Syrians and finally returning to Kearney, just in time for the flu outbreak to hit the town. The local and state governments imposed a quarantine. Some of Fr. Nicola's parishioners were sick, and despite the quarantine, Fr. Nicola took the reserved sacrament and began going house to house, anointing them and giving them communion. A young man in the parish died, and then a toddler. Father Nicola served the funerals. More and more people came down with the flu. Father Nicola's own health continued to deteriorate—he was weak, his breathing worsened. He had to have known that he was dying.

But he did not rest. I wonder if it even occurred to him to rest—would it have even been a temptation to a priest who had already so crucified his own will, his own self-interest, for the sake of Christ and his flock? A lesser man—a normal man, really—could have rationalized the need for rest. After all, he had great responsibilities—his parishioners needed him, and so did all the other Syrians throughout mid-America. His grandchild would be born any day. His family needed him. But Fr. Nicola did not stop visiting his people, anointing them, giving them communion, helping them either to heal or to prepare for death.

This, in fact, was his own preparation for death. He ministered to his people until he physically could not continue and collapsed. This calls to mind the Lord Himself, whom Fr. Nicola imitated and served—having loved His own, He loved them to the end (John 13:1). Father Nicola's last words to his sons were, "Keep your hands and your heart clean." He died at midnight, as October 28 turned to October 29.

The local Kearney newspaper reported, "During the past week Rev. Yanney worked faithfully among his parishioners here, many of them being stricken with the influenza. Considerable exposure to the disease was inevitable and although he had complained of not being [in] the best of health he continued his work uninterrupted until the last." The Brooklyn Arabic newspaper *Al-Nasr* wrote of Fr. Nicola's death, "It was the worst hour when we received the telegram from the children of Father Nicola. They told us that we had lost him because he was always the first to serve the people and the congregation."

Father Nicola lived in the United States in the twentieth century. He was not given the opportunity to die a martyr's death. But we cannot doubt that he would have embraced martyrdom. And the manner of his death echoes the martyric end of another great Antiochian saint, Joseph of Damascus, dean of the patriarchal cathedral where St. Raphael's parents were parishioners. In 1860, Druze madmen rioted and massacred Orthodox Christians in Damascus. Amidst this chaos and bloodshed, St. Joseph took the reserved sacrament and jumped from rooftop to rooftop, going into the homes of his parishioners to prepare them for martyrdom. When he was finally cornered by the Druze, St. Joseph consumed the rest of the sacrament, moments before he was brutally murdered.

Father Nicola was not killed by an anti-Christian mob, but his faithfulness, his courage, his patient endurance of suffering, his selflessness, and his devotion to his people to the very end demonstrate without question that he would have embraced martyrdom had he been presented with the opportunity.

What, then, is the legacy of Fr. Nicola? He was a pioneering priest, a founder of parishes, a moderately notable historical figure for Antiochian Orthodoxy in America. But to me, his legacy is much more than that: he is an icon of what a priest should be and a model for all of us—clergy and laity, married and celibate, all Orthodox of whatever jurisdiction—for all of us, he is a model of what true faith looks like in practice.[1]

---

1   For a fuller treatment of Fr. Nicola's life, see *Apostle to the Plains: The Life of Father Nicola Yanney*, by the Saint Raphael Clergy Brotherhood (AFP, 2019).

CHAPTER FORTY

Saint Raphael's Greek Priest

Father Joseph Xanthopoulos

E VERYONE THOUGHT FR. Joseph Xanthopoulos was half
Syrian. But he wasn't. Born sometime between 1880 and 1886
in Tripoli, in what is now Lebanon, Fr. Joseph spoke perfect Arabic, but his parents were Greeks (hence the Greek last name). His
father was an import-export trader whose job took him all over
the Mediterranean. The family owned large estates in the Mount
Lebanon region, where Fr. Joseph grew up, and in time he went
to school at the Balamand Monastery, then to a French academy
for five years, and finally to Holy Cross Seminary in Jerusalem.
In Palestine, he met and married his wife Helen, also a Greek
from an expat family living in Palestine. He spent time studying
in Athens, too, where he took up Latin. Finally he returned to
Tripoli and followed in his father's footsteps, becoming a merchant. His wife bore him two children.

At one point, during his business travels, Joseph heard that
a Greek Orthodox man was being held in a Turkish prison,
where he'd become very sick and needed someone to care for him
overnight. Joseph volunteered to do this, helping the man survive. Another time, Joseph's two brothers, George and Sophocles, found themselves on the run from the Turkish authorities.

According to family lore, Joseph tracked them down and led them in a march across the desert, saving their lives.

In September 1911, the Italian army invaded Libya, which was then part of the Ottoman Empire. The resulting Italo-Turkish War intensified the already strained relationship between the Christian minorities of Turkey and their Muslim overlords. Over in Lebanon, Joseph was "persecuted on the street by his Moham-medan neighbors, left his store standing, and fled to Jerusalem."[1] Joseph, Helen, and their children moved into her father's house in Jerusalem for a couple months. Then, Joseph—a polyglot who reportedly could speak eight languages—left his family in Jeru-salem and went to the war zone in Libya, where he spent three months working as a translator for the Italian army. Then it was back to Jerusalem to retrieve his family, and finally off to New York, where he arrived at the end of May, 1912.

When the family reached Ellis Island, there was a problem: a relative was supposed to meet them at the immigration station to sponsor their entry into the United States, but he didn't show up. The immigration officials began to give them trouble. As Joseph was going back and forth with the officials, a Greek-American man who was sponsoring some other immigrants overheard the conversation and recognized Joseph: improbably, it was the same man whom Joseph had nursed back to health in a Turkish prison years before. The man returned the favor, sponsoring the Xan-thopoulos family into the country.

Immediately, the Syrian bishop of Brooklyn, St. Raphael, caught wind of the fact that a seminary-educated, Arabic-speaking layman had just arrived in America. Saint Raphael was always on the lookout for gifted priestly candidates, and soon he ordained Fr. Joseph and put the word out to his parishes that he had a new priest available. The community in Wilkes-Barre, Pennsylvania, responded, asking for a trial period to see if he

---

1 *Wilkes-Barre Record* (August 8, 1912), 11.

would suit them. Saint Raphael agreed, and Fr. Joseph arrived in the summer of 1912. By the end of August, it was clear that this arrangement was a good one, and Fr. Joseph was made the full-time pastor of the church.

From the beginning, his ministry was unique. There were a lot of Greeks in Wilkes-Barre, and Fr. Joseph considered them to be part of his flock, too. Before this, the Wilkes-Barre Greeks had relied on visiting priests, most notably Fr. Demetrios Petrides of Philadelphia (profiled in chapter 29). Now they could have regular services in Greek led by Fr. Joseph. In time, a separate Greek parish was established in Wilkes-Barre—with Fr. Joseph as pastor of both churches, the Syrian and the Greek. In 1915, the Xanthopoulos family moved into the Greek church building, which was a two-story house, with the church on the main floor and the priest's residence upstairs. Later, Fr. Joseph was involved in pastoring both the Greek and Syrian churches in neighboring Scranton, Pennsylvania. In this confusing period of American Orthodox history, jurisdictional affiliation was secondary to local needs, and Fr. Joseph was unusually well equipped to care for both the Syrians and the Greeks in his area.

An incident occurred in 1916 that tells us something about Fr. Joseph's courage. He'd betrothed a young woman, Bella Alexandria, to a local Greek barber. But when Bella's cousin Constantine, in New York City, heard the news, he was enraged: apparently he'd already decided that Bella should marry some friend of his, and he rushed to Wilkes-Barre to try to get her to break the engagement and return with him to New York. She refused, and then Fr. Joseph got a call from the barber fiancé, who was afraid that Bella wasn't safe at home. Father Joseph told her to come to the Xanthopoulos house, which she did.

At eight-thirty the next morning, Constantine, the New York cousin, showed up at the house, declaring that if Bella wouldn't give in, he would kill her, her fiancé, and himself. Father Joseph tried to reason with the man, to no avail: Constantine ripped open his shirt, beat his chest, and boasted that he'd already been shot several times and cared nothing for his own life or anyone else's. Then he stormed off, but he was back that afternoon.

At this point Fr. Joseph was teaching some of the children at the parish school. One of the boys alerted the priest that Constantine was approaching the Xanthopoulos house. Father Joseph rushed over to meet him. Constantine began to make a scene, cursing Bella and her family. Father Joseph ordered him out of the house; Constantine responded by brandishing a knife and slashing himself across the chest. Somehow remaining calm, Fr. Joseph grabbed him, pushed him outside, locked the door, and called the police. Bella and Fr. Joseph's wife, Helen, had both fainted. The police arrived, and the whole episode ended without further incident.[2]

ooooo

THROUGHOUT HIS MINISTRY, Fr. Joseph paid special attention to engaging young people in the life of the church. The Wilkes-Barre Antiochian parish website tells us that Fr. Joseph's "strong voice rang out in Byzantine chant. Many young people learned to chant with him, and he started a Syrian school for them." By 1927—with the Syrian/Antiochian jurisdictional situation in chaos—Fr. Joseph found himself in the Greek Archdiocese, where he became pastor of Holy Trinity Greek Orthodox Church in Bridgeport, Connecticut. As soon as he arrived, he established the E Mirofori Society, an organization for single girls who wanted to serve the church. (E Mirofori is a reference to the myrrhbearing women.) The girls formed the first parish choir, which is particularly notable because in this era, parish choirs with both male and female members were a pretty new

2   *Wilkes-Barre Times-Leader* (June 27, 1916), 20.

phenomenon. Until this time, church music was provided mainly by male chanters. The society was still in existence twenty years later, when they had an anniversary celebration and invited Fr. Joseph back as a guest of honor. Eventually, the E Mirofori Society became the local branch of the Greek Archdiocese's Young Adult League (YAL), which still exists today.

After a decade in Bridgeport, Fr. Joseph was transferred to Holy Transfiguration in Lowell, Massachusetts. Lowell had one of the largest concentrations of Greek people in America and actually had three Greek parishes (one of which was under the schismatic hierarch Christopher Contogeorge and the other two under the Greek Archdiocese). Father Joseph did his usual thing, working with the youth, running a parish school, establishing an Orthodox cemetery, and so forth. He also sponsored a youth football team, the Blackhawks. According to the *Lowell Sun* (Sept. 11, 1937), Fr. Joseph "will provide medical care for the players and will supply equipment." I don't know if that means that Fr. Joseph himself had medical training or just that he was going to pay for medical care (probably the latter). The next year, he formed Boy Scout and Girl Scout troops for the parish children. Atypically, Fr. Joseph did not establish a young women's organization in Lowell—but that was only because one already existed when he arrived. He was enthusiastic about the group, the Muses of Helicon, and seems to have been a big supporter of organizations for Orthodox girls wherever he went.

Once, Fr. Joseph was asked to perform an exorcism: the daughter of a Greek Orthodox grocer was possessed by demons. Father Joseph went to the house and performed the exorcism, and the girl was immediately healed. Many decades later, when Fr. Joseph died, the family sent a large wreath to the funeral with a sign saying, "Thank you Fr. Joseph for 'The Miracle.'"

While Fr. Joseph was now part of the Greek Archdiocese, he didn't forget his Antiochian roots. In 1939, Antiochian

Metropolitan Antony Bashir visited Lowell, and Fr. Joseph was on hand for the events.

His time in Lowell was busy, but it was also brief — just two and a half years. In September 1939, Fr. Joseph—by now well into his fifties—was transferred to St. George in Springfield, Massachusetts. It was his final parish assignment, although he had an extraordinarily long retirement. But let's not get ahead of ourselves.

According to the history on the St. George parish website, "By the 1920s, the Greeks of Springfield were joined by a sizeable, Arabic-speaking, Lebanese Orthodox population. Together they grew and shared the church that, by then, grew to several hundred families." The Springfield Orthodox community went through various divisions and reunifications in the 1920s and early 1930s, but by the time Fr. Joseph arrived in 1939, everyone was worshipping together at St. George Church. Father Joseph was the ideal priest for this situation. From the parish website: "Fr. X., as he was affectionately known, was half Greek and half Lebanese and spoke Greek, Arabic and English fluently. For close to twenty years, he held the community together and dramatically increased the participation of the laity in various programs and ministries."

He was not actually half Greek and half Lebanese—but the fact that he was routinely mistaken as such tells us something about his pastoral versatility.

In 1940, Fr. Joseph orchestrated the purchase of a beautiful old Congregationalist church building, designed by the famed architect Richard Upjohn and big enough to accommodate the growing Orthodox parish. The church was built for Congregationalists, so the choir and organ were located where Fr. Joseph wanted to put the Orthodox sanctuary. The parish removed the choir section, moved the pipe organ, and added iconography to the walls and ceiling.

One of Fr. Joseph's parishioners in Springfield was Andrew Georgaroudakis, who was born in 1933 (and thus was about six years old when Fr. Joseph arrived). Father Joseph had a profound influence on Georgaroudakis, who went on to become a priest. In a December 3, 1960, article in the *Mason City Globe-Gazette*, the newly ordained Fr. Andrew talked frankly about his relationship with Fr. Joseph:

> [T]he real model for his life is an elderly priest, now retired, who recognized and channeled his boyhood desire for the priesthood. That priest, Father Joseph Xanthopoulos, was the Springfield pastor, and from the age of 8 until entering seminary Father Andrew was with him at every opportunity, learning whatever he could.
>
> "I was constantly living in his image—in his shadow," Father Andrew said. "He is the most inspiring person I have ever met."

ooooo

FATHER JOSEPH RETIRED in about 1960, or perhaps a year or two earlier. One of his daughters moved to Chicago after getting married, and Fr. Joseph moved along with her. His final years were spent in Chicago, first at Assumption Greek Orthodox Church in Chicago proper, and later at St. John the Baptist in Des Plaines, Illinois.

During his long retirement, Fr. Joseph apparently spent many hours in prayer, praying every day for every person he had ever known. His grandson and namesake, Joe Xanthopoulos, recalls, "At night every night he would go to bed around 8 PM but he would go to sleep hours later. I would peek into his room and he was on his knees praying. I asked him once how come his prayers take so long. He said, 'I have lived many years and know many people. I pray for each of them as well [as] considering issues of

the world, asking God for direction and giving thanks to him."'[3]
Father Joseph died on July 22, 1981, in a nursing home in Des Plaines, a suburb of Chicago. He was somewhere around 94 to 98 years old—the last surviving priest ordained by St. Raphael and one of the most remarkable figures in American Orthodox history.

---

3   Joe Xanthopoulos, "Recollections of My Grandfather: Fr. Joseph Xanthopoulos," Orthodox History (October 28, 2014), https://orthodoxhistory.org/2014/10/28/recollections-of-my-grandfather-fr-joseph-xanthopoulos/.

Epilogue

THE RUSSIAN REVOLUTIONS of 1917 threw the Russian Orthodox Church into an existential crisis that deeply affected its archdiocese in North America. Subsidies from the Russian government vanished overnight, creating a financial catastrophe. The ruling archbishop, Evdokim Meshchersky, was in Moscow for the All-Russian Council when the Bolshevik Revolution erupted in the fall, and he never returned to North America. In his stead, the bishop of Alaska, Alexander Nemolovsky, took the reins of the archdiocese, but he was completely unable to manage the crisis. In time, one of the former archbishops of North America, Platon, came to the United States as a refugee, and in 1922 Alexander handed the archdiocese over to him. Metropolitan Platon led the transformation of the archdiocese into an independent North American metropolia, which, many decades later, would become the Orthodox Church in America (OCA). Platon's tenure in the 1920s and '30s was one of near-constant turmoil, rocked by lawsuits and battles over church property with representatives of the Soviet-backed Living Church and, later, the semi-functional Moscow Patriarchate.

As the Russian Archdiocese was struggling to come to grips with its unpleasant new reality, the Church of Greece elected a new metropolitan of Athens, Meletios Metaxakis, perhaps the most influential and (in many quarters) infamous man in modern

Orthodox history. Shortly after his election in 1918, Meletios traveled to America and began organizing the tangle of Greek parishes into an archdiocese. He appointed his ally, Bishop Alexander Demoglou, as the first hierarch of this new Greek Archdiocese. But Meletios was closely linked with the sometime Greek prime minister Eleftherios Venizelos, and the Greeks—both in Greece and America—were divided into factions, some favoring Venizelos and others supporting King Constantine (these being dubbed the Royalists). Meletios's fortunes rose and fell with those of Venizelos, and by 1921, Venizelos was out of power and Meletios found himself ousted from Athens. He returned to America, where he oversaw the formal incorporation of the Greek Archdiocese.

Metropolitan Platon

Late that year, he was—somewhat surprisingly—elected ecumenical patriarch, at which point he rescinded the 1908 tomos that had transferred the Greek diaspora to the Church of Greece, and he and his patriarchate laid claim to jurisdiction over all the so-called "barbarian lands" around the world, including the United States. Despite the presence of the new Greek Archdiocese, other Greek churches tried to claim jurisdiction in America, too—a situation that wasn't fully resolved for several decades.

By the mid-1920s, there were multiple competing jurisdictions for the Greeks, Russians, and Antiochians. The churches of Serbia, Romania, and Bulgaria sent their own bishops in the twenties and thirties. The tangle of jurisdictions that we know today attained a recognizable form in this interwar era.

This coincided with the end of the Ellis Island era of immigration. The Immigration Act of 1924 capped the number of immigration visas issued per year at two percent of the total number of people of each nationality in the United States, based on the 1890 census. Orthodox Christians in America were now here to stay, and no new blood was coming over. Immigrant communities redoubled their efforts to Americanize, embracing American culture. Men joined fraternal organizations (including the Freemasons). Parishes began to add Protestant and Roman Catholic elements such as pews, organ music, and mixed choirs. Priests increasingly cut their hair and beards and traded cassocks for the clerical suits common among heterodox clergy. For better or worse, American Orthodoxy entered a new phase in the years following World War I, a phase that shaped the direction of the Church in the United States in the century that followed.

By the time World War II came, Orthodoxy in America had put down roots. The three major seminaries—Holy Cross, St. Vladimir's, and St. Tikhon's—were all established in the late 1930s. In the forties, several jurisdictions made an initial attempt at pan-Orthodox collaboration, forming a short-lived, voluntary pan-Orthodox federation. In 1960, a new push for cooperation resulted in the founding of SCOBA—the Standing Conference of the Canonical Orthodox Bishops in the Americas. Now decades removed from large-scale immigration, some—especially younger people—pushed for more use of the English language in church services and even hoped that SCOBA might evolve into a proper synod of bishops for a unified American Orthodox Church. In 1963, a coalition of youth leaders from seven jurisdictions organized the largest pan-Orthodox event in American history—a gathering of some twelve thousand Orthodox youth in Pittsburgh, Pennsylvania, with a vespers service in a jampacked arena, with a hundred fifty priests and a thousand-person youth choir.[1]

---

1   For more, see my article "The Biggest Pan-Orthodox Event in American History," Orthodox History (August 5, 2019), https://orthodoxhistory. org/2019/08/05/the-biggest-pan-orthodox-event-in-american-history/.

But a fully unified American Orthodox Church was not to be. In the 1960s, the dynamics in the Greek Orthodox Archdiocese changed dramatically with the arrival of a new wave of immigrants fleeing unrest in the Old World. Meanwhile, the Russian Metropolia spent the better part of the decade negotiating peace with its estranged mother, the Moscow Patriarchate, which issued a tomos of autocephaly in 1970, transforming the Metropolia into the Orthodox Church in America (the OCA). The creation of the OCA was an earthquake in pan-Orthodox relations. Some saw it as a great opportunity: now the various jurisdictions could simply join up with an autocephalous American Church, ending jurisdictional overlap. But for others, the creation of the OCA out of just one of the many jurisdictions represented a major setback, a unilateral action where collaborative decision-making was needed. In the end, the OCA has not fulfilled the hopes of its founders and remains just one star in the constellation of Orthodox canonical structures in America.

While a single Orthodox Church structure in America didn't happen, Orthodox unity in America became more visible. Various schisms within ethnic groups were healed—the two rival Antiochian archdioceses united; so too, in time, did the rival Serbian jurisdictions. In 2007, the Russian Orthodox Church Outside of Russia (ROCOR) reestablished communion with the Patriarchate of Moscow. Among the jurisdictions, pan-Orthodox collaboration increased. International Orthodox Christian Charities (IOCC) was formed in 1992 as an agency of SCOBA. The Orthodox Christian Mission Center (OCMC), originally a department of the Greek Archdiocese, was transferred to SCOBA; later, the same occurred with Orthodox Christian Prison Ministry, which had been founded under the Antiochian Archdiocese. In 2010, in preparation for the hoped-for Holy and Great Council of the Orthodox Church and at the behest of the overseas patriarchates and other autocephalous church structures, SCOBA was transformed into the Assembly of Canonical Orthodox Bishops. Whereas SCOBA had been composed of jurisdictional primates, the Assembly would include all active canonical bishops. At the local level, parish associations and clergy brotherhoods have emerged, fostering cross-jurisdictional cooperation.

The latter decades of the twentieth century witnessed an increasing flow of converts into the Orthodox Church that continues to this day. Some of this was spurred on by the 1976 decision of the Episcopal Church to begin ordaining women to the priesthood, which caused many disillusioned clergy and faithful to look elsewhere—in some cases, to the Orthodox Church. Separately, a big infusion of converts occurred in 1987, when a large portion of the formerly Protestant group of parishes known as the Evangelical Orthodox Church joined the Antiochian Archdiocese en masse. This would have a transformative effect on the archdiocese, and today, a strong majority of Antiochian clergy are converts. Across all jurisdictions, converts to Orthodoxy now make up around thirty to forty percent of the total Orthodox population, with a growing number of "cradle" Orthodox whose parents or grandparents converted to Orthodoxy but who have no ethnic ties to the Church.

Conversions to Orthodoxy have become more common in part because Orthodoxy is more visible to Americans than it was before. Whereas in the early years, hardly any Orthodox books were available in English, today, dozens and dozens of Orthodox books are published every year, with websites, podcasts, and videos making it increasingly easy for inquirers to learn facts about the Orthodox Church. The publisher of this book, Ancient Faith Ministries, is a prime example of this phenomenon.

∞∞∞

BACK IN 1975, Fr. Alexander Schmemann looked back on the early days of Orthodoxy in America with lament—he saw the turn of the twentieth century as a kind of lost golden age and our jurisdictional jungle as the result of a tragic fall:

> [U]nity did exist, was a reality, [. . .] the first "epiphany" of Orthodoxy here was not as a jungle of ethnic ecclesiastical colonies, serving primarily if not exclusively the interests of their various "nationalisms" and "mother-churches," but precisely as a local Church meant to transcend all 'natural' divisions and to share all spiritual values; [. . .] this unity was broken and then arbitrarily replaced with the unheard-of principle of "jurisdictional multiplicity" which denies and transgresses every single norm of Orthodox Tradition; [. . .] the situation which exists today is thus truly a sin and a tragedy.[2]

As we've seen throughout this book, the truth is much more complicated—the founding era of Orthodoxy in the United States, like every era of church history dating back to ancient Israel, was a mix of good and bad, of sinners and saints. Today is and, I daresay, the future will be much the same.

---

2 Fr. Alexander Schmemann, "To Love Is to Remember," in Constance J. Tarasar, gen. ed., *Orthodox America: 1794-1976* (Syosset, NY: OCA Dept. of History & Archives, 1975), 12.

Annotated Bibliography

on American Orthodox History

General Histories

John H. Erickson, *Orthodox Christians in America: A Short History* (Oxford University Press, 2007).
This book is great if you're looking for a brief but informative overview of American Orthodox history. It's part of a series called Religion in American Life, and the intended audience is Americans who aren't necessarily familiar with Orthodoxy.

Thomas E. FitzGerald, *The Orthodox Church: Student Edition* (Praeger, 1998).
Like Erickson's, FitzGerald's intended audience isn't primarily Orthodox Christians but outsiders who are interested in the history of Orthodoxy in America. FitzGerald covers ground that Erickson doesn't, and vice versa; between the two of them, you'll get a solid handle on the basic story of American Orthodoxy.

Alexei Krindatch, ed., *Atlas of American Orthodox Christian Churches* (Holy Cross Orthodox Press, 2011).
Built around data from Krindatch's 2010 census of American Orthodox churches, this atlas includes some valuable historical material, including an overview of the historical narrative, a timeline, and introductions to all the different jurisdictions.

Mark Stokoe and Leonid Kishkovsky, *Orthodox Christians in North America 1794–1994* (Orthodox Christian Publications Center, 1995).

This book is out of print, but the entire text can be downloaded as a PDF on the OCA website. It's a brief work, 145 pages in book form and 66 in the PDF, and it presents a rather OCA-centric history of American Orthodoxy, including the now-debunked myth that all Orthodox Christians in America were unified under the Russian hierarchy prior to the Bolshevik Revolution.

Archimandrite Serafim (Surrency), *The Quest for Orthodox Church Unity in America* (Saints Boris and Gleb Press, 1973).

This one is a classic—imperfect in all sorts of ways, but full of information you won't find anywhere else. Unfortunately, it's been out of print for decades, and it's what they call in the copyright world an "orphaned work," still technically under copyright and thus unable to be reprinted without permission, but without any clear copyright owner to grant that permission. If you can track it down, grab a copy.

Specific Histories

Lawrence Barringer, *Good Victory* (Holy Cross Orthodox Press, 1995).

Long out of print, this book tells the story of how the American Carpatho-Russian Orthodox Diocese came into being, focusing on its first hierarch, Metropolitan Orestes Chornock. I mention it here because it's important to remember that not all the Uniates converted to Orthodoxy in the St. Alexis Toth-led wave at the turn of the twentieth century. Many remained loyal to Rome, and in the case of the parishes that would become ACROD, they resisted the russification that came along with membership in the Russian mission in America, instead joining the Ecumenical Patriarchate decades later.

Antony Gabriel, *The Ancient Church on New Shores: Antioch in North America* **(Borgo Press, 1996).**
Billed as "a comprehensive history" of the Antiochian Archdiocese of North America. The book is full of the author's biases and it's missing all sorts of details, but it remains the best attempt to sum up Antiochian history in North America.

Alexander Kitroeff, *The Greek Orthodox Church in America: A Modern History* **(Northern Illinois University Press, 2020).**
A solid overview of the history of the Greek Orthodox Archdiocese of America. My one quibble with this book is that it does a pretty weak job of telling the story of Greek Orthodoxy in America prior to the foundation of the Archdiocese. In many respects, it's a modern successor to George Papaioannou's now out-of-print *From Mars Hill to Manhattan: The Greek Orthodox in America under Athenagoras I.*

Paul G. Manolis, *The History of the Greek Church of America in Acts and Documents,* **vols. I–III (Ambelos Press, 2003).**
Now out of print, this is a 2,367-page, three-volume collection of primary sources on the history of Greek Orthodoxy in America. The sources are mostly a mix of Greek and English.

Michael J. Oleksa, *Orthodox Alaska: A Theology of Mission* **(St. Vladimir's Seminary Press, 1993).**
Father Michael Oleksa has long been regarded as the leading authority on Alaskan Orthodox history, and this book is the starting point if you want to delve into that topic.

Maxim L. Vasiljevic, ed., *The Serbian Christian Heritage of America: The Historical, Spiritual, and Cultural Presence of the Orthodox Diaspora in North America, 1815–2019* (Sebastian Press, 2019).

This monumental work by Bishop Maxim is over a thousand pages long and covers the history of Serbian Orthodoxy in America in great detail. It's expensive, but if you want to know this history, there is nothing better.

Lives of the Saints

The Monastery of St. John the Forerunner of Mesa Potamos, *Glorified in America: Laborers in the New World from Saint Alexis to Elder Ephraim* (Holy Trinity Publications, 2023).

If you want a detailed account of the lives of most of the saints who labored in America during the period covered by my own book, get this one. St. Alexis Toth, St. Tikhon, St. Raphael, St. Alexander Hotovitzky, St. John Kochurov, St. Sebastian Dabovich . . . all their life stories in one place.

The Saint Raphael Clergy Brotherhood, *Apostle to the Plains: The Life of Father Nicola Yanney* (Ancient Faith Publishing, 2019).

Written in an engaging, novel-like style, this is a deep dive into the remarkable life of Fr. Nicola Yanney.

Jane Swan, *Chosen for His People: A Biography of Patriarch Tikhon* (Holy Trinity Publications, 2015).

To date, this is the only complete biography of St. Tikhon. Before publication, it was revised by Scott Kenworthy, the foremost expert on St. Tikhon's life. I eagerly await the publication of Scott's much more ambitious work on St. Tikhon. If you want more on St. Tikhon, check out *Instructions and Teachings for the American Orthodox Faithful (1898–1907)*, a collection of St.

Tikhon's writings and homilies from his time in America, translated and edited by Alex Maximov and David Ford and published by St. Tikhon's Monastery Press in 2016.

Fr. Serge Veselinovich, *The Life and Works of Saint Mardary of Libertyville and All-America* (Diocese of New Gracanica & Midwestern America, 2019).

One of my regrets is not writing anything about St. Mardarije, a Serbian priest in the Russian mission who went on to become the first Serbian Orthodox bishop in America, under the Serbian Patriarchate. This book tells his story.

About the Author

MATTHEW NAMEE HAS run OrthodoxHistory.org since 2009. He's given numerous talks on church history over the years at most of the major Orthodox institutions and venues in the United States. In his day job, Matthew is an attorney working exclusively on Orthodox Church matters for a nonprofit ministry. He also serves as director of the Orthodox Studies Institute at Saint Constantine College. He lives in Washington State with his wife Catherine and their seven children.

We hope you have enjoyed and benefited from this book. Your financial support makes it possible to continue our nonprofit ministry both in print and online. Because the proceeds from our book sales only partially cover the costs of operating **Ancient Faith Publishing** and **Ancient Faith Radio**, we greatly appreciate the generosity of our readers and listeners. Donations are tax deductible and can be made at **www.ancientfaith.com**.

To view our other publications,
please visit our website: **store.ancientfaith.com**

 **ANCIENT FAITH RADIO**

Bringing you Orthodox Christian music, readings, prayers, teaching, and podcasts 24 hours a day since 2004 at **www.ancientfaith.com**